A Garland Series

# Accounting History and the

*A thirty-eight-volume facsimile series*

# )evelopment of a Profession

*Edited by Richard P. Brief,* NEW YORK UNIVERSITY

# The History of The Institute of Chartered Accountants in England and Wales 1870–1965

*Sir Harold Howitt*

GARLAND PUBLISHING, INC.
NEW YORK & LONDON 1984

For a complete list of the titles in this series see the final pages of this volume.

This facsimile has been made from a copy in a private collection.

Reprinted by permission of The Institute of Chartered Accountants in England and Wales.



**Library of Congress Cataloging in Publication Data**

Howitt, Harold, Sir, 1886–1969.
The history of the Institute of Chartered Accountants in England and Wales, 1870–1965.

(Accounting history and the development of a profession)
Reprint. Originally published: The history of the Institute of Chartered Accountants in England and Wales, 1880–1965, and of its founder accountancy bodies, 1870–1880. London : Heinemann, 1966.
Bibliography: p.
Includes index.
1. Institute of Chartered Accountants in England and Wales—History. I. Institute of Chartered Accountants in England and Wales. II. Title. III. Series.
HF5601.I7736H68 1984 657'.06'042 83-49113
ISBN 0-8240-6329-5 (alk. paper)

The volumes in this series are printed on acid-free, 250-year-life paper.

Printed in the United States of America

# THE HISTORY OF THE INSTITUTE OF CHARTERED ACCOUNTANTS IN ENGLAND AND WALES 1870–1965

The Coat of Arms of the Institute

# *The history of* THE INSTITUTE OF CHARTERED ACCOUNTANTS IN ENGLAND AND WALES 1880-1965 *and of its founder accountancy bodies* 1870-1880

*The growth of a profession and its influence on legislation and public affairs*

HEINEMANN
LONDON

William Heinemann Ltd
LONDON MELBOURNE TORONTO
CAPE TOWN AUCKLAND

*First published* 1966


*Printed and bound in Great Britain by*
THE SHENVAL PRESS
*London, Hertford and Harlow*

# Foreword

BY THE PRESIDENT OF THE INSTITUTE,
ROBERT MCNEIL, F.C.A.

THIS HISTORY only purports to deal with The Institute of Chartered Accountants in England and Wales, with its founder bodies, and with the development of accountancy and its related professional services in that area. The histories of chartered accountant bodies formed in other parts of the United Kingdom – in Scotland earlier and in Ireland later – are accordingly not dealt with here.

Chartered accountant bodies (whether formed under Royal Charter or not) have been established in many other parts of the British Empire and Commonwealth. They have, however, always been autonomous bodies and their past records are not reviewed in detail in this history though the Institute keeps close touch with them.

The history attempts to make some record of the emergence and development of a vigorous profession, which has already reached considerable dimensions, and shows every sign of further substantial expansion. It does not attempt to deal in detail with technical matters nor with the detailed administration and rules of the Institute, for information on which reference should be made to its *Members' Handbook* and other publications.

There is no particular reason why this history should be written now, except that as the years tick along available records become dustier, and so do available memories. It may be hoped perhaps that it will be revised for the centenary of the Institute and that another chapter may then be added for the period 1965–80. Chartered accountants are not allowed to prophesy, so no attempt will be made at a forecast for that period, fascinating though it would be. If, however, a peg is required on which to hang a justification for present issue, the year 1965, even perhaps more than a special birthday (and several existing firms have already celebrated their centenaries), marks a milestone in the development of the Institute in certain important respects:

(a) The recent amendment of the Charter to cater for the increasing activity of members in management accounting and consultancy; a significant and major development in the activities of chartered accountants, and the first time the Institute has co-operated with other accounting bodies in post-final examinations in a specialist field.

(b) The temporary movement of the Institute's headquarters, preparatory to the redevelopment of its Hall and offices in Moorgate Place.

(c) In this year the membership of the Institute reached a total of 40,000 though it is recognized that numbers are not the all-important factor.

At the request of the Council, Sir Harold Howitt, a leading figure in his profession and a most distinguished past President, undertook, in his retirement, the arduous task of compiling this history and in so doing has again rendered great service to the Institute. He has been chiefly helped by two other members, W. G. Campbell and, until her death in 1963, Miss Ethel Watts, with the assistance also of Miss V. M. Snelling, a former editor of *The Accountant*. The information herein recorded has been collated from the records of the Institute, from members of its Council, past and present, from its staff, from members of its district societies, and from the volumes of *The Accountant* from 1874 onwards. To all who have contributed in this way our thanks are offered.

President
The Institute of Chartered Accountants
in England and Wales

*August* 1965

# Contents

## Part II. Special features

# Illustrations

# Introduction

ACCOUNTANCY, as a profession, is of comparatively recent origin, though, as an occupation, it has existed since earliest recorded days. None of us (and certainly not our wives) can free ourselves from its exacting clutches. It is referred to in the Bible, in early Roman history, in Shakespeare and indeed throughout the ages. And yet it was not until after the middle of the nineteenth century that the professional accountant really saw the light of day. From 1870 to 1877 Institutes and Societies of Accountants were formed in London, Liverpool, Manchester and Sheffield. In 1872 the Society of Accountants in England was established. The Royal Charter of the Institute of Chartered Accountants in England and Wales (the first national charter for accountants), with which this history is primarily concerned, was granted on May 11, 1880.

The honour of the earliest reference to the handiwork of accountants, namely organized book-keeping, is always attributed to Italy. A treatise entitled *Summa di Arithmetica* by Pacioli, published in Venice in 1494, can be seen in the Institute's library, along with other interesting records, some of which are referred to later in this history. The history of accounting is, however, much older. Indeed it may be claimed that among the earliest surviving examples of writing of any kind are the records of temple incomes kept by priests in lower Mesopotamia in the fourth millennium B.C.

The art of accountancy, if so it may be described, has gone through many developments, changing in form, from the handwritten books (or even papyrus leaves) to loose-leaf records, mechanical accounting and computers and, in purpose, from a record only of past events and current position, to assistance of management in promoting efficiency and forecasting over the whole field of industry, commerce and finance.

An attempt will be made in these pages, at least in outline, to trace the development of the profession in this country, the urge to be organized into a national chartered body, the circumstances which have led to its subsequent rapid growth, the role which it has been called upon to play in the community; and to provide a record, necessarily brief, of the Institute's administrative problems, of its old-established firms and of a few of its prominent past leaders.

It is difficult in reviewing the activities of the early days to do more than scan the proceedings of annual and other meetings, and the remarks thereat of Presidents and other important members. It is unfortunately impossible to invoke the help of the old stalwarts of those days and it would be unprofitable and laborious, both to writer and reader, to go into detail concerning the technical problems that arose, the development of legislation in which the Institute was vitally affected and in which it took an active part, and the domestic disputes. It is probably better to endeavour to deal with these early periods by selecting from the records the chief items of subject matter which seem to have engaged the attention of our forebears.

The first periods selected (Chapters One and Two of Part I) deal with the years 1870 to 1890 which take us from the events leading up to the Charter of 1880 to the closing years of the nineteenth century; they cover much of the active lives of the founders of the Institute and the early problems of its first Councils.

The later chapters of Part I continue the story chronologically in what appear to be convenient periods dictated very largely by the advent of two world wars and by integration with the Society of Incorporated Accountants. In these chapters reference is also made to the underlying events of legislation, commercial development and internal professional problems which have played so large a part in the history of the Institute and of the profession.

As many of the internal matters referred to recur repeatedly throughout the narrative and were the subject matter of discussion at successive annual and autumnal meetings, it has been thought appropriate to summarize the more important of them in Part II even though this must result in some repetition.

Finally one reflects on the origin of the title 'Chartered Accountant' and on the right of members of the Institute to regard their calling as a profession. Many definitions may be attempted of the term 'profession' and of the requirements of those who practise it – a skilled occupation tested by examination, practice and research; a high degree of integrity, independence and hard work; the client-adviser relationship, entailing the placing of client before self, and so on; but in the last resort the real test is whether the calling is accepted by the public as a profession. Members of the Institute can but hope they have long ago gained this recognition and the privilege which it brings.

The designation 'Chartered Accountant' derives from the Royal Charter, and was not therefore used south of the Border till 1880, although attempts to obtain such a Charter had been made since the early 1870s and in the face of discouragement from Ministers of State.

The designation had been used in Scotland since it was adopted in the Bye-laws of the Royal Charter of 1854 which established the Society of Accountants in Edinburgh, but it was not included in the title of that Society nor of that of either of the two other Scottish bodies for which Charters were subsequently granted, the Glasgow Accountants and Actuaries (1855) and the Accountants in Aberdeen (1867). These bodies also used the designation 'Chartered Accountant' for their members. The three Royal Charters were applied for separately by accountants practising around the cities named, and were national neither in scope nor intention. At no time during the nineteenth century, nor during the first half of the twentieth century, was there an Institute of Chartered Accountants in Scotland. It was not until 1951 that the Edinburgh Society was renamed and reconstituted by Charter as the Institute of Chartered Accountants of Scotland. It thus became the nucleus of a national Scottish Institute, completed by the surrender of their

Charters by Glasgow and Aberdeen, whose members became members of the reconstituted Institute.

The designation was, therefore, first used on a national basis, that is to say as part of the title of a national body, in 1880 by the Institute of Chartered Accountants in England and Wales. It was subsequently adopted on a national basis in Ireland in 1888 and in Scotland in 1951, as set out above.

The membership of the Institute by March 1965 had reached 40,000, of whom nearly 5,000 were not resident in the United Kingdom. If this be compared with its opening membership of about 600 some eighty years earlier, and if it be recalled that prior to 1870 there was no public accountancy body at all in England or Wales, a striking indication is given of its rate of growth and of the growth of the demand of the public for the services of a new profession.

# Part I
# Narrative

The Accountant's Bank Note Office, Bank of England, 1882–91.
*Courtesy Radio Times Hulton Picture Library*

# Chapter One

# 1870-1880

*The founder bodies and the emergence of public accountancy as an organized profession. The grant of a Royal Charter.*

OWING TO the Industrial Revolution, England was the workshop of the world in the nineteenth century. In 1845 Great Britain produced 34,000,000 tons of coal against 5,000,000 produced by France. By 1848 nearly 5,000 miles of railway lines had been laid. The production of pig iron in 1839 was twenty times greater than it had been in 1788. In the cotton industry Great Britain supplied 60 per cent of the world consumption in 1835. In addition England was the greatest moneyed country in the world in the nineteenth century. According to the figures given in Bagehot's *Lombard Street*, the known deposits in banks, that is to say 'borrowable' monies were:

| | | |
|---|---|---|
| London | (December 31, 1872) | £120,000,000 |
| Paris | (February 27, 1873) | £13,000,000 |
| New York | (February 1873) | £40,000,000 |
| German Empire | (January 31, 1873) | £8,000,000 |

This country was rich and led the world in commerce.

It was therefore natural that the services of accountants should become essential to the community. According to Holden's triennial *Directory of London, Westminster and Southwark*, first published in 1799, they numbered eleven at that date, and some of the existing firms of the Institute (see Section II) can trace their origins back to the eighteenth century. In England and Wales in 1793 the names of only three 'accomptants' can be traced, one resident at Liverpool and the other two at Bristol; there is no mention of any accountant in practice in London at that time. In a speech given by Frederick Whinney in 1887 on the occasion of

Queen Victoria's Jubilee he stated that the number in London had grown to 464 when the London Institute was founded in 1870.

It has been suggested that the growth of country banks made the services of accountants widespread. Whinney attributed the early growth of the profession not only in audits but also in winding-up of companies to the railway mania of 1845, and said that additional work had followed as the result of the Winding-Up Acts of 1848 and 1849. The succession of Companies Acts following the Limited Liability Act of 1855 had increased very largely the demand for the services of accountants. Firms, however, worked in isolation and there was no required standard of skill. Some practitioners were generally held in esteem as is shown by the appointment in 1864 of Robert Palmer Harding, head of the firm of Harding Whinney & Co., to be a Commissioner to inquire into the working of the Bankruptcy Acts. On the failure of the banking firm of Overend, Gurney & Co., he and William Turquand were appointed liquidators in 1865.

The need to combine, to improve the status of accountants by the introduction of rules of professional conduct and a required standard of skill, became evident. As Whinney said in 1887, the work available had resulted in a great influx of persons 'who thought they had nothing whatever to do to become accountants but to put up a plate and designate themselves as such, in order to become rich men'. Some firms combined accountancy with other businesses, some shared their profits with other people and direct and indirect advertising was indulged in. In spite of the eminence of some practitioners Mr Justice Quain, a judge of the Queen's Bench, in the trial of a fraudulent bankrupt at Bristol Assizes, complained that the trustee, who was a professional accountant, had wasted the time of the Court. The learned judge referred to solicitors as gentlemen and gave it as his opinion that the encroachments into bankruptcy cases by 'an ignorant set of men called accountants' was 'one of the grossest abuses ever introduced into law'.

The first steps towards combination were taken in 1870 when the Incorporated Society of Liverpool Accountants was formed in

January and the Institute of Accountants in London in November. The latter began as an informal committee of nine men who met on June 8, 1870, at 3 Moorgate Street, London – the offices of Quilter, Ball & Co. William Quilter was voted unanimously into the chair, on the proposition of Samuel Lowell Price, of Price, Holyland, Waterhouse & Co., seconded by William Turquand, of Turquand, Youngs & Co. The six others were Quilter's partner, John Ball; Turquand's partner, John Young; J. B. Gibbons of Harding, Whinney, Gibbons & Co.; G. A. Cape of Cape & Harris; Robert Fletcher of Robert Fletcher & Co.; and Charles Fitch Kemp of Kemp, Cannan, Ford & Co.

The object of those present was expressed in two resolutions which were carried unanimously:

(1) 'That it is highly desirable, in order to maintain and secure the efficiency of the profession, that steps be taken to form an Association of Accountants, to be incorporated by Royal Charter.'

(2) 'That the gentlemen now present be a Provisional Committee for the promotion of the aforesaid object, with power to add to their number.'

Thomas Abercrombie Welton, who was at that time a clerk employed by Quilter, Ball & Co., was appointed honorary secretary of the committee.

Turquand applied immediately to G. J. Goschen, President of the Poor Law Board in Gladstone's first Cabinet, for advice about a Charter and was informed by letter that difficulties were likely to arise. The Minister said that for the past two years the Privy Council had declined to grant charters and he suggested that for the sum of five guineas a Memorandum of Association could be registered with the Board of Trade under Section 23 of the Companies Act, 1867. 'For all practical purposes,' he wrote, 'there seems to be no difference between the old "Charter" and the present "Memorandum of Association".'

The Committee was disappointed when the letter was read at the second meeting held a week later. It resolved that it would be inadvisable to register a Memorandum of Association with the Board of Trade, lest such action should prejudice the possibility of applying successfully for a Charter later if the Government's attitude should change, and it was decided unanimously that a voluntary association should be formed to be known as the Institute of Accountants in London. A sub-committee, consisting of Turquand, Ball, Price, Gibbons and Fletcher, was appointed to draw up draft rules and regulations with the aid of a solicitor. As soon as the sub-committee had completed its work, all the leading accountants of London (in number sixty-three) were summoned to a meeting at the City Terminus Hotel, Cannon Street, on November 29, 1870.

Quilter, who had been voted into the chair, explained how the movement for the formation of an Institute of Accountants in London had been initiated. The draft rules and regulations which had been circulated defined the object of the Institute as follows:

'To elevate the attainments and status of professional accountants in London, to promote their efficiency and usefulness, and to give expression to their opinions upon all questions incident to their profession.' After discussion it was decided that the object and the rules should be approved and adopted 'subject to such modifications as the Council may, under legal advice, consider necessary or desirable'. It was agreed that membership of the Institute should be confined to professional accountants in London and no provision was made for practitioners in the provinces, an omission which was not remedied until 1872.

Membership of the Institute of Accountants in London was divided into two classes, Fellows and Associates. It was provided that until July 1, 1871, the Council should be empowered to admit as Fellows, if otherwise eligible, all persons who had been in uninterrupted practice as accountants since January 1, 1866. After July 1, 1871, except in special cases, Fellows were to be elected only from the body of Associates.

Fellows admitted after July 1, 1871, without first becoming Associates, were required to pay an entrance fee of 50 guineas. Associates paid an entrance fee of 25 guineas, and a further 25 guineas if and when they were subsequently admitted as Fellows. The annual subscriptions of Fellows and Associates were fixed respectively at 5 and 3 guineas.

Thirty-seven accountants affixed their signatures to a copy of the draft rules and regulations and on the proposition of S. L. Price, seconded by A. A. James, of James, Edwards, Cash & Stone, the first Council of the Institute of Accountants in London was constituted. It consisted of the following twelve members:

John Ball, of Quilter, Ball & Co.
G. A. Cape, of Cape & Harris
H. Croysdill, of Croysdill, Saffery & Co.
W. W. Deloitte, of Deloitte, Dever, Hollebone & Griffiths
R. Fletcher, of Robert Fletcher & Co.
J. B. Gibbons, of Harding, Whinney, Gibbons & Co.
R. P. Harding, of Harding, Whinney, Gibbons & Co.
C. F. Kemp, of Kemp, Cannan, Ford & Co.
S. L. Price, of Price, Holyland, Waterhouse & Co.
William Quilter, of Quilter, Ball & Co.
William Turquand, of Turquand, Youngs & Co.
John Young, of Turquand, Youngs & Co.

Three trustees were then nominated. They were:

W. H. Holyland, of Price, Holyland, Waterhouse & Co.
A. A. James, of James, Edwards, Cash & Stone
Alexander Young, of Turquand, Youngs & Co.

Finally, Henry Chatteris, of Chatteris, Nichols & Chatteris, and Frederick Whinney, of Harding, Whinney, Gibbons & Co., were appointed as honorary auditors.

At the first meeting of the Council, held on December 13, 1870, Quilter was formally appointed President and Turquand Vice-President of the Institute of Accountants in London. Welton, who was confirmed in his office as secretary at an annual salary of £100, read out the names of those who had signed the rules and regulations since the general meeting on November 29. On February 8, 1871, the Council formally adopted the report of the sub-committee on rules and regulations and gave instructions for 300 copies to be printed. A new sub-committee, consisting of Gibbons, Fletcher and Ball, was appointed to take and furnish offices for the Institute, to establish a library and to be responsible for publicity work. John Ball then presented, as a first contribution to the proposed library, an edition of Dr Johnson's dictionary in four quarto volumes.

The stipulated entrance fee for Associates operated as an effective bar to the admission of many struggling but reputable and competent practitioners. However, the London Institute was successfully launched with sixty Fellows and eighteen Associates on April 19, 1871.

Quilter, who was entirely self-made, possessed the gift of taking quick and sound decisions. He was a born leader, upright, independent, and conscientious. He and his able partner, John Ball, did much to lift the profession morally and intellectually. When, on Quilter's retirement in 1877, William Turquand took over the office of President of the London Institute, Ball succeeded Turquand as Vice-President.

The first committee of examiners appointed by the Council of the London Institute consisted of John Ball (chairman), J. B. Gibbons, who died in July 1872, and Robert Fletcher. They examined candidates *viva voce* for admission as Associates. At the first Annual General Meeting of the Institute, which was held in 1872, Quilter was able to report that the membership had increased to 134, namely, seventy-four Fellows and sixty Associates.

In the meantime, in response to complaints from influential accountants practising in the provinces, the Council received, early in 1872, a deputation of seven provincial accountants to discuss the project of extending the scope of the London Institute to cover the whole country. Four members of the deputation came from Newcastle upon Tyne, and one each from Huddersfield, Hull and Southampton. At a meeting of the Council on May 7, a letter was read from the Manchester Institute of Accountants, which had been formed on February 6, 1871, expressing the unanimous view of its members that a national organization was needed to represent the profession. A letter from George William Spence, of the

Newcastle firm of Gillespie, Swithinbank & Co., was also read. In the view of the writer 'the best country practitioners who would be eligible for the Institute, have not joined the new Society of Accountants. The course taken recently by that Society in opening its doors so extremely wide convinces us of the desirability of the Institute taking some decided course in order to maintain a high standard.' This new body was the Society of Accountants in England, which was in course of formation and was constituted in 1872. Both letters made a strong impression, and it was resolved that a special meeting of the Council should be summoned to consider the desirability of complying with the representations of accountants from the provinces.

The special meeting was held on May 21, 1872, under the chairmanship of William Turquand. A letter was read which had been signed by thirty-nine accountants practising in Blackburn, Bradford, Brighton, Bristol, Halifax, Hull, Leeds, Manchester, Newcastle, Portsea, Preston, Southampton, Wolverhampton, and Worcester, calling upon the London Institute, for the sake of the profession and of the public, to widen its rules in order to admit 'properly qualified' accountants, that is to say those who fulfilled certain conditions as to experience and length of time in practice, from the provinces. The canvass had been organized by the Newcastle accountant, G. W. Spence, in response to a hint conveyed to him by T. A. Welton, the secretary of the London Institute, in a private letter. Spence was the principal figure among those provincial accountants of standing who desired to see the scope of the London Institute extended to cover the country as a whole. It was clear that there was a widespread desire among nearly all leading provincial accountants that the scope of the London Institute should be widened.

Membership of the London Institute was accordingly made available to accountants in all parts of the United Kingdom and the name was changed from 'Institute of Accountants in London' to 'Institute of Accountants'. These changes, with consequential alterations to the rules, were approved at a special general meeting of the newly named Institute in July 1872, and confirmed at the

A counting-house scene from *'t Recht Gebruyck van't Italiaens Boeck-houden . . .*, Amsterdam, 1672. (In the Institute's Library.) (Enlarged.)

general meeting in October. There was no suggestion that any change should be made in the rule which restricted membership to professional accountants and excluded all 'official' accountants employed by railway, dock or other companies, even when, as often happened, such accountants engaged in outside professional work with their employers' consent.

The immediate result of the change in the constitution of the London Institute was disappointing. Few provincial accountants applied for membership and in 1874 only thirteen had joined the Institute. The requirement in the new rules that all applications for membership should be accompanied by a recommendation signed by three Fellows possessing professional as well as personal knowledge of the candidate, presented a more serious bar to the admission of provincial members than had been anticipated. The Council, nevertheless, was unwilling to modify that requirement, stating in its report that it afforded 'the only real security for the professional competence and status of candidates'. Advertising was rife among those who chose to call themselves accountants but could not support their claims with either knowledge or experience. *The Accountant* of November 1874 quoted one gentleman who wrote round to prospective clients: 'I take the liberty of enclosing my card. I have recently commenced business as Law Stationer, Law Bill Clerk, Public and Private Auditor and Accountant, House, Land and Estate Agent, Rent and Debt Collector, and Trustee in Bankruptcy.' Both the public and the genuine accountant needed protection.

The minute books show that there had been a decline in the original enthusiasm which had led to the successful launching of the Institute. On March 10, 1874, the Council resolved to invite four leading provincial accountants, Harmood Walcot Banner of Liverpool, Henry Webster Blackburn of Bradford, Edward Carter of Birmingham, and George Edwin Swithinbank of Newcastle upon Tyne, to serve as additional members of the Council. The invitations were accepted and the appointments were confirmed at the annual general meeting in April 1874.

Nevertheless the membership of the Institute failed to increase substantially, the Provincial Societies continued their separate existences, and the Society of Accountants in England continued to be openly hostile to the Institute of Accountants on two grounds. It maintained that the financial and other conditions governing admission to the Institute were arbitrary and unfair and that they had been deliberately framed with the object of excluding many competent accountants. It maintained also that the Institute had been formed without any attempt to consult the whole body of the profession and, in particular, without taking provincial interests into proper consideration. Membership of the Society rose much more rapidly than membership of the Institute, reaching 220 in 1877 and 286 in 1880. Membership of the Institute stood at 154 in 1877 and 188 in 1880. The Society advertised regularly in *The Accountant*, which was started as a monthly publication in October 1874, and changed to a weekly in January 1875. The Institute seldom advertised because it felt that its membership constituted the cream of the profession, and that it was derogatory and unnecessary to appeal for recruits.

The able and courageous founder and the first editor of *The Accountant*, Alfred Gee, pressed resolutely for a Charter. In the first issue of the paper, which was and still is a private venture, he urged 'all respectable accountants' to 'lay aside petty jealousies and co-operate together to obtain the sanction of Parliament to an association of which membership would be a guarantee of reputation'. In 1877 he wrote: 'We have all along advocated the desirability of an amalgamation of all accountants' societies, so that, when necessary, the opinion of the profession might be given with no uncertain sound. That this will come in the process of time we entertain no manner of doubt. But, for the present, there are forces at work which tend to keep asunder for a while the two great London societies of accountants; and, this being so, we can scarcely find fault with country members of the profession if they manifest an inclination to form local societies of their own.'

In February 1875, Gee wrote to the secretary of the Institute to beg the Council to reconsider its attitude on the question of advertising in his paper, saying, 'Quite apart from the monetary considerations, I should be glad to be allowed to insert an advertisement from you, as it would tend to negative an idea which, I learn from my canvasser, now exists amongst some members of the profession, that because the Society of Accountants in England advertises, the paper is in some respects the particular organ of that Society.' In response to Gee's appeal the Council's attitude relaxed slightly; it advertised from time to time but not on the scale adopted by the Society, and its outlook and methods were still felt in some quarters to be unprogressive.

In those circumstances Frederick Whinney presented to the Council in 1876 a requisition signed by twenty-six members of the Institute asking for a special general meeting to be called for the purpose of enlarging the Council by the election of three additional members who would, it was hoped, constitute a 'ginger' group. That subject had been discussed at the fifth Annual General Meeting of the Institute in April 1876. The meeting had been adjourned until July 1 when William Turquand, who was in the chair, stated that the resolution calling for an enlargement of the Council by the appointment of three additional members was out of order and that such a resolution could not be raised under the rules until the next annual general meeting.

However, Frederick Whinney and two of his friends were elected members of the Council at the Annual General Meeting in April 1877. Their election was proposed by William Turquand, who had been elected President of the Institute in February 1877, after William Quilter, at the January meeting of the Council, had announced his resignation of that office on the plea of advancing years. Quilter distrusted the new outlook and particularly the decision to reduce the entrance fees of Fellows and Associates. He resigned his seat on the Council and, in May 1877, his membership of the Institute. This inflexible attitude was characteristic of a number of the original members.

Under Turquand's presidency the Institute entered upon a period of renewed activity which culminated three years later in the grant of the Charter. At the Annual General Meeting on April 26, 1877, it was resolved that any member of the Institute who should, in future, share with a solicitor, broker, auctioneer or other agent any commission arising out of the business of any estate in the administration of which the services of the accountant, or those of his firm, were employed, should be deemed to be guilty of unprofessional conduct and should be liable to expulsion from the Institute. That resolution replaced a strong but less emphatic condemnation of such practices which had been adopted in 1873.

Further indications that a new spirit had been breathed into the policy of the Institute were seen in the vigorous action taken by the Council in matters of first importance to the profession. During the year 1877 Disraeli's Government introduced a new Bankruptcy Bill, and appointed a Select Committee of the House of Commons to consider and report on the Companies Acts of 1862 and 1867. The Secretary of the Institute was instructed to attend the meetings of the Select Committee at the House of Commons and to take a note of the proceedings in the interests of the profession. T. A. Welton had resigned the office of secretary in June 1876, but he agreed to serve until February 1877, when W. G. Howgrave succeeded him. One of the first important matters that confronted the new secretary was the statement made by a witness at a meeting of the Select Committee that the sums of money in the hands of liquidators in the form of undistributed assets amounted to 'millions sterling', and that, as a general rule, no notice was given to creditors of the declaration and payment of dividends in respect of bankrupt estates.

All members of the Institute were circularized and it was found that on June 30, 1877, the aggregate total of undistributed assets in their hands, and in those of their firms, amounted to £66,487 18s 10d and the total of unclaimed dividends amounted to £3,596 10s 9d. It was found, moreover, that notice was invariably given to creditors whenever dividends were declared and paid. That information was communicated by the President to the Chairman of the Select Committee.

The President, accompanied by S. L. Price and R. P. Harding, gave evidence before the Select Committee. They were examined on their experience in connection with the conduct of liquidations, and Turquand did his profession good service by the forthright manner in which he spoke.

He admitted that if the conduct of liquidations was permitted to fall into bad hands it would be impossible to check accurately the declared amount of time taken by trustees in finishing their work, but he effectively refuted false impressions about the existence of widespread malversation in the administration of insolvency, and he gave no countenance to the suggestion that the profession of accountancy was in any sense on its trial before the Committee.

The struggle lasted for many years and the Bankruptcy Act, 1883, established the office of Official Receiver in disregard of the objections of all leading professional accountants. Nevertheless, the resolute action of the Institute, and the measures which were taken in good time to bring its views to the notice of all concerned, convinced many of the value of an organization which could speak with authority. The struggle also indicates the importance of insolvency work to the profession in those days.

In June 1877, it was announced that the Institute had taken a twenty-one years' lease of new offices on the ground floor of 3 Copthall Buildings at a rent of £300 a year, in place of its previous office which had been on the second floor at 8 Old Jewry. The original office consisted of rooms over a shop at 30 Moorgate Street. The Council proceeded immediately to buy the whole of the Authorized Law Reports from the date of their first publication in 1865. The Secretary was instructed to prepare an index of all cases affecting the profession, and to purchase a variety of useful law books and works of reference. He was instructed also to endeavour to obtain copies of the accounts of all the leading railway, banking, and other public companies. Within a few months the accounts of more than seventy companies, many of them covering a large number of years, had been conveniently arranged in the Institute's library. A clerks' register was established for the convenience alike of principals and of unemployed clerks. At the same time a system of examinations for admission to associate membership was inaugurated.

At the first meeting held by the men who founded the Institute of Accountants in London, it had been resolved that steps should be taken to form an association of accountants incorporated by Royal Charter, but they had been discouraged by the reply from G. J. Goschen. With the early history in mind it was decided in 1878 to make another attempt to obtain incorporation by different means. The Council of the Institute resolved on May 3, 1878, that 'it is desirable that the Institute should endeavour to obtain an Act of Parliament incorporating it under the title of "The Incorporated Institute of Official Accountants" or some other title, and providing rules for the regulation of such Incorporated Institute'. That resolution proposed by Frederick Whinney and seconded by J. J. Saffery was carried unanimously. Whinney then read some headings for such an Act which he had prepared with the aid of the Secretary. A fortnight later the work was begun of preparing a Bill based on Whinney's suggestions.

The draft of the proposed Bill was read to the Council in November 1878, together with a notice which had, by statute, to be published in the *London Gazette*. The secretary reported that the secretary of the Society of Accountants had called upon him and left a copy of a memorial which the Society proposed to present to the Lord Mayor and Corporation of London, asking them to constitute 'a body of sworn accountants'. The Council of the Institute resolved that, while it was unable to co-operate with the Society in that action, the Society and all provincial organizations of accountants should be invited to comment on the proposed Bill.

On December 31, 1878, the Council of the Institute received a deputation from the Society of Accountants who argued that it was highly desirable that the Institute and the Society should amalgamate if satisfactory terms could be arranged. Accordingly, at the Council Meeting in January 1879, the proposal of the Society of Accountants in England to amalgamate with the Institute was formally considered. It was unanimously resolved that such an amalgamation would be desirable in principle and that a joint meeting of the Councils of both bodies should be held to discover whether a satisfactory basis could be arranged. The joint meeting was fixed for January 16, 1879. Two days earlier, the Council of the Institute received deputations from the Liverpool Society, the Manchester Institute, the Sheffield Institute (formed on March 14, 1877), and the newly formed Accountants' Incorporation Association.

The chairman, John Young, said that the Council of the Institute considered that the local societies should continue in existence, but that they should be affiliated to the Incorporated Institute. He added that some accountants engaged in business as auctioneers or brokers had been admitted to the provincial associations and he did not think that such men would be eligible for admission to the Incorporated Institute, because they were not *bona fide* accountants according to the rules of the Institute of Accountants. On the other hand, it was stated that many of the most respected members of the Sheffield Institute were brokers as well as accountants, and that the Sheffield Institute would become 'perfectly useless' if an attempt were made to penalize accountants who were also in practice as brokers.

At the joint meeting on January 16, 1879, the Council of the Institute and the Society of Accountants in England, who were represented by their President, John Bath, and four other members, discussed the question of the admission to the Incorporated Institute of accountants who were also auctioneers or brokers. The Society was in a stronger position than any of the provincial organizations to negotiate on equal terms with the Institute. It was finally resolved that the meeting should be adjourned, that the Council of the Institute should meet for the specific purpose 'of discussing the question of the admission of accountants engaged as auctioneers or stock and share brokers, or other business', and that, as a preliminary measure, the secretaries of the two societies should carefully scrutinize the lists of members of both bodies.

The Council of the Institute met again on January 22, 1879, with Turquand in the chair. It was argued that it ought not to go on record as having entertained, even for a moment, the suggestion that accountants engaged in business other than that of public accountancy could be regarded as qualified for admission to the Incorporated Institute. The minutes were read but not confirmed, and a motion was carried unanimously: '*That the Council, after careful deliberation, considers that the true interest of the profession requires that eligibility for membership should be limited to persons whose only business is that of public accountant.*' The secretary was instructed to send copies to the Society of Accountants in England and to the various country societies.

At a meeting of the Council held on February 4, 1879, a committee consisting of W. Turquand, John Ball, A. Cooper, G. A. Cape, E. Hart, G. A. Ladbury, T. A. Welton, F. Whinney and John Young was constituted to settle the clauses of a draft Bill, to watch its progress through Parliament, and to report to the Council.

The Liverpool Society was unique among the provincial bodies in expressing unqualified approval of the resolution passed by the Council of the Institute on January 22, 1879. The Sheffield Institute drew up a formal petition against the draft Bill believing, the chairman wrote, that such a petition 'might be of assistance to the Society of Accountants in their opposition to the Bill', and objecting to the proposal that accountants who were also stockbrokers or auctioneers should be ineligible for admission to the Incorporated Institute.

The Society of Accountants also drew up a formal petition against the Bill. It objected that the Bill, if passed, would tend to place members of the Institute 'in a better position than other accountants, and give them the monopoly of the business in the Court of Chancery and other official departments of the Crown, to the prejudice of other gentlemen of equal eminence and respectability'. Members of the Society were informed, at a meeting in London in February 1879, that negotiations for effecting an amalgamation between the Institute and other bodies of accountants had broken down on the question of the admission of accountants who were in practice also as brokers or auctioneers. The Society maintained that the Institute was trying to force a private and selfish version of an incorporation Bill through Parliament, and to ride roughshod over the Society which 'largely surpassed the Institute in numbers and was not less fortunate in ability'. Its

President said that the Society was quite as anxious for a Bill as the Institute could be, but that the Bill drafted by the Institute was intolerable and must be opposed.

During the twelve months which followed, every effort was made to reconcile outstanding differences among existing bodies of accountants in England and Wales. The negotiations were hard and feeling, at times, was bitter, but the English genius for compromise prevailed and an agreement was slowly hammered into shape around the conference table. The original draft Bill of the incorporation of the Institute of Accountants was amended to meet the objections of the Society of Accountants in England as well as those of other bodies, and in consequence the petitions lodged against it were withdrawn.

The amended Bill was entrusted to Lord Redesdale in the House of Lords, and to Sir John Lubbock (later Lord Avebury) in the Commons. Lord Redesdale consulted the Duke of Richmond, who was Lord President of the Council in Disraeli's Government. The Duke expressed the view that the Institute would be well advised to drop the Bill and to petition the Queen in Council for a Charter of Incorporation. Lord Redesdale reported that a petition to that effect would be more in accordance with precedent, and that he had reason to think that it would be successful. The Government would not be willing to make time available for a Bill unless it should become clear that the Privy Council was unwilling to advise the Queen to grant a Charter.

It is notable that the Council was now advised to apply for a Royal Charter, which had been its original object. Among the great advantages of Charters were the fact that the tradition surrounding them dated back to the fourteenth century, the prestige attaching to them and the characteristics of monopoly they conferred.

A draft petition having been prepared and read to the Council of the Institute on July 31, 1879, its terms were approved by all the existing bodies of accountants. It was signed by the Presidents of the Institute of Accountants, the Society of Accountants in England, the Manchester and Sheffield Institutes, and the Liverpool

Society, and by two well-known Manchester practitioners (Edwin Guthrie and Charles Henry Wade) on behalf of the Accountants' Incorporation Association. It was then forwarded to the Privy Council together with a draft of the proposed Charter.

The application set out the objects of the proposed Institute as follows:

> 'That the said societies were not established for the purpose of gain nor do the members thereof derive or seek any pecuniary profit from their membership but the societies aim at the elevation of the profession of public accountants as a whole and the promotion of their efficiency and usefulness by compelling the observance of strict rules of conduct as a condition of membership and by setting up a high standard of professional and general education and knowledge and otherwise.
>
> 'That in the judgment of the Petitioners it would greatly promote the objects for which the said societies have been instituted and would also be for the public benefit if the members thereof were incorporated as one body as besides other advantages such incorporation would be a public recognition of the importance of the profession and would tend to gradually raise its character and thus to secure for the community the existence of a class of persons well qualified to be employed in the responsible and difficult duties often devolving on Public Accountants.'

By the terms of the Charter the bodies who signed the application were to merge their separate identities in the Institute of Chartered Accountants in England and Wales, which all their members became entitled to join. All members of the first Council of the new body and all who were, at the date of the Charter, Fellows of the Institute of Accountants, of the Society of Accountants in England, or of the Manchester and Sheffield Institutes, were entitled to become automatically Fellows of the Institute of Chartered Accountants in England and Wales. The Liverpool Society, which had only twenty-nine members, had never differentiated between Fellows and Associates. Its members, accordingly, were given the right to become Fellows if they had been in practice for five years immediately preceding the date of the Charter, otherwise they had the right to become Associates. All Associate members of the other four accountants' organizations at the date of the Charter were entitled to become Associates.

Candidates for admission to Fellowship who, at the date of the Charter, were not members of any of the five original bodies of English accountants, were required to have been in practice as public accountants on January 1, 1879, and subsequently for five years continuously up to the date of the submission of their applications for admission, or to have been Associates of the new body and in continuous practice for five years. The Council of the proposed corporation was empowered in all cases to decide whether or not the specified condition had been satisfied.

Applicants who were not members of any of the five original bodies of English accountants at the date of the Charter and who desired to become Associate members of the new body were required to pass the final examination specified in the Charter; or to have passed, at some time, the final examination specified by the rules of any of the five original bodies. They were required to have been in practice as public accountants for three years immediately preceding the date of the Charter or to have had five years' service as clerks (or partly as principals and partly as clerks) immediately preceding the date of the Charter. In the case of graduates of a University in the United Kingdom, the five years' period of service was reduced to three years. But it was provided that five years after the date of the Charter, or three years in the case of university graduates, the term 'service' was to be construed to mean service under articles to a member or members of the proposed corporation in practice in England and Wales. Entrance fees and annual subscriptions were fixed on a moderate scale, and Fellows and Associates were authorized to use the distinguishing initials, F.C.A. and A.C.A.

It was provided that no member of the new corporation should allow any person, not being his partner or a member of the Institute, to practise in his name as a public accountant, and that he should not share any professional remuneration with a solicitor, auctioneer, broker, or other agent. Further no member who was not in practice as a public accountant at the date of the Charter should follow any business or occupation other than that of a public accountant, or some business which, in the opinion of the Council, was incidental thereto or consistent therewith. The last phrase covered the compromise by which certain firms who combined the business of public accountancy with some other business were not to be penalized.

Provision was made in the Charter for the exercise by the Council of the Institute of specific disciplinary powers, with appropriate sanctions, as well as for the exercise of general powers of superintendence, management and control. The Charter was applicable only in England and Wales; it was not applicable in Scotland or in Ireland.

Before the Charter was granted, the Institute of Accountants suffered a grievous loss by the death, in August 1879, of its Vice-President John Ball. A correspondent writing in *The Accountant* said that 'no man better succeeded in combining an inflexible adherence to just principle with that disposition to concede as far as possible, and to allow full consideration to the case of an adversary, which is so sure to win regard'. All the influence and the persuasiveness of the Vice-President had been used in the efforts to reach an accord with the Society of Accountants during the difficult and critical months of negotiation in the first half of 1879. Despite failing health he had driven himself unsparingly until the last. The Council of the Institute passed a resolution in October 1879:

> 'The Council desire to express the deep sorrow with which they received the announcement of the death of the late Vice-President, John Ball, Esq., and to record their grateful recollection of the energy and judgment which he brought to bear in the formation of the Institute. . . . They further wish to express their high appreciation of the ability, integrity and courtesy which made him so generally esteemed. . . .'

The Charter, incorporating into one body nearly all the members of the five separate institutes and societies of accountants which were in existence in 1879, was submitted to the Queen in Council on March 24, 1880, and was approved on that date. A visit to the Continent by Her Majesty delayed the signature of the Order in Council until May 11, 1880. It appears from a comment in *The Accountant* that the delay may have given rise to an unfounded rumour that there had been a hitch in the proceedings. By its terms the new body was entitled The Institute of Chartered Accountants in England and Wales.

Clause 1 of the Charter provided that the first Council of the Chartered Institute should consist of forty-five members; Clause 2 listed the names, and specified those of William Turquand and Robert Palmer Harding as President and Vice-President.

At the date of the Charter the Institute of Accountants had 188 members. It was allotted twenty seats on the Council of the Chartered Institute, including both the Presidency and the Vice-Presidency. The Society of Accountants in England, which had 286 members, was allotted fourteen seats. The Manchester Institute, with 103 members at the date of the Charter, was allotted three seats. Two other Council members from Manchester were Guthrie and Wade, who, as already noted, had joined the Presidents of the five original bodies of accountants in signing and presenting the petition for the Charter. They had not been members of the Manchester Institute but both enjoyed large practices in Manchester, where they had organized the Accountants' Incorporation Association. The Sheffield Institute, with 32 members, and the Liverpool Society, with 29 members, were each allotted three seats on the Council.

The five original bodies of English accountants had 638 members between them at the date of the Charter; of that total, 587 became members of the Institute of Chartered Accountants under the terms of the Charter, and 606 further individuals were admitted by the Council. On January 1, 1882, a year and half after the date of the Charter, the membership had thus risen to 1,193, consisting of 489 Fellows, 512 Associates in practice, 160 Associates not in practice, and 32 Associates not resident in England and Wales.

Public reaction to the Charter was generally favourable. The *Law Times* called it 'a step in the right direction'. There was some opposition based mainly on the fact that length of service in the profession did not necessarily indicate good repute. A correspondent in *The Accountant* said that in almost every town in England there were people describing themselves as accountants who obtained work by 'touting' and other disreputable means. *The Accountant*, in a leading article, agreed that it was impossible to prevent the assumption by quacks and rogues of the designation of accountant but that the public would, for the future, be well advised to employ only the services of members of the Institute of Chartered Accountants and to look for the initials 'F.C.A.' or 'A.C.A.' after their names.

The eighth decade of the nineteenth century is remarkable for the number of inventions and new ideas it brought into being, many destined to have profound influence throughout the world in the years to come. By 1880, for example, the internal combustion engine and the gramophone had begun to make their voices heard and, only a month or two before the Institute received its Charter, the first telephone exchange had been opened in London, with less than ten subscribers. It may be inferred that they had not seen the comment of an eminent scientist, the third Lord Rayleigh, who, on having the new invention demonstrated to him by Alexander Bell, wrote, 'It is truly extraordinary! From the top floor of my house I could distinctly hear Mr Bell who was talking to me from the ground floor. It is a surprising instrument, but I don't suppose it will ever be very useful.'

There is evidence that a similar cautious reservation would have been made by many, both within and outside the accountancy world of that day. Even the stalwarts who had striven, so long and resolutely, successfully to advance their calling to the status of a profession could not have anticipated how important and widespread that new profession was destined, like Lord Rayleigh's 'surprising instrument', to become in less than a generation.

## Chapter Two

# 1880-1890

*The early organization of the Institute, the establishment of standards of professional conduct, and the acquisition of headquarters.*

THE FIRST meeting of the Council of the Institute of Chartered Accountants in England and Wales was held on May 26, 1880. Four members of the Council who had previously been members of the Institute of Accountants were authorized to sign cheques, and W. G. Howgrave was appointed secretary at an annual salary of £400 with a clerk to assist him who was paid 18s a week. The Council took over the offices of the Institute of Accountants at 3 Copthall Buildings and agreed to buy the furniture and library for the sum of £400. In July 1880 it was arranged that the funds of the Institute of Accountants after its affairs had been wound up (which included the repayment of the entrance fee and one year's annual subscription to all living members of the original Institute) should be handed over to the new body to be used for the formation of an adequate library. It was also decided that the sum of 200 guineas should be presented to Messrs Gee & Co. for services rendered by *The Accountant* to the profession, and a like sum to Howgrave for the additional work he had done in connection with the obtaining of the Charter.

A great deal of work was involved at the beginning in dealing with claims for membership, and a number of applicants, whose qualification was found to be inadequate, were rejected. In April 1882, an examination committee was appointed. It recommended annual examinations at preliminary, intermediate and advanced levels and the report was accepted unanimously. The first examinations were held in July 1882, at which five of the thirteen candidates taking the preliminary examination and fifteen of the twenty-five candidates taking the final examination were successful. The Annual Report for 1882 states 'No intermediate exam has yet been held, as only persons who commenced service between May 11th and second week of June 1880, would have been entitled to present themselves in December 1882.' The final examination occupied three days and was divided into six papers covering book-keeping, auditing, the adjustment of partnership and executorship accounts, the rights and duties of liquidators, trustees and receivers, bankruptcy and company law, and mercantile law with the law of arbitration and awards. Candidates were required to define the chief aim and object of a book-keeper; to state the object of a profit and loss account, the nature of the items of which it is composed, on which side such items are recorded, and how the final balance of such an account is disposed of; to describe the accounts that executors should keep; to give a short statement of the duties of a receiver in bankruptcy, to state briefly the rules relating to fraudulent assignments and fraudulent preferences, and to say whether partners, by any form of agreement among themselves, could limit their liability for the debts of their firm to third parties. An opinion was expressed in some quarters that the first examinations held by the Institute had not been sufficiently searching. The standard of the examinations was borne in mind and, at the third Annual General Meeting in 1884, Frederick Whinney (the Vice-President) observed that he had no apology to offer for the alleged stiffness of the examination papers, and candidates who wished to become members of the Institute would be 'obliged to fit themselves for entrance rather more than those who have been with us for some time'.

Settlement of the bye-laws took care and consideration and they were finally approved by the Privy Council in March 1882.

The Council's policy from the beginning was to stamp out advertising and touting for business. A Fellow of the Institute was formally censured in April 1881, for canvassing by means of post-cards for proxies in bankruptcy and liquidation cases, and a committee of the Council was appointed to consider and report upon the question of touting by members of the Institute. The committee reported in November 1881. The secretary of the Institute was authorized, in all cases in which advertisements issued by members of the Institute came under his notice, to communicate with such members and to inform them that the Council considered such advertising to be unprofessional.

In connection with advertising a difficulty arose in the case of some chartered accountants who were secretaries of trade protection associations. They pleaded that they had a duty to promote the interests of their associations by advertising for business. The Council, nevertheless, passed a resolution in March 1882, strongly disapproving of such activities by members of the Institute, and it was made clear that trade protection societies would in future be faced with the necessity either of ceasing to advertise for bankruptcy business, or of ceasing to employ chartered accountants as secretaries or managers. The committee on touting was ordered to keep a constant and vigorous watch on every aspect of that question.

Although officially abolished, advertising continued, and in 1887 the President drew attention to a number of cases where members had used circulars or space in the Press, and said it was essential that such practices should cease. In spite of the risk that the penalties provided by the Charter would be put into operation, the problem remained and it was over twenty years before the practice entirely died out.

In domestic matters there was criticism of the composition of the Council. It was advanced that the affairs of the Institute were being handled by too small and privileged a circle, and at the second Annual General Meeting in 1883 a motion was proposed to prevent any firm of accountants from being represented by more than one member on the Council. It was pointed out on behalf of the Council that the three vacancies which had occurred in 1882–3 had been filled by accountants from Bristol, Manchester and Newcastle upon Tyne. The question remained a contentious one and in 1889 *The Accountant* questioned the stability of the Institute in view of the lack of proportion in representation, stating that Sheffield was over-represented and Manchester under-represented on the Council.

The Council was also criticized on the ground that London interests took precedence over local interests and it was urged to encourage the formation of branches of the Institute in important towns. There was also a demand for an autumn meeting of members of the Institute outside London. Such a meeting was arranged at Manchester in 1886 and the next at Birmingham in 1888. Both meetings were felt to be successes and the policy of holding them regularly was established. The members were received by the Mayor at Manchester and the Mayor elect at Birmingham and the President of the Institute gave an address. This was followed by papers on topical matters. At Manchester Frederick Whinney, the President, took as his subject 'The Origin, Purpose and Future of the Institute'. The papers that followed dealt with 'Corporation Accounts', 'Our Status and Obligations', 'Chartered Accountants as auditors of Companies' and 'Insolvency'. In 1888 the address of the President, William Deloitte, centred on the enhanced position of the profession of accountancy in England, which he attributed to the 'vast expansion of the commerce of the country and the appreciation by the public of the services of the profession'. He stated that business arising out of the Companies Act had become of such importance that a permanent committee of the Council had been set up to watch all legislative proposals on the subject. In the afternoon Frederick Whinney gave a paper on the Companies Act in which he argued that auditors were not responsible for the accounts which they checked, that they were totally independent of directors, and that it was improper for the directors to require them to report in any particular way.

*The Accountant* was often critical of the Council. In order to placate members it was decided, in July 1883, that a summary of the proceedings of the Council should be inserted in *The Accountant*, but the Council continued to be attacked frequently in that journal on the ground that its policy was not sufficiently democratic. In February 1885, *The Accountant* suggested that the Council was taking too narrow and exclusive a view of the interests of the profession as a whole, and that it was too much afraid of lowering the status of the profession to take adequate account of the plight of the small men after the loss of so much insolvency business. *The Accountant* considered that the illiberal policy of the Council was responsible for the formation on February 11, 1885, of the Society of Accountants and Auditors, 'to fill', as its chairman, C. E. Trotter, affirmed, 'a void that the existing Institute does not fill'. One of the Society's declared aims was 'the protection of the interests of accountants, accountants' clerks, efficient book-keepers, and others who are not members of the Institute of Chartered Accountants'. It was perhaps not surprising that a request from the proprietors of the paper that the Council should assist them to obtain a larger circulation was rejected in April 1885, the Council giving as its opinion that it did not approve of the way in which the paper was conducted.

In 1886, it was announced that a Chartered Accountants' Benevolent Association had been formed and that 139 members had promised support. The first report of the Association was published in 1887, and the President stated that it had been authorized to use the services of the secretary and clerks of the Institute. In the same report he referred to the Students' Society in London, founded in 1883, which was in a flourishing condition, and stated that a students' library and reading room had been opened in Manchester.

A sustained effort was made in the period 1880 to 1890 to acquire premises suitable as a headquarters. In 1880 the headquarters consisted of the offices at 3 Copthall Buildings held on lease, and a committee to consider plans for more suitable premises was set up almost immediately. This was not announced at the first Annual General Meeting as the Council had had to face some criticism of extravagance. However, at the next Annual General Meeting in 1883, the President stated that a plan to purchase or rent a site for the erection of a hall was under consideration. This statement was amplified in 1884, when it was explained that the retention of the offices at 3 Copthall Buildings after June 1885 was not recommended because better accommodation was necessary. The members were promised that they would be consulted before a large sum of money was spent on new offices. At the sixth Annual General Meeting in 1887, the President, Frederick Whinney, reported that a site had been found in Moorgate Place and that a provisional agreement had been signed subject to confirmation by members of the Institute. A special meeting was held in July 1888, when William Deloitte put the motion to approve the acquisition of the site at Moorgate Place on a 999 years lease at a ground rent of £900 per annum. It was carried by a large majority.

Six architects were asked to submit competitive designs for a hall and offices, and the design submitted by John Belcher, F.R.I.B.A., was judged the best. It was estimated to cost £17,250 and the Council commissioned Hamo Thornycroft, R.A., to execute a sculptured frieze at an additional cost of £3,000. At a special general meeting held in August 1889, the Council's action in putting the work out to tender was sanctioned. The lowest tender received was £22,996, and in view of the cost of the sculptured frieze, architect's fees and other items, a total sum of £32,000 was approved. Delay occurred, however, because a receiving order was made against the contractors and it was necessary to engage a new firm, Messrs Colls & Sons. The terms of the lease were altered by the reduction of the ground rent to £472 for twenty years and £786 thereafter in return for the surrender of part of the site required for widening Great Swan Alley. This caused no hindrance, having been foreseen in the original plans. The foundation stone was laid by J. J. Saffrey in July 1890. Under the stone a jar was placed containing the current issues of *The Times* and *The Accountant*, a copy of the Charter and the Bye-laws, a list of members and a specimen of each of the current silver and copper coins of the realm. By a curious sense of economy specimens of the gold coins were omitted. At a social meeting held after the ceremony *The Accountant* remarked 'it was a pleasant sight to watch the President and ex-President and members of the Council hobnobbing with more ordinary Fellows and Associates'. It declared also, with truth, that the laying of the stone was:

> 'the actual and visible embodiment of the astonishing growth of a profession, young, but already of commanding power, and capable of practically unlimited extension.'

The building was completed in May 1893.

The Council continued to keep watch on commercial legislation affecting the profession, which meant at that time largely legislation affecting bankruptcy.

At the second meeting of the new Council, held in June 1880, a committee was appointed to watch the progress of a new Bankruptcy Bill which was being proposed, and it suggested to the promoters of the Bill that no one should be appointed as a professional trustee unless he were a chartered accountant. The suggestion was not accepted, but the views of the Institute were submitted to the Board of Trade, and Joseph Chamberlain, its President, who introduced the Bill into Parliament, received deputations from the Council of the Institute on a number of occasions. As a result many alterations which the Council advocated were incorporated in the Bill, and after it became law in 1883 the Council was afforded full opportunity to consider the draft of the Bankruptcy Rules and Regulations. Many of the suggestions and alterations which it proposed were adopted by the Board of Trade. One of the members of the committee appointed by the Council was Arthur Cooper, President in 1883, who took a great deal of trouble to secure amendments to the Bill, and a lawsuit to which he was party at that time – Titterton v. Cooper – resulted in the establishment of an important principle. Arthur Cooper was the trustee of a bankrupt who had pledged a lease to a creditor. As the law then stood the trustee could not disclaim the lease without injuring the creditor with whom it was pledged. The landlord sued the trustee for rent and dilapidations, and the trustee was held personally liable. Arthur Cooper brought the position to the notice of the Board of Trade and, although the Bankruptcy Bill had then already passed the Commons, Chamberlain arranged for an amendment to be added by the House of Lords to enable a trustee, with the leave of the Court, to disclaim his interest. In making a report in 1884, Frederick Whinney said that the President of the Board of Trade had been extremely helpful while the Bankruptcy Act was passing through Parliament, and he claimed that the Council's efforts had 'prevented the whole business of . . . winding up bankrupts' estates being taken away from accountants'. The Bankruptcy Act was avowedly experimental, its operation was being carefully watched and if it was found to be defective there was reason to believe that its defects would be remedied by Parliament.

At the seventh Annual General Meeting, held in 1888, Whinney reported that bankruptcy matters had again occupied much of the Council's time and attention, and that a complaint had been addressed to the President of the Board of Trade on the subject of the employment of solicitors and others to prepare debtors' statements of affairs. The Minister had been informed that such statements presupposed an expert knowledge of book-keeping and accounts, which solicitors were unlikely to possess, and that statements prepared without that knowledge often gave a totally inadequate view of the true state of a bankrupt's estate. The Council had asked that 'for the future, none but persons who from their profession and training might be competent to prepare such accounts should be employed to assist debtors for such purpose'. In 1890 the President, J. J. Saffery, said that the Council was endeavouring to obtain amendments to a Bill which would have the effect of altering the Bankruptcy Act of 1883. If the new Bill became law the position of non-official receivers in bankruptcy would be made much more difficult. The Council had also given careful consideration to the Companies (Winding-Up) Bill which the Government had introduced. The effect of that Bill would be to place liquidators under the control of the Board of Trade, and to permit officials to become liquidators of companies. The Council was endeavouring to obtain important amendments to the Bill.

The Council was also greatly concerned with the proposal to transfer the audit of municipal corporation accounts from elected auditors to district auditors. It reported in 1888 that it had proposed that the Local Government Bill constituting the County Councils should contain a clause that all such accounts should be audited 'only by properly qualified accountants'. In the following year it reported that it had failed to persuade the President of the Local Government Board to accept the amendment.

A picture of the growing importance of chartered accountants was given by the President, Frederick Whinney, in 1887, at a meeting held in honour of Queen Victoria's Jubilee. He pointed out the vast amount of work that had come to them not only from the Winding-Up Act of 1849 but also from the succession of Companies Acts. While admitting that accountants could not regard themselves 'as on a line with the old professions', he added: 'But I think we have a perfect right to say that the exigencies of modern life have called into existence certain semi-professions of which we form one, and that not the least distinguished.' He went on to predict that 'as our commercial affairs grow, and they have the tendency to become more complicated, honest and able men, who are skilled not only in accounts but also in commercial questions, will continue to flourish and increase, and that there is a great future for the profession of commercial accountants'.

The increase in numbers of chartered accountants was very striking. The Institute began with 587 members in 1880. The number had grown to 1,678 in 1890. It was not only that work was waiting to be done, but there was a prestige attached to the qualification of chartered accountants known to every well-informed person. They were regarded as experts, their service as arbitrators was in demand and their opinions were respected by Judges.

A great part had been played by the Presidents and members of the Council. It was no easy task to weld a body of practitioners of different levels of education and skill into a professional body, but it could be said that by 1890 the Institute was important commercially and held in respect by government officials. In the period 1880 to 1890 there were six Presidents, starting with William Turquand who had been one of the original members of the 1870 committee, and including Frederick Whinney who was held in such esteem that he was elected to serve four terms in office.

Before leaving the 'eighties some reference should be made to a movement which, although it was of Scottish origin and was destined to fail, aroused interest in the profession south of the Border during several years.

In February 1884, *The Accountant* recorded that the Scottish Institute of Accountants – a body which had been formed in 1880 with the same objects as the Society of Accountants and Auditors and subsequently became the Scottish branch of that Society whilst retaining its own name – had applied for a charter. When the application was gazetted in March, *The Accountant* observed that it would 'probably be a pure matter of form', which implies at least a not unfavourable reaction to the request in London. At a General Meeting of the new English and Welsh Institute on March 4, 1885, D. G. Hoey, who was a member of that Institute and was also secretary of the said Scottish Institute, addressed the meeting. In the course of his speech he said that, in England, with their great national organization, the profession was far in advance of Scotland. This belief cannot have endeared him to the members of the three Scottish chartered societies, but *The Accountant* discussed the movement in two lengthy articles following the meeting. After noting that 'their desire is to found a national Institute for Scotland, just as in England and Wales', the articles went on 'Many members of the Scottish Institute are original members of the English Institute and indeed continue to express regret that it does not embrace all the members of the profession in the United Kingdom. We cannot but echo this regret.'

For the next few years references are few but they indicate the determined opposition which, in Scotland, the Scottish Institute was facing. Early in 1889 *The Accountant* warned its readers that 'Unless the three chartered bodies and the new Institute are agreed no national charter will be obtained.' This implies that the Societies of Edinburgh, Glasgow and Aberdeen were all unwilling to unite nationally, but the members of the last named may have changed their views, because the final notice for the movement, which appeared in *The Accountant* of July 26, 1890, reads: 'We understand that the Society known as The Institute of Scottish Accountants, which lately applied to the Privy Council for a Royal Charter, has been defeated in that respect by the Institutes of Chartered Accountants of Edinburgh and Glasgow.'

Over sixty years were to pass before the profession in Scotland became united in a national Institute, but the scanty evidence now available proves the existence of many accountants in the United

Kingdom, even in those earliest years, who looked ahead, dissatisfied with regional restrictions within the Kingdom.

In the meantime the social side of professional life was not neglected and the Chartered Accountants' Dining Club was founded as early as 1888. It rapidly grew in numbers, the hundred mark being passed early in 1891. Membership is limited to 150 practising members of the Institute, in addition to any Council members who 'shall signify their wish to become members of the Club'. In one important respect the Club was in advance of its time. From the earliest days an absolute ban on after-dinner oratory was imposed and has remained an inflexible, although unwritten, rule ever since. It is reasonably certain that this rule contributed greatly to the success, immediately established and continuously maintained, of the Club. Of the rules, which are few, a written one reads oddly today: 'No dice or game of hazard shall on any account be permitted nor shall any higher stake at whist than one shilling points be played for.' There is no record that this rule has ever been invoked but it does, by its existence, shed some light on the habits of the time – as also does a copy of the menu, reproduced opposite, of one of the Club dinners at the old Monico Restaurant in 1898, at a cost of 12s 6d per head inclusive of wines, coffee and cigars.

For the first thirty years no lady guests were entertained but, since the 'twenties, special 'Ladies' Nights' have been successfully held at intervals. Lady members of the Institute have also since 1945 had their own Women Chartered Accountants' Dining Society. The President of the Institute and other favoured individuals are on occasion privileged to be guests with their wives and, unlike the men's Club, the women's Society allows speeches.

Apart from dining, several other very successful clubs for activities such as golf, rugby football and hockey have been established in London and in provincial centres, with intent to keep members together on a social and athletic basis. Perhaps special reference should be made to the Chartered Accountants' Golfing Society formed in 1898 and still 'going strong'. Cups for its various meetings have been presented by past presidents – Turquand, Young, Ernest Cooper and A. O. Miles; and two past

# CHARTERED ✦ ACCOUNTANTS DINING CLUB.

*PRESIDENT* - - FREDERICK WHINNEY, Esq.

*Tuesday, November 1st, 1898.*

## Menu.

Hors-d'œuvre variés

Consommé Marquise    Bisque d'écrevisses

Turbot au court bouillon, sauce Sauterne

Eperlans Colbert

Ris de veau Soubeyrand

Chartreuse de foie gras

PUNCH à la PRUNELLE

Carré de pré sale bouquetière

Faisan à la broche
Salade

Celeri à la moelle

Gâteaux mon plaisir

Sujet de glace à la Monico

Petits fours

DESSERT.

*AFTER dinner Mr. FREDERIC UPTON will give some humourous sketches.*

"The Monico." Egyptian Saloon.

PRINTED ON THE PREMISES. G.C.N. 4108

Entertainments at which we have never assisted: 'Balancing the Books' at the Annual Dinner of the Society of Chartered Accountants. By George Morrow. *Reproduced by permission of Punch.* 1931.

presidents also have been captains of the Society, Clare Smith and D. V. House.

It is interesting to reflect what office work and conditions were like, particularly in an accountant's office, in these early days of the Institute and indeed earlier. Some pen-pictures of this may be gleaned from the details and anecdotes of the old-established firms whose histories are recorded later in Section II: no taxis or cars, but instead open-top horse buses and four-wheeler or hansom cabs with the proverbial comments and language of their drivers, and for many a member a ride on horseback to the office; no telephones or electric light; no typewriters and no typists – indeed the very thought of women in the office was anathema to most of the old die-hards till a much later date; steel pens only just replacing the quill, and handwriting, an art seldom seen today; the letter press the only means of copying letters, and many members still in practice remember that their early duties included the swinging of those heavy screw tops; the background of audits largely the tick, and they were no doubt conducted with a solemnity in keeping with the top hats that many, even of the juniors, were required to wear on visiting a client's office; the size of fees an insult by present standards, but the rates of income tax a dream.

## Chapter Three

# 1890-1914

*The growth of the influence of the Institute on commercial legislation and public affairs. Attempts to unify the profession.*

THE PERIOD 1890 to 1914 saw chartered accountants recognized as having a well-established place in the national economy. This was perceived early in the period by J. J. Saffery who, presiding at the Annual General Meeting in 1891, said, 'We are recognized now in ways in which we were never recognized or referred to before,' and two years later by Edwin Waterhouse, who stated, 'The duties and responsibilities of our profession, more especially as auditors, are as yet hardly appreciated even by the commercial world. . . . The vast extension of joint stock enterprise consequent on the legislation of 1862 not only produced an immense increase in the volume of business done, but brought about new methods of business. . . . The use of our Institute as an informal court of appeal on questions of principle arising not only in audits, but in the method of stating assets and liabilities, and of drawing up statements, is daily becoming more evident. . . . Our Institute was designed, and our Charter was granted us, for the purpose of providing the education necessary to qualify our members for their responsible duties.' The legal profession accepted them at least in after-dinner speeches. Judge Snagge said at a dinner given by the Council in 1894 that the Institute had 'found the accountants of England a scattered host, and had made them into an organized army, trained, disciplined, drilled, and banded together to do battle for the great principle of commercial and financial integrity in this country, while preserving the thorough efficiency and the unsullied character of a great and growing profession'. Two years later at the autumn meeting of the Institute at Sheffield the

Recorder said that no society had 'worked so much good and given so much valuable assistance to the legal profession as the Institute of Chartered Accountants'.

The Council felt it to be imperative to keep watch over legislation affecting commercial interests and it showed increasing activity in tendering advice. One of its objects was the necessity, as it thought, to fight officialdom. The views generally held were that expansion of commerce rested on individual freedom; those engaged in the work understood the problems; and properly qualified accountants experienced in general auditing were superior to Civil Service auditors. It was largely on this ground that the Council approached the Bill later enacted as the Bankruptcy Act of 1890. In its original form it was regarded as giving rise to an increase of official interference. The Council's suggestions, which effected many alterations in the original draft, resulted in legislation which was regarded as a great improvement on the Act of 1883. At the Annual General Meeting of 1893 the President, Edwin Waterhouse, made a point of the continued 'interference of the State in the management of private business', and in the following year the then President, C. Fitch Kemp, referring to the Board of Trade and bankruptcy administration said, 'Our contention is that it is impossible for a great public department to satisfactorily administer the affairs of public companies.' In his speech in 1896 he was able to say, 'I may refer, I will not say with exultation – for Heaven forbid that any of us should exult over the misfortunes of others – but at all events I will say this, that it is a legitimate ground of remark that the Board of Trade have not been successful in making their bankruptcy department pay. I believe firmly and strongly that accountants with their vast amount of practical experience connected with the administration of failed estates, can afford to carry out the administration of estates on terms which ought to shut the Board of Trade out from any competition with yourselves.'

A fundamental reason for the increase in the importance of chartered accountants was the growth in the number of limited liability companies. Limited liability had been established in 1855, and now in the commercial and industrial field the days of partnerships, with partners conducting their own businesses, were beginning to disappear, their place being taken by businesses owned by shareholders and managed by directors, both alike being fluctuating bodies. The statistics are revealing. It is estimated that in 1880 there were 6,300 limited companies with a total capital of £380,000,000; in 1900 the comparable figures were 29,730 companies with an aggregate capital of £1,622,000,000. One result of this change was that the services of experts, including those of members of the Institute, were in constant demand. Undoubtedly the most significant piece of legislation from the Council's point of view was the Companies Act of 1900. Its importance to the profession was that it required every limited company to appoint an auditor and gave the auditor statutory rights, including the right of access to books and papers and the right to require directors and officers to supply information and give explanations. These terms were repeated in the Companies (Consolidation) Act of 1908, which, also closely watched by the Council, was intended to codify the law, sixteen amending Acts having been passed between 1862 and 1908. The concept of the private company had also been introduced. A company's auditor was required to report to the shareholders whether the balance sheet was properly drawn up and true as shown by the books and the information provided. The requirement that an auditor should be appointed by every company had less value to the shareholders than appeared on the surface. His report could be appended to the balance sheet or referred to in it, and it was possible to obey the letter of the law whilst preventing shareholders from knowing that an adverse report had been given; nevertheless the requirement was a considerable advance and brought increased work and responsibility to the profession.

As an example of the way shareholders might be misled a member recalls that as a young man in those days he did the audit of a notorious company whose chairman subsequently had a holiday at His Majesty's expense. The audit report was a 'stinker', and according to the company's articles it did not have to be circulated but had to be read at the annual meeting. The member was sent to see this done and rather sensed that the packed room contained several queer characters. When the chairman called upon the secretary to read the audit report, these gentlemen got up and in loud voices asked all manner of irrelevant questions. The audit report was duly read and no one heard a word of it. Such practices were, however, exceptional.

The position of chartered accountants as auditors and advisers having become generally recognized, industrial concerns realized more and more that their professional training fitted them also to play a valuable part in management. Accordingly they were appointed in growing numbers to the post of secretary or accountant of companies, a trend that has gathered momentum during the intervening years and shows no signs of falling off.

Much time and attention were given by the Council to the Companies (Winding-up) Act of 1890, in connection with which the Board of Trade promulgated a set of rules which was regarded as very onerous. The Council was able to announce in 1892 that new rules had been authorized which were to a great extent in accordance with its views. In 1893 it was reported that Bills relating to building societies were being watched; forms of account had been drawn up and the Council had suggested that the accounts of such societies should be audited by qualified accountants. It unfortunately failed to secure an amendment to the audit section of the Education Act 1902 in favour of professional accountants. That section provided that the income and expenditure of Borough Councils so far as it related to the Act should be audited by auditors of the Local Government Board. The question arose with special force in relation to local government audits. A committee appointed by the Local Government Board recommended in 1903 that the existing system of audits applicable to Corporations, County Councils and Urban District Councils in England and Wales should be abolished and that the audits should be conducted by selected members of the Institute of Chartered Accountants or the Incorporated Society of Accountants and Auditors.

In 1905 the Council was watching the False Statements (Companies) Bill and the Public Trustee and Executor Bill, both of which were before Parliament, and in 1906 the Limited Partnership Bill and the Prevention of Corruption Bill. When the Public Trustee Act became law it submitted to the Lord Chancellor amendments to the draft rules for carrying into effect the objects of the Act. Certain of the suggested amendments were incorporated in the Limited Partnership Bill which was passed in 1907.

In addition individual chartered accountants came into public notice by their achievements in public affairs. John George Griffiths, who had investigated the Egyptian debt problem prior to 1882, acted for many years as joint honorary secretary of the King Edward's Hospital Fund for London and designed a standard system of hospital accounting. He served for forty-two years on the Council of the Institute. Edwin Waterhouse was appointed to the committee which framed the Companies Act of 1900. He and Frederick Whinney were asked to report on the accounts of the Ordnance Department. At a dinner given by the Council in 1894 Lord Randolph Churchill pointed out that they had taken only four months to complete their 'lucid and valuable' report and all their recommendations had been adopted. William Plender acted for the Metropolitan Water Board in 1903 in connection with the acquisition of the property of the London Water Companies. At the Annual General Meeting in 1906 it was reported that John Gane was serving on a committee of the Local Government Board which was inquiring into the system of local government accountancy, that W. B. Peat was serving on a committee appointed by the Board of Trade to inquire into the laws relating to insolvent estates, and that Edwin Waterhouse was a member of another committee set up by the Board of Trade to study the working of the Companies Acts. In 1908 William Plender assisted in the establishment of the Port of London Authority. In 1911 he was appointed a member of the committee set up to inquire into Irish finance and also of the Advisory Committee of the National Health Insurance Commission. Walter Knox was appointed to help in the investigation of the accounts of David Lloyd George and Sir Rufus Isaacs in the notorious 'Marconi' case. These are a few examples of the reliance coming to be placed on chartered accountants for skilled advice in public matters, and it is noteworthy that in 1902 the Institute was for a period appointed the examining body in book-keeping of candidates applying for higher division clerkships in the Inland Revenue Department.

A very important problem which occupied the Council and members during this period was that of registration of accountants in order to bring the profession into line with older professions such as those of law and medicine. When the Charter was granted in 1880 it was believed that all possible steps had been taken to combine accountants belonging to reputable bodies and to abolish competition. The formation of the Society of Accountants and Auditors in 1885 negatived that belief, and addressing the Annual General Meeting in 1892 the President, T. A. Welton, had accepted the position in his remark, 'I presume that a body so solid as ours must not think it surprising that it has a shadow; but I think if anyone will get out statistics showing the audits held by our members and by those of the other Society, the contrast will be found to be very great.' The great difficulty which had to be faced in any combination with that Society was that it admitted to membership persons who would not have been admissible to membership of the Institute. It became apparent that it was impossible to fulfil the hope which had been expressed by the President, J. J. Saffery, at the Autumn Meeting of 1890, namely 'The time is not distant when a clause will find its way into every Act of Parliament enacting that in any and every case when the appointment of a public auditor, liquidator, trustee or receiver is required, that official shall be a chartered accountant, so that confidence in his training, experience, position, ability, and integrity may be assured to those whose interests are at stake.'

The first steps were reported to the Annual General Meeting held in May 1893. Edwin Waterhouse explained that a draft Bill had been prepared with the object of securing the public registration of members of the Institute and of excluding unqualified persons from practising as public accountants, and that the Law and Parliamentary Committee under the chairmanship of Frederick

Whinney was working energetically to secure this result. It was recognized by the Council that 'as a condition of registration we should be required to open our doors, for the moment, to all other practitioners who might be held properly qualified, such as the practising members of the Society of Accountants and Auditors – a body to some extent competing with ourselves, and attracting within its membership some who, under our bye-laws, could not be admitted into the Institute'. The President said that the Society had drafted a Bill of its own and the position was that both Bills were before the House of Commons, and if they passed their second readings they would be referred together to the same Select Committee. In conclusion Waterhouse said that the matter could be fully discussed at a Special General Meeting to be held a fortnight later.

At the Special General Meeting the President stated that every effort had been made to reach agreement with the Society of Accountants and Auditors but that negotiations had broken down. The suggestion of the Institute was that members of the Society who were properly qualified, and who could show that they had been in practice for two years or more, should become members of the Institute. Waterhouse concluded 'if restrictive legislation is to be obtained, the Society of Accountants and Auditors must be provided for. We feel that this Society, which was not in existence when the Institute obtained its Charter, is a growing body, and that the longer legislation of this nature is delayed, the greater will be the difficulty for the future.'

He was followed by Frederick Whinney who recalled that the Institute had been formed 'to elevate the whole body of accountants' and said that it was not 'for the good of accountancy as a profession that there should be two bodies existing in the City of London, both of which represent accountants'. He urged that it would be impossible to obtain the approval of Parliament to the proposed draft Bill unless it covered all who were practising efficiently as public accountants, and that meant including members of the Society.

After a long debate it was resolved:

(1) That it is desirable to promote legislation which shall restrict public accountancy to existing and future chartered accountants;

(2) that if restriction cannot be obtained, then it is desirable to legislate to protect our title of 'chartered accountant';

(3) that it is desirable, with a view to the above legislation, that arrangements be made with the existing societies of accountants;

(4) that having regard to the foregoing resolutions, this meeting approves of the Council taking legislative action in the direction indicated.

Accordingly, on May 30, 1893, the Council resolved that its draft Bill should be withdrawn, conditionally on the draft Bill prepared by the Society of Accountants and Auditors being withdrawn also; and that a joint Bill should be drafted in agreement with the Society.

At the following Annual General Meeting held in May 1894, the Council reported without comment that it had proved impossible to reach agreement with the Society regarding a joint Bill and that the matter had been dropped for the time being.

In 1895 the Council reported that it had been arranged to introduce a Bill into Parliament for the purpose of establishing a register and protecting the title of chartered accountant. The problem of men who called themselves chartered accountants without being members of the Institute had a habit of cropping up. In the same year the Council secured an injunction from the High Court to restrain a non-member from describing himself as a chartered accountant, and in 1899 it secured similar injunctions against two non-members. It proved impossible, however, to obtain the consent of Parliament to permit the Bill to go forward.

The question of organizing the profession was reopened in 1897 at a Special General Meeting attended by some 300 members. Proposals were placed before the meeting based on the resolutions carried in May 1893, the President, G. W. Knox, stating that the Council was itself divided. There were certain new features in the draft Bill, namely:

(1) All existing members of the Society of Accountants and Auditors in practice should be placed upon the Register and they should become members of the Institute upon payment of half the usual entrance fee.

(2) All persons who could satisfy the Council that they had been in business as accountants for the whole of the three years immediately preceding January 1, 1897, should be entitled to registration as members of the Institute.

(3) A person who had not been in practice for three years on that date would be entitled to practise without being registered and without being challenged, until January 1, 1908, and would become entitled to registration after he had been in practice for ten years, if three-fourths of the Council of the Institute voted in his favour.

(4) The admission to the Institute of other members of the Society by categories and subject to conditions.

These proposals in effect amounted to the amalgamation of the two bodies.

Frederick Whinney spoke strongly in favour, and urged the necessity of the leading body of accountants taking the initiative. He was opposed by Ernest Cooper who stated that he regarded the proposed legislation as unnecessary. He said that he was sorry to find himself in conflict with his old friend, but he could not understand Whinney's statement that legislation might be forced upon the Institute if it failed to take the initiative. He saw no evidence of any public demand for such legislation; nothing had appeared about it in the Press and he thought that Whinney was utterly mistaken in suggesting that there was need for legislation of any kind. Most speeches were against the Bill and the result of a postal ballot was 1,046 against and 613 in favour.

In 1898 a Bill was placed before Parliament by the Scottish Institute of Accountants. The object of the Bill was to place all professional accountants practising in the United Kingdom on a common register and to constitute a central authority. The effect would have been to place the representatives of the Institute (in England and Wales) in a minority and the Council was therefore opposed to it. In 1899 it reported its opposition to a Bill introduced by the Scottish Chartered bodies, which placed no restrictions on Scottish Chartered Accountants who decided to practise in England but required English Chartered Accountants who decided to practise in Scotland to pass an examination in Scottish Law. At the Annual General Meeting held in 1900 a new Bill sponsored by the Society was reported as being vigorously opposed by the Council.

The problem of organizing the profession in general was referred to by the President, W. N. Fisher, in 1902 when he said it was necessary 'to try to secure a legal and governing recognition by Act of Parliament of our professional standing and status, defining our rights and responsibilities on the same lines as the legal and medical professions. This can only be done by working hand in hand with our Scotch and Irish friends, and it must also be in a spirit of generosity, fairness, and consideration for the claims of practising accountants other than chartered accountants. I believe the longer we defer moving in the direction I am advocating, the greater will be the difficulties to surmount.' At the same meeting Frederick Whinney said, 'Not so long ago there was an institute, so-called, in the Isle of Man. Its members described themselves as "chartered accountants". Men who went over to the Isle of Man became members of that institute, returned to this country, and dubbed themselves "chartered accountants". That is altogether wrong. . . .' The question was assuming an urgency because of the number of practising accountants. There were approximately 4,000 in England and Wales of whom 2,700 were chartered accountants. The debate sprang into life again in 1907 when the President, W. B. Peat, advocated registration. He argued that the exclusive policy pursued by the Institute since its foundation was becoming an anachronism, and that steps should be taken to cooperate with the other bodies of accountants so long as they adhered to reasonable standards of qualification, for the purpose 'of promoting registration for the profession'. He made no attempt to minimize the difficulties, and he pointed out that registration in itself could not be 'a panacea for all evils'.

In 1908 negotiations with the Society of Incorporated Accountants and Auditors (the new name of the Society) were reported. A draft Bill was laid before the members in 1909 and the discussion was led by W. B. Peat. He argued that so long as chartered accountants retained their distinctive title, they had little to lose from legislation which would subject other accountants to discipline and accord them a recognition which had hitherto been withheld. The status of the profession would be enhanced, and chartered accountants would remain the cream of the profession. The fact that there was no serious opposition to the proposed Bill was attributed to the force and persuasiveness of Peat's speech. He also carried the meeting in regard to clause 17 which provided for the admission of women, a clause which was advocated by Winston Churchill, then President of the Board of Trade. In 1910, however, the Council had to report the withdrawal of the Bill after opposition in the House of Lords. It was stated to be undergoing remodelling and no further information was given, but it was resubmitted with amendments in 1911 and was then stated to have been read a second time in the House of Lords. This time, however, it was blocked in the House of Commons, and in 1913 the Council reported to the Annual General Meeting that the Bill had not been reintroduced into Parliament owing to the congested state of public business.

In fact enthusiasm for registration was decreasing. William Plender, the President, said in 1911 that the members of the Institute could not expect to gain anything directly, since their status and financial position were unassailable, and that the sole reason for the Bill was the protection of the public. According to statistics given at the Autumn Meeting in 1913, fifty-nine out of every sixty public companies which submitted their accounts to professional auditors employed some member or members of the Institute. The life dropped out of the issue so far as the Institute was concerned for the following thirty years.

Great care was taken to encourage and support the provincial societies of the Institute. The dates of the formation of these societies and other details are given in Section 2. It was appreciated that the Institute derived much of its strength from the *esprit de corps* of members of local societies. Financial grants were made for their administration, to their libraries (in which the Council reported that it had renounced its proprietary interest in 1899) and to students' societies. The policy of holding autumn meetings in the provinces was maintained. The procedure was for the local society to arrange for the members to be welcomed by a man of standing associated with their district and to give a dinner at which their own President took the chair. The President of the Institute gave a speech in which he made a statement of policy, and eminent members read papers on matters of interest. The meeting included social activities such as visits to places of interest in the neighbourhood.

In this connection it should be mentioned that criticism continued regarding the composition of the Council. At the Annual General Meeting held in 1901, a member protested against the practice of the Council of filling vacancies in its membership without reference to the wishes of members attending the meeting. The reply given was that the method suggested by the objector was likely to result in the representation of London at the expense of the provinces, and the policy of the Council was to try to secure the services of the best available members and to have regard to a balanced representation of provincial centres. This statement was amplified at the Annual General Meeting held in 1908, when the President said that when a vacancy occurred, if a local society existed in the district where the former member had practised, its views were invariably ascertained.

The maintenance of discipline with a view to preserving a professional standard was carefully watched. Advertising had been officially abolished in 1882, but it still appeared in indirect forms and once again in connection with trade protection societies. In 1902, the President reported that the Council had been making inquiries into the connection between certain members of the Institute and a particular trade protection society. It had been found that no such society existed and it was only a means of canvassing for business. The Council laid it down that a professional connection between a member and a trade protection society was only permissible in circumstances where the society was controlled by an independent committee representing the trade interests it purported to protect. The matter of advertising was referred to by the President in 1911, when he said that the Council would have to consider making greater use of the penalties provided by the Charter if complaints of advertising were found to be justified. In 1899–1900 it had been found necessary to expel six members for professional misconduct, and there was great regret when in the following year two members of the Institute who had been auditors of Dumbell's Bank in the Isle of Man were imprisoned for misconduct in connection with the audit.

A special method of assisting members was announced in 1892, when the Council decided to offer financial assistance to certain members who were engaged in four complicated, important and expensive test cases which had come before the courts in regard to trusteeships and liquidations; and in 1895 the President stated that where it was desirable in the interest of the profession it was the policy of the Council to assist members financially in test cases. At the same time the Council was opposed to the idea of promulgating fixed rules for the guidance of members in conducting audits because circumstances varied too greatly. The President, C. Fitch Kemp, had stated at the Autumn Meeting held in 1894 that in his opinion, which agreed with that of his friend, Edwin Waterhouse, 'examined and found correct' was as satisfactory a certificate as an auditor could possibly give, provided it was given by a person of integrity.

The increase and the widespread nature of commerce made the position of accountants in the Dominions and Colonies of great importance to the Institute. The President said in 1904 that English capital was being poured into every quarter of the globe, and wherever capital went chartered accountants followed. In general terms members of the Institute desired to be as free to practise in the Colonies as in the United Kingdom. However, Dominion and Colonial legislation were not in accord and the problem was one which frequently occupied the Council. In 1904 it was stated that the Institute was prepared to assist in every possible way the establishment or extension of the work of overseas institutes or societies of chartered accountants, if they could prove that they had reached a standard equivalent to the English Institute. At the Annual General Meeting held in 1907, the President, W. B. Peat, emphasized that members of the Institute ought to be free to establish themselves in the Dominions and Colonies and in general to exercise throughout the Empire the functions which they exercised in the mother country. In order to carry out its policy the Council appointed solicitors in the more important Colonies to watch the interests of members. It was able to report in 1910 that amendments proposed by the Institute had been incorporated in an Act for the registration of accountants in Natal, and that an association of chartered accountants had been formed by members of the Institute in the Straits Settlements (Malaya). In 1911, however, it had to report its failure to persuade the legislature of Ontario, Canada, to incorporate amendments suggested by the Institute in an Act recently passed to amend the Chartered Accountants Act of 1883. In this case the title 'chartered accountant' was derived from the provincial legislature and not from a Royal Charter. It was also reported that the terms of a Registration of Accountants Bill in Canada, which was about to be promoted, were being studied by the Council. In the following years steps were taken to protect the interest of members in their capacity as auditors of public companies in India.

The Institute was also active at international conferences. In 1905 F. W. Pixley represented the Institute at the International Congress of Accountants at St Louis, USA, organized by the Federation of Societies of Public Accountants in the United States. In 1909 the report included a statement that the President, John Ball – nephew of the John Ball who had been so instrumental in the founding of the Institute – and William Plender had been the representatives of the Institute at a congress of Accountants held at Atlantic City, New Jersey, USA, to celebrate the twenty-first anniversary of the American Association of Public Accountants. At the Annual General Meeting held in 1913 it was reported that H. Woodburn Kirby had represented the Institute at the twenty-fifth anniversary of the same body in Chicago.

There were certain alterations to the bye-laws during this period concerned with the terms of admission and allowing some elasticity as regards qualifications. In 1891 it was announced that the bye-laws had been revised to allow candidates who had been in practice or in service prior to March 21, 1882 (the date on which the bye-laws came into force) and had so continued, to take an examination 'equal to the Final Examination'. It was in fact the ordinary final examination and was so described because the candidates had not served under articles. There was a wider overhaul of the bye-laws in 1904 and the suggestions of the Council were passed by a postal ballot and authorized by the Privy Council. They came into force on January 1, 1905, one of the important results being to admit to membership until the end of 1906 persons who had been in practice as accountants for ten years and had passed the final examination. At the same time clerks who had served chartered accountants for ten years and who were 35 years of age were exempted from the preliminary examination. All 'ten-year men' were interviewed by a special committee.

The admission of women was raised on two occasions. The Council reported in 1895 that it was unwilling to petition the Privy Council for an amendment to the Charter for this purpose; and the President said that it would be so embarrassing to manage a staff composed partly of women that he would rather retire from the profession than contemplate such a position. It is interesting, if irrelevant, to wonder whether the 'loud laughter' with which this statement was greeted may not have been occasioned by the knowledge that he had married young and had ten children. In 1909 the proposal was put forward in the President's address in connection with the subject of registration of the profession. As has been stated earlier the suggestion had come from Winston Churchill, the President of the Board of Trade, but probably the members felt it was not a matter of much importance as it was believed that there were at most six women in practice as professional accountants in England and Wales. The proposal was dropped with the withdrawal of the draft Bill for registration.

The Chartered Accountants' Benevolent Association grew slowly over this period. One of its energetic workers was William Deloitte, to whose efforts the President paid tribute in his annual address in 1890. As part of the celebrations of Queen Victoria's Diamond Jubilee in 1897 a Jubilee Fund was opened which resulted in a sum of approximately £1,700 being raised in support of the Benevolent Association. By 1901 the Funds amounted to over £8,000. Then, as now, it was only supported by a small proportion of the membership, estimated at that date at 14 per cent of the total.

In June 1906, twenty-three prominent members of the profession, who were also Masons, founded the Chartered Accountants' Lodge. The Lodge has never been a large one – its highest membership having been sixty-six – but it has provided many Masons of senior rank, including in particular Sir Sydney White, for many years Grand Secretary of the United Grand Lodge of England. Nine presidents of the Institute have been amongst its members, as also have been three Lords Mayor of London.

The library of the Institute made notable strides. One of its greatest benefactors was F. W. Pixley, President in 1903. Under his care it grew to be the most complete collection of books relating to accountancy in the world. The office of Librarian was regarded at first as a part-time task. Edward Taylor, who was also chief clerk, became Librarian in 1897 when R. B. Fellows resigned. The post became a full-time one when T. A. Onions succeeded Edward Taylor in 1900. T. A. Onions resigned after twelve years' service and Cosmo Gordon of King's College, Cambridge, was appointed.

The secretary of the Institute, W. G. Howgrave, who had been appointed in 1877, served until 1899 when the Hon. George Colville, barrister-at-law, succeeded him. Perhaps it may be mentioned here that it was not until 1913 that the Council announced they had decided to pay in the usual way for the services of the auditors, which had previously been honorary.

In 1895 it was announced that the President and all surviving ex-Presidents had subscribed to present to the Institute a diamond studded gold badge to be worn by the President on all suitable occasions. The dinner held at the Merchant Taylors' Hall to celebrate the Diamond Jubilee in 1897 was honoured by the presence of many distinguished guests. Lord Halsbury, who was now Lord Chancellor, mentioned that accounts were the one subject with which Judges were 'not even supposed to be familiar'.

This supplied an opportunity for *The Accountant* in its report of the dinner to suggest that a capable assessor should be appointed in all complicated cases involving questions of account to assist Her Majesty's Judges. As previously stated the paper was entirely independent and relations between it and the Council had not always been harmonious. In the matter of policy it always pointed out the benefits that would accrue to the profession if it were organized as a whole. The Council, while stressing the fact that *The Accountant* was an independent publication, realized that it could be a very useful organ to the profession. Members were urged in 1890 to become subscribers and to assist the paper by submitting letters, reports and the like. The Council also arranged with the paper to extend its coverage of law reports.

# Chapter Four

# 1914-1938

*The First World War and its influence on the profession. The developing call on chartered accountants. Their participation in public affairs. The Companies Act, 1929. The Royal Mail and other cases. Registration becomes a dead issue.*

THE YEARS covered by this chapter can be seen in retrospect as a period leading from one world war to another, for there was little interval between the Armistice signed in 1918 and the course of events which moved inexorably towards another great conflict.

For the accountancy profession in general and the Institute in particular they were years of extraordinarily rapid development, due in great part to the far-reaching effects of the 1914–18 war, which disrupted the life of the whole nation. It soon became clear that the conduct of the war required nothing less than the mobilization of the whole of the man-power and the industrial and financial resources of the country, and to this end a number of new Government Departments were brought into being and a vast amount of emergency legislation was passed, including the Defence of the Realm Acts and the innumerable regulations under them, which together became popularly, if not affectionately, known as DORA. The interpretation of the new laws, many of them inevitably brought on to the statute book in haste, gave rise to continual difficulties, and a special Court of Appeal was set up. Recruitment for the forces was at first on a voluntary basis, but under the National Registration Act of 1915 there was compulsory registration of all persons between the ages of 15 and 65. In a nation-wide recruiting campaign in the following year the War Office included an appeal to men over age, or physically unfit to fight, to come forward to replace in essential jobs those who joined up.

In anticipation of hard times to come a fund known as the

Prince of Wales' National Relief Fund was formed, and a Board of Audit Control was appointed to supervise the monies received for the fund and distributed through the agency of the Soldiers' and Sailors' Families Association. The President of the Institute, H. Woodburn Kirby, was chairman of this board and working with him were the Vice-President, A. H. Gibson, six members of the Council, and the Secretary of the Institute, who acted as its honorary secretary. District committees were established throughout the country, with nearly 900 district and divisional auditors, the majority of whom were members of the Institute, and all of whom acted without remuneration.

The reaction of the financial world to international events is always swift, but never before had there been so many complicated questions to be faced at short notice. Even before war on Germany had been declared on August 4, 1914, a moratorium postponing the payment of certain negotiable instruments was brought into force by a Royal Proclamation, issued on August 2, and subsequently confirmed by the Postponement of Payments Act, 1914; it remained in operation until December 4. It was the first time within living memory that such a step had been taken. The London Stock Exchange, having closed for the Bank Holiday weekend on July 31, did not open its doors again until January 4, 1915, and then carried on business only under severe restrictions agreed between the Stock Exchange Committee and the Government. Something had to be done to meet the difficulties caused by the collapse of the foreign exchanges, and the Bank of England agreed to provide funds to allow payment to those who had accepted bills before the moratorium. The interests of British firms had to be protected, and with the authority of the Treasury advances were permitted to traders against debts due by foreign nationals, while the Courts (Emergency Powers) Act, 1914, gave protection to debtors in the United Kingdom who could prove that their inability to meet their obligations was due to the war. Most important of all, the defence of the realm required that the activities of enemy controlled banks and firms in this country should be strictly supervised, and trading with the enemy through neutral countries prevented. Under the

Trading with the Enemy Act, 1914, and four subsequent Acts, the Board of Trade was empowered to take the necessary steps to investigate the affairs of businesses that came under suspicion, and to make application to the High Court for the appointment of controllers of enemy concerns. This body of legislation imposed many new obligations upon firms, companies and financial institutions, and among the precautions necessary was the appointment of a Custodian of Enemy Property with wide powers and duties. At the same time new responsibilities were placed upon everyone who had to deal with dividends, trusteeships, executorships, enemy property, debts and shares, and many doubtful points arose upon which advice had to be sought from both lawyers and accountants.

From the first it was apparent that by reason of their training and qualifications accountants could make a significant contribution to the war effort in a variety of ways, and as time went on and months lengthened into years, their services were in demand as never before. Many leading members of the Institute were called in at top level as controllers, advisers and organizers, the hard and ungrateful task of Controller of the German, Austrian and Turkish Banks licensed to carry on business in this country being entrusted to Sir William Plender, assisted by Ernest Cooper, Lionel Maltby, William Cash, Edward Davis and Edward Dexter as official supervisors.

It is only possible to mention a few of the important appointments held by members of the Institute. Arthur Whinney acted first as Adviser on Costs of Production to the Admiralty and later became Assistant Accountant-General of the Royal Navy; S. H. Lever was appointed Consulting Accountant to the Government in connection with the control of the railways, and from 1917–19 was Financial Secretary to the Treasury; Gilbert Garnsey was Deputy-Director of Munitions Accounts in 1917 and later Controller of Munitions Accounts and Finance Member of the Munitions Council; Mark Webster-Jenkinson was Controller of the Department of Factory Audit and Costs, Ministry of Munitions; Harry Peat was Financial Secretary and Accounting Officer to the Ministry of Food from 1917–20; Arthur Roberts was Assistant

Director-General of the Royal Army Clothing Department and later Chairman of the Financial Board of Control at the Air Ministry; Albert Wyon was Government Auditor of Railways and of the Irish Railways, and Government Accountant of Controlled Canals. All of these were knighted for their services.

A large number of members of the Institute and their staffs were wanted for work in Government Departments. The War Office needed them as temporary officers in branches of the Army Service Corps, the Admiralty required them as Assistant Paymasters in the Royal Navy and also for their costing investigation department, and in addition to a strong cost accounting branch, the Ministry of Munitions had a factory accounting branch, and an audit section, in all of which accountants were required. An advertisement for 'Smart Men' as Assistants to Regimental Paymasters is some indication of the conditions of work fifty years ago. They were required to be 'personally smart, industrious, quick and obedient'. Pay was '5s a day and no overtime allowed, although a good deal of overtime will have to be worked including Sundays'. The President of the Institute in 1915 asked for volunteers for Government service from members having knowledge of shipping and armament accounts for the period of the war and six months beyond, and he was also asked to recommend a few qualified men for permanent positions in Government posts. In the same year a memorandum was sent by the Institute to the Home Office in support of the contention that, as professional accountants and their staffs were of vital importance to the finance and commerce of the country, it was desirable that they should receive special treatment by the tribunals appointed under Lord Derby's attestation scheme. When in 1916 the stress of events led to the introduction of conscription and a list of certified occupations was issued, the work of chartered accountants was recognized as being of national importance; qualified men of 31, if married, and 41, if single, were exempted from military service provided that it could be shown that their principal and usual occupation was that of an accountant and unless, at the hearing of an application for exemption, the local military representative could prove that the applicant's current work was not essential in the national interest. A committee of five members of the Council of the Institute was appointed in 1916 at the request of the military representative for the City of London to advise him on the cases of members, and their qualifications, which were the subject of appeal before the City of London Tribunal. This committee met under the chairmanship of Thomas Wise on 125 occasions and dealt with 927 claims. There was considerable criticism in some quarters of the inclusion of accountants in the list, due probably to lack of knowledge and understanding of their work, with the result that they were removed from the revised list that appeared some months later, the general powers of the tribunals being regarded as sufficient to grant exemptions where justified. The calls upon professional accountants, however, continued to grow, and the third revised list issued in 1917 reinstated them, though the conditions for exemption were tightened up. Two Military Service Acts were passed in 1918 and, although the second raised the age limit for conscription to 50 and in a national emergency to 55, the position of qualified practitioners and their clerks remained unchanged.

The cost of the war was tremendous, reaching a total of £7,750,000 a day. State expenditure was governed by the necessity to 'deliver the goods' to the men at the front, and all other considerations went by the board. With little or no incentive to economy, wages, profits and prices all rose steadily, and the knowledge that many people were making fortunes out of the misfortunes of their country created considerable unrest. From time to time demands were heard for more efficient control and costing methods, particularly in connection with the manufacture of munitions, the cost of which trebled in one year between 1915 and 1916. A general campaign for economy led to the appointment of a Select Committee on National Expenditure in the latter year, Mr Herbert (later Lord) Samuel being chairman. The committee found evidence of gross profiteering on the part of some manufacturers, and referred to the savings effected through accountants' cost investigations. The much criticized cost-plus contract system was condemned, and the work of the Joint Committee of Accountants in the War Office, the Admiralty, and the Ministry of Munitions in agreeing in principle the treatment of wages and oncost was commended. It was in these years that the importance of cost accounting began to be more generally recognized, and the subject gradually assumed the prominent place in the training of accountants that it was later to occupy.

In the field of taxation the work of accountants increased every year with the passing of successive Finance Acts and their accompanying Statutory Rules and Regulations. Not only were there wide extensions of indirect taxation and steep rises in the rates of income tax and super-tax, but two entirely new taxes were introduced, the Munitions Levy and the Excess Profits Duty, both designed to prevent excessive profits being made out of the war effort. The Munitions Levy, which came first and was later merged with the Excess Profits Duty, applied to Government-controlled undertakings engaged in the manufacture of munitions, while the Munitions (Limitation of Profits) Rules governed the ascertainment of profits in controlled establishments and prescribed the manner in which the profits to be retained and the levy payable to the Exchequer should be determined. Under these rules the accounts were to be audited by a chartered or incorporated accountant or an accountant approved in any particular case by the Board of Trade. The Excess Profits Duty, introduced by the Finance (No. 2) Act, 1915, cast its net much more widely. It originated in the fertile brains of Mr Josiah (later Lord) Stamp and Mr (later Sir) William Coates, both of whom were in the Inland Revenue Department, and was aimed at exceptional profits derived from the manufacture of war supplies and abnormal trading and business gains, whether directly attributable to the war or not, agriculture, employment and the professions being excluded.

The rate of duty started at 50 per cent and rose by two stages to 80 per cent. Standard profits were calculated according to a prescribed method, or the standard could be a statutory percentage on the capital employed, namely, 6 per cent for companies and 7 per cent for other businesses. A Board of Referees appointed by the Treasury, on which the accountancy profession was well represented, considered individual cases. They could increase the statutory percentage or vary the statutory standard, and deal with such matters as depreciation, wear and tear, and exceptional statutory requirements. It can justly be said that the successful working of this tax depended to a great extent upon the co-operation of the accountancy profession with the Revenue. Although the Chancellor of the Exchequer announced in 1921 the Government's intention to abolish the Excess Profits Duty after it had run its normal course, all businesses except those begun after the war had to pay the tax for a period of seven years dating from their first accounting period, and the result was that it dragged on as part of the taxation system until it was brought to an end by the Finance Act, 1926. Sir John Harmood-Banner, a member of the Institute and an M.P., once described this tax in the House of Commons as the most 'infamous, unenlightened, extravagant, ruinous and demoralizing measure' ever brought before the country, and its passing was unlamented.

During the slumps which followed the war members of the Institute took a prominent part in the rationalization and reorganization of British industry. This close contact with industry has since continued in ever increasing volume and importance.

It must not be thought that members of the Institute did not take their full share in the fighting lines. 1,625 members and 1,803 articled clerks served in the armed forces. 184 members and 326 articled clerks were killed in action, and decorations for gallantry were awarded to fifty-eight members and seventy-one articled clerks. One member, A. C. Herring, and one articled clerk, R. L. Haine, won the Victoria Cross and both happily survived. Several members of the staff of the Institute, including the Librarian (Cosmo Gordon), also joined the colours. In 1922 a War Memorial in the entrance hall of the Institute was unveiled. It was in the form of two tablets inscribed with the names of those who gave their lives in the cause of freedom, and a brief ceremony of dedication was performed by the Dean of St Paul's, the Very Reverend W. R. Inge, C.V.O., D.D.

The citations for the awards of the Victoria Cross were as follows:

*R. L. Haine* (on April 28–9, 1917)

'Second Lieut. Reginald Leonard Haine, 1st Battalion Honourable Artillery Company for most conspicuous bravery and determination when our troops occupying a pronounced salient were repeatedly counter-attacked. There was an ever-present danger that if the enemy attack succeeded the garrison of the salient would be surrounded.

'Second Lieut. Haine organized and led with the utmost gallantry six bombing attacks against a strong point which dangerously threatened our communications, capturing the position together with fifty prisoners and two machine-guns.

'The enemy then counter-attacked with a battalion of the Guards, succeeded in regaining his position and the situation appeared critical.

'Second Lieut. Haine at once formed a block in his trench and for the whole of the following night maintained his position against repeated determined attacks.

'Reorganizing his men on the following morning he again attacked and captured the strong point pressing the enemy back for several hundred yards and thus relieving the situation.

'Throughout these operations this officer's superb courage, quick decision and sound judgment were beyond praise and it was his splendid personal example which inspired his men to continue their efforts during more than thirty hours of continuous fighting.'

*A. C. Herring* (on March 23–4, 1918)

'Temporary Second Lieut. Alfred Cecil Herring, 6th Battalion Northamptonshire Regt, for most conspicuous bravery, initiative and devotion to duty when after severe fighting the enemy gained a position on the south bank of the canal. His post was cut off from the troops on both flanks and surrounded. Second Lieut. Herring however immediately counter-attacked and recaptured the position together with twenty prisoners and six machine-guns. During the night the post was continually attacked but all attacks were beaten off. This was largely due to the splendid heroism displayed by Second Lieut. Herring who continually visited his men and cheered them up. It was entirely due to the bravery and initiative of this officer that the enemy advance was held up for eleven hours at an exceedingly critical period. His magnificent heroism coupled with the skilful handling of his troops were most important factors leading to success.'

The contribution of women to the war effort was immense. That they should work in military and auxiliary hospitals and in canteens was taken for granted, but at the beginning of 1916 a complete revolution in ideas regarding women's work took place. From that time on they were to be found replacing men in the forces in practically every occupation, and doors hitherto closed to them were suddenly opened wide. They made munitions, took jobs in industry and agriculture, and appeared in the uniforms of postmen, ticket collectors, guards on the underground railways and bus conductors; some even became labourers in gasworks. They were taken on to the staff in every professional and business office and worked as accountancy and audit clerks in Government Departments, banks and insurance offices. It is amusing to note that in 1865 a Society for the Employment of Women advertised in the *Daily Telegraph*. It offered instruction to young women in 'commercial handwriting, arithmetic and book-keeping', and invited applications from 'tradesmen who required well-taught female clerks and book-keepers'. This shadow of the future was at last overtaken by events.

The Representation of the People Act passed in 1918 gave the vote to all men of 21 years of age and upwards and all women of 30 years of age and upwards. The Sex Disqualification (Removal) Act passed in 1919 had a still more important effect, for it opened membership of professional bodies to women. One woman, Miss Harris Smith, who had been in practice as a public accountant since 1878, was at once admitted to Fellowship of the Institute and occupied the proud position of being the first and only woman chartered accountant in the world. At the annual meeting in 1920, the President stated that five articles of clerkship for women had been registered since the passing of the Act. In 1924 Miss Ethel Watts, who until her death in 1963 helped materially with the compilation of this history, became the first woman to be admitted a member of the Institute by examination.

As has been noted in the previous chapter, enthusiasm for registration of the accountancy profession gradually waned and for many years it ceased to be a live issue so far as the Institute was concerned. Yet it was never so dead that it could not raise its head from time to time, and it did so in various forms and places, so that a writer in the *Financial Times* could say in 1915 that there were 'forty different species (of auditor) most of them with their own Registration Bills'.

The matter came up very frequently in connection with the audit clause in municipal corporation bills. Following a statement by the Chairman of the Local Legislation Committee of the House of Commons in 1914 that the standard of auditors' qualifications was that of the Institute and the Society, the usual form of the clause provided for the audit to be carried out by members of these bodies. Attempts to widen it to include other societies of accountants were by no means infrequent and the Institute and the Society acted together in opposing any alteration. They were successful for a good many years, but it was a costly and lengthy process on each occasion, and a considerable amount of time had to be given by Parliamentary Committees to hearing the arguments on both sides. It was small wonder that they found it both irritating and time wasting to be called upon to pronounce on questions which were quite outside their knowledge and experience. After the House of Commons Committee had dismissed a petition by the London Association of Accountants Ltd on the Chester Corporation Bill in 1929, the Chairman, Sir Thomas Robinson, spoke out strongly. Sound and reliable accounting, he said, was of paramount importance to industry, commerce and the investing public, and the committee considered that the time had come to establish a register of properly qualified persons on the lines of the law and medicine, and the accounting world should seriously consider the matter.

In these circumstances the President of the Institute undertook that the matter would again be considered by the Council and joint discussions took place between the Institute, the Scottish bodies and the Society, which resulted in the President of the Board of Trade being asked to set up a Departmental Committee to go into the whole question. He consented and on February 7, 1930, a committee under the chairmanship of Lord Goschen was appointed: 'To consider and report whether it is desirable to restrict the practice of the profession of accountancy to persons whose names would be inscribed in a register established by law, and if so to report on the method by which such register should be established and controlled.'

The views of the Institute Council on the subject had been embodied in a resolution passed after consultation with the provincial societies of Chartered Accountants and of the Scottish bodies. It stated that there was no public demand for registration and that it would not be in the public interest. Further, if Parliament were to insist on a system of registration for practising accountants, the Council asked that members of the Institute should be exempted from the provisions of any such legislation and that 'the separate entity of the Institute with the rights, powers, examinations and other privileges which are assigned to it by the Royal Charter, should be preserved'. This was not favourably regarded by the Society.

The Institute's case was presented by Sir William Plender and William Cash, both of whom gave oral evidence, as did the secretary of the Institute, the Hon. George Colville. Plender emphasized the wish of all the Chartered bodies to remain outside any scheme of registration and to be allowed to continue using the description of, and practising as, chartered accountants. In the course of the hearing it became clear that the word 'accountant' by itself was almost meaningless, but that the description accompanying it was all-important; yet to define what was covered by the term 'accountancy' was impossible. It was not surprising, therefore, that the committee reached the conclusion that registration would create more problems than it would settle, and accordingly unanimously decided that on the evidence before them it was not desirable.

Meantime, the discussions arising out of Corporation Bills went on interminably, making confusion worse confounded. After the Departmental Committee had been appointed, but before it reported, the Cardiff Corporation Bill went before the House of Commons Local Legislation Committee and this time the petition of the London Association to be included in the audit clause was allowed, the Institute and the Society taking no part in the contest owing to the setting-up of the Departmental Committee. When, however, the Bill went to the House of Lords, they petitioned that the clause should be restored to its original form. Their Lordships refused to interfere with the decision of the Lower House, although when the Reading Corporation Bill had been recently before them, they had declined to include the London Association. The audit clause in the Tamworth Corporation Bill in 1931 provided for the appointment of members of the Institute, the Society or the London Association, and the House of Commons Select Committee on Private Bills allowed a petition by the Corporation of Accountants Ltd for the inclusion of their members.

In view of the unsatisfactory position thus created the Municipal Corporations (Audit) Bill introduced as a private member's Bill in 1933 was of particular interest. Its object was to enable municipal corporations to provide for the audit of their accounts and the accounts of their officers by district auditors 'or by other qualified accountants', instead of by borough auditors as provided by the Municipal Corporations Act, 1882. In spite of Mr George Lansbury's contention that 'The fact that you have a professionally trained mind on the subject is not a guarantee that you will not have professionally trained nonsense. . . . I am aware that chartered accountants are wonderful jugglers of figures, but when it comes to deciding whether tiles are better than painted walls, I think I am as capable of judging that as the most learned chartered accountant in the world', the Bill passed its third reading. The provisions of this Bill eventually became part of the Local Government Act, 1933, which provided, that unless an alternative method of audit was in force or adopted, there should be in every borough elective auditors and the Mayor's auditor but the Council might, by resolution passed by two-thirds of the members voting and duly confirmed, adopt as an alternative either district audit by the Ministry of Health, or professional audit. Where the latter was adopted, no person was qualified for appointment as auditor unless he was a member of one or more of the following bodies:

The Institute of Chartered Accountants in England and Wales;
The Society of Incorporated Accountants and Auditors;
The Society of Accountants in Edinburgh;
The Institute of Accountants and Actuaries in Glasgow;
The Society of Accountants in Aberdeen;
The London Association of Certified Accountants Ltd;
The Corporation of Accountants Ltd.

The Council of the Institute gave much consideration during the war to plans for helping students serving with the forces on their return to civil life. The conditions controlling exemption from the preliminary examination were made easier in some respects, and a resolution passed at the Annual General Meeting in 1917 authorized a grant not exceeding £10,000 to be made from the Institute funds to provide special educational facilities for students. Many of the younger men were not demobilized for some time as they were required for the Army of Occupation in Germany, and, pending their return, correspondence courses were organized. A new bye-law which came into effect in August 1919 made it possible for the Council to grant a reduction in the term of service under articles for clerks who had served in the forces. J. W. Woodthorpe became chairman of a Chartered Accountants' Board of the Appointments Department of the Ministry of Labour, which for some time held weekly meetings to consider applications from ex-Service men for maintenance and training grants.

The education of articled clerks continued to be the subject of many discussions and gave cause for deep thought to those who had the future of the profession at heart. The Union of Chartered Accountants' Students' Societies took the initiative to ensure that proper methods of training were adopted. They produced a comprehensive scheme embracing the whole of the areas covered by the Students' Societies and making provision for students whose geographical position made membership of a local society impracticable. It included revision lectures in the fourteen days preceding each examination, and a complete correspondence course prepared by highly experienced tutors and edited by an advisory committee appointed by the Union. The Institute substantially increased the total subsidies granted to the Students' Societies. It was felt that the scheme would ensure that the theoretical training of articled clerks and the inculcation of the ethics of the profession would be in safe hands and would be carried out on the right lines.

The well-known coaching firm of H. Foulks Lynch & Co. were appointed official tutors under the scheme, but strong exception to this was taken by a member of the Institute, E. Miles Taylor, principal of the British College of Accountancy. The Annual Meeting of the Institute in 1937 produced some stormy scenes when Miles Taylor contended that the Institute grant for tuition purposes was not expenditure within the Council's powers. He proposed an amendment to the resolution for the adoption of the Report and Accounts for the year to December 31, 1936, by adding the following words:

> 'Subject to the exclusion of the sum of £3,500 shown in the accounts as allowances to provincial Students' Societies and the London Students' Society for tuition, pending a complete inquiry into and report on the circumstances in which those allowances were voted and the publication of the report of the inquiry.'

This episode was not without its amusing side. A poll showed a majority of two to one against Taylor's amendment, but by an unfortunate mistake in the voting papers they were stated to be returnable on May 18, whereas it should have been a day later. Taylor thereupon applied to the Court for an injunction restraining the Institute from giving effect to the poll. Mr Justice Bennett granted the injunction, but the Court of Appeal discharged it, holding that it was a matter concerning the internal management of the Institute and the general body of members and that it was not competent for Taylor, as an individual member, to sustain his action.

The tumult and the shouting had hardly died down, when the second war itself intervened on an even higher note. Controversies were, however, renewed thereafter as will be later related.

Early in 1918 the general trend of events indicated that it was not too soon to begin some constructive thinking about the many problems that would have to be faced at the end of the war. Among those most nearly affecting the accountancy profession were the changes that would be required in company law when normal trading relations with other countries could be resumed, and the activities of foreign nationals would no longer be subject to such severe restriction.

In April of that year, therefore, the Board of Trade appointed a Departmental Committee 'to inquire what amendments are expedient in the Companies Acts, 1908–17, particularly having regard to circumstances arising out of the war'. The chairman was Lord Wrenbury and the committee included no fewer than four leading accountants: Sir William Plender, James Martin, F.S.A.A., A. W. Tait, C.A., and G. W. Currie, M.P., C.A. The scope of the inquiry was much wider than that of previous committees on the same subject, the committee being called upon to consider questions that belonged to the domain of political science, economics and international statesmanship, as well as those relating to company administration and business.

The committee was particularly anxious not to allow its findings to be influenced by the nationalism that had been inflamed by the war nor by the extreme caution that had necessarily governed the actions of the legislature during the past three years. It desired to conserve what was good in the existing system and only to restrict such facilities as might possibly be used against essential national interests. The question of the employment of foreign capital was of prime importance in its investigations. In considering whether aliens should be permitted to hold shares or debentures in British companies, it had to bear in mind the desirability of attracting foreign capital to this country, and to recommend nothing that would make it difficult for London to maintain its position as the financial centre of the world. It therefore expressed the opinion that anything which would have a severely restrictive or deterrent effect should as far as possible be avoided. It recommended that the nationality of alien directors, shareholders and owners should be disclosed, recognizing at the same time that the enforcement of such disclosure would be difficult. Even in shipping and other key industries the total exclusion of aliens from ownership was considered neither essential nor commercially expedient, though the committee recommended that not more than 20 per cent of the power of control should be in the hands of aliens.

On matters relating directly to the accounts and audit of companies the committee had little to say. It did not enter into the question whether auditors should be required to have some professional qualification, and therefore made no recommendation; nor, rather surprisingly, did it feel able to recommend that a profit and loss account should be required to be included in the annual accounts summary which had to be filed, since such a requirement might give individual traders an unfair advantage over companies. It did recommend that the balance sheet should be included in the Annual Summary and should state the amounts or rates of dividend that had been paid since the last balance sheet. Private companies, the committee thought, had justified their existence and should be left undisturbed. The identity of shares by their distinctive numbers should be retained, and payments to directors free of income tax or super-tax should be forbidden.

This committee had obviously not said the last word on company law, and its report did not result in any new legislation. Not many years passed before the subject was again to be referred to a committee but in the meantime, 1925, a case arising out of the winding-up of the City Equitable Fire Insurance Company Ltd was to cause difficulties to the accountancy profession, and emphasize very strongly the need for giving details of assets in the balance sheet, particularly in the case of banking and insurance companies.

In this case the auditor had made his report in the usual form and had further committed himself to the statement that the stock exchange securities had been taken at or under cost price and that in his belief the assets set forth in the balance sheet were 'in the aggregate fully of the value as stated therein'. It subsequently transpired that certain of the securities were at the date of the balance sheet pledged to a considerable extent with the chairman's firm; that under the heading 'loans at short notice' in the balance sheet, a large personal loan to the company's manager was included, and that by the purchase of Treasury Bills at the end of the financial year by way of 'window-dressing', the assets were represented to be much larger than was really the case. The Crown was apparently content with the theory that the chairman was the master mind and that others concerned were his tools, and on an appeal by the Official Receiver, as liquidator, the Court of Appeal confirmed this view. An immunity clause in the company's articles exempted directors and officers of the company from liability for loss except if due to wilful default, and the Master of the Rolls said in effect that here there was no wilful default, but the auditor, having been deceived by the cunning of a dishonest chairman, had taken as trustworthy that which had in fact proved not to be trustworthy. It appeared that the auditor had proceeded in his audit according to the standard of care ordinarily observed in the accountancy profession. The winding-up of the City Equitable was one of many instances of liquidations where the Official Receiver acting as liquidator applied to the Court for leave to employ chartered accountants to assist him in unravelling and resolving the complex affairs of large companies. And it became not infrequent for chartered accountants to be appointed Inspectors by the Board of Trade under powers contained in the Companies Act to investigate allegations affecting the conduct of directors in the administration of their companies' affairs.

New questions were also being raised by the tendency of business towards combination and the consequent multiplication of holding companies, a trend which was likely to continue and to make growing demands on the skilled assistance and specialized knowledge of qualified accountants.

The time was obviously ripe for amendment of the existing laws and in January 1925 the President of the Board of Trade appointed a strong committee under the chairmanship of Wilfrid Greene, K.C., an acknowledged authority on company law, afterwards Lord Greene, Master of the Rolls. Its task was to consider what amendments were desirable in the Companies Acts, 1908–17, and the members of the committee included William Cash, Sir James Martin, F.S.A.A., and Sir William McLintock, C.A. Once again the committee was anxious not to make the honest – who were in the great majority – suffer for the sins of the dishonest few. Its report was issued in 1926 and formed the basis of the Companies Act, 1929, a most important measure with far-reaching effects on the accountancy profession.

The Greene Committee had taken the view that in general the law with regard to the powers of auditors was satisfactory, and had therefore recommended little alteration. The Act did, however, strengthen the position of auditors by specifically empowering them to attend the general meeting of the company and to make statements or give explanations. A company was prohibited from acting as auditor and, except in the case of private companies, partners and employees of directors or other officers of the company came under the same prohibition. The thorny question of professional qualifications was once more left untouched, and a proposal that auditors should state their qualifications when signing reports was not adopted.

Hitherto companies had been under no statutory obligation to keep proper accounts, but after the 1929 Act the directors were obliged to see that they did so. They were also to lay a profit and loss account and balance sheet before the company at the annual general meeting and, except in the case of private companies, to send the balance sheet and the directors' and auditors' reports to members. Some of the professional evidence given to the Greene Committee had been definitely adverse to insisting on the issue of a profit and loss account or to defining the amount of disclosure to be made in a balance sheet. While the Act gave no substantial guidance about the contents of the profit and loss account, it prescribed that the balance sheet must contain a summary of the share capital, an indication of the general nature of the liabilities and assets, and as to how the value of the fixed assets had been arrived at; goodwill, preliminary expenses, and the aggregate of loans to directors were to be stated separately; if a liability was secured a note was necessary, but not of the relevant asset. Investments in, and loans to or from, subsidiary companies (as defined in the Act) were in the aggregate to be stated separately. Consolidated accounts were not made compulsory, but the Act did for the first time tackle the question of the profits and losses of subsidiary companies, and required that there should be annexed to the accounts a statement as to how these had been dealt with, but without requiring that their amount should be disclosed. Private companies that were subsidiaries of a parent company retained their privileges, including exemption from filing accounts.

Creditors were given two valuable safeguards under the Act. The period before the commencement of a winding-up which rendered invalid a floating charge (unless the company was solvent when the charge was created) was extended from three to six months; and a modified procedure was introduced to give creditors effective control in a voluntary winding-up if the company were insolvent.

On the whole the Act was regarded as a sound one, reflecting the best professional practice. It introduced very important changes relating to the preparation and audit of balance sheets, and the Council of the Institute thought it right to obtain and publish to members a joint opinion given by three eminent counsel, Wilfrid Greene, Cecil W. Turner and Walter Monckton, on the sections vitally affecting the duties of the auditors.

But excellent though the 1929 Act was so far as it went, accountants did not have long to wait before having it painfully brought home to them that it did not go far enough. The Royal Mail Steam Packet case in 1931 shook the whole business world and caused great distress and anxiety throughout the profession. Lord Kylsant, chairman of the RMSP, a company incorporated by Royal Charter, was charged with making and issuing annual reports of the directors of the company for the years 1926 and 1927 which he knew to be false in a material particular with intent to defraud the shareholders, and H. J. Morland, the auditor of the company, a distinguished member of the Institute, of outstanding character and held in the highest respect, was charged with aiding and abetting him. The item in the published profit and loss account which gave rise to the charge was: 'Balance for the year, including dividends on shares in allied and other companies, adjustment of taxation reserves less depreciation of fleet, etc.' This item included a transfer of an undisclosed amount from a previous provision no longer required. The company had suffered from the general depression in the shipping industry and the fact that it had made a loss in the two years in question was not indicated. The words 'including adjustment of taxation reserves' had been inserted at the suggestion of the auditor. After a trial at the Central Criminal Court lasting nine days, at which expert evidence was given by Lord Plender, H. L. H. Hill (the President of the Institute), Henry Morgan (the President of the Society of Incorporated Accountants and Auditors) and Sir William McLintock, C.A., the auditor was acquitted. The chairman was also acquitted on that particular charge, but was found guilty on a further charge of making and publishing a prospectus which he knew to be false in a material particular.

Though the acquittal of the auditor was received with general satisfaction, the accountancy profession had had a shock, and it had been brought home to all concerned with companies that further amendment of the law might be necessary to make compulsory the issue to shareholders of informative profit and loss accounts. The Royal Mail Steam Packet Company, as a Chartered Company, was not within the requirements of the Companies Acts, but it now appeared desirable that such companies should be placed on exactly the same legal footing in the matter of accounting requirements as any other public company.

The question of secret reserves came up for discussion whenever accountants met together. Mr Justice (afterwards Lord) Wright who heard the Royal Mail case made some comments on the subject which aroused considerable interest. He said:

'It was said by a very learned Judge on one occasion, by way of observation and not by judgment, that a company, that is to say the shareholders, could not complain if the position of the finances of the company was better than the accounts disclosed. That has been quoted from time to time as a justification for this method of keeping reserves secret. But there may be very great evils if those who have the control and management of the companies, and who control and manage companies for the benefit of the shareholders who entrust their monies to companies, have very large portions of the companies' assets left in the secret disposition of the managing authority. It may work very well in many cases; no doubt it does. It is a practice which is being followed, no doubt, by many concerns of the highest standing. On the other hand it may be the subject of almost intolerable abuse. Such a system may be used to cover up negligences, irregularities, and almost breaches of faith. It is said to be a matter of domestic concern between the company and the shareholders, but if the shareholders do not know and cannot know what the position is, how can they form any view about it at all?'

The comments of the Council of the Institute upon this important and difficult case were eagerly awaited by members. The learned Judge had emphasized that a statement true in every published particular might nevertheless give a false impression as a result of the suppression of material information. In his speech at the Annual General Meeting in 1932, the President, H. L. H. Hill, explained that the Council had decided to issue no directive to members and was not prepared to lay down general principles for guidance arising out of the circumstances of the Royal Mail case. The Council had been advised not to make any official pronouncement on matters which by their very nature were incapable of reduction to exact formulae. Distinguished counsel had been consulted and the President said that, while it was clear that a need existed for raising the standard of disclosure practised in connection with company profit and loss accounts, the Council of the

Institute thought that any reform should be effected through the influence of individual members and that there was no need for further legislation. Expressing his personal opinion he added:

> 'In my view the dangers arising from publishing more informative accounts have been overstated and the legitimate claims of shareholders have not received adequate recognition. . . . I feel that we can do nothing better calculated to maintain and increase the confidence we now enjoy than to use our influence to make the profit and loss account increasingly valuable as some guide to earning capacity.'

In some quarters, however, there was considerable pressure for further reform of the law. Losses by the investing public due to a number of causes had to some extent destroyed public confidence and lent force to the arguments of those who advocated a new inquiry. There was, in fact, a sharp division of opinion. On the one hand there was a strongly supported view that amendment of the 1929 Act would be premature and have a harmfully restrictive effect; on the other a special committee of the Society of Incorporated Accountants and Auditors had come out strongly in favour of amendment in some important respects, and this view also commanded a large measure of support. The Executive Committee of the Association of British Chambers of Commerce urged amendment of the law in conformity with present-day experience.

The general effect of the Royal Mail case was to induce the boards of a number of companies to present more informative accounts and it strengthened the hands of auditors in advising as to the extent of the information to be given. There was also a markedly increasing tendency to appoint accountants to boards of directors, the best evidence that the value of accountancy was much better appreciated than it was before the war; but the prevailing opinion was that new legislation should be deferred until further experience had been accumulated.

It is interesting to note here that the accounts of the Dunlop Rubber Company Ltd for 1933 were in many ways a landmark in accountancy history. The company, of which a member of the

Institute, F. R. M. de Paula, was Controller of Finance, realizing that if the principle of consolidation was confined to the balance sheet, a large part of its practical value was lost since the reader could not draw the right conclusions from it, presented a statement of consolidated earnings. This departure from the normal practice was widely welcomed and the company was hailed as a pioneer in the presentation of more informative accounts. For a number of years prior to this Sir Gilbert Garnsey had emphasized the need for consolidated accounts to explain the real position and earnings of holding company groups. He was largely responsible for putting consolidated accounts on the accountancy map of Great Britain. He lectured, spoke and wrote about this subject from 1922 onwards and one of his books became the standard work on the subject prior to the Second World War. T. B. Robson, who took over responsibility for the book on Garnsey's death in 1932, made the first serious attempt to develop, in a lecture at Manchester in 1936, a professional technique for consolidated statements.

There are other cases which must be mentioned, if only briefly, because although they did not directly relate to company accounts, they were of such magnitude that they contributed largely to a feeling of unease and insecurity in financial matters and among shareholders generally. Moreover, accountants, in their capacity of business doctors, were inevitably called in.

In the first, the Hatry case (1929), the four defendants themselves, Clarence Hatry and three associated directors in the Hatry Group, first brought accountants on the scene. Finding themselves in difficulties from which there was no escape, they went to Garnsey and confessed to frauds involving conspiracy and the forgery of scrip certificates to a huge amount. Garnsey was thus faced with a most serious responsibility, and he later had the task of investigating the affairs of the companies concerned, a task described by the Attorney General as 'of immense magnitude'. Heavy sentences of imprisonment were passed on the four men. Their defalcations were possible as the result of collusion and could hardly have remained undetected when the accounts of the various concerns came to be audited.

In the Kreuger case of 1932, which was an international affair, irregularities extending over a long period remained undetected. In this case also members of the Institute played the principal part in unravelling the threads and exposing the ways in which the frauds had been perpetrated.

The Pepper Pool case which was heard at the Old Bailey in February 1936 ended with the conviction of three City financiers for issuing a prospectus false in a material particular.

A case of importance to auditors in view of the increasing use of loose-leaf books was Hearts of Oak Assurance Co. Ltd v. Flower in October 1935. Mr Justice Bennett held that a loose-leaf record was not a 'book' within the meaning of S.120 of the Companies Act, 1929, which required that 'every company shall cause minutes to be entered in books kept for that purpose'.

The Institute consulted counsel, who took the view that auditors might accept for the purposes of audit, as part of 'the information and explanations' they required, documents that might not be evidence in a Court of Law; and that S.123 of the Companies Act giving an auditor the right of access to a company's books included the loose-leaf forms upon which records were kept.

As well as the reform of company law, amendment of bankruptcy law was undertaken in 1924. A committee, including Sir James Martin, F.S.A.A., and A. O. Miles, was appointed to 'consider and report what amendments to the Bankruptcy Act 1914 recent experience has shown to be desirable, more particularly in regard to the provisions for the discovery and punishment of offences'. The most important section of the Committee's report (issued as a White Paper early in 1925) was that dealing with the keeping of books by debtors. Under the existing law, failure to keep books was an offence only in second or subsequent bankruptcies. The Committee advocated extension of the offence to all bankruptcies, subject to the exception that two years' grace should be allowed after the passing of the Act, and that bankruptcies of professional men or traders involving unsecured liabilities not exceeding £500 should be excluded. This report included a number of the amendments suggested by the Association of Chambers of

Commerce, and a Government Bill was introduced which came into operation as the Bankruptcy (Amendment) Act, 1926.

A matter of considerable interest and importance to the whole accountancy profession came up in 1926 in connection with a Bill promoted by the Scottish Widows' Fund and Life Assurance Society under which they sought power to undertake the offices of liquidator, receiver, trustee in bankruptcy or auditor. The Scottish Chartered Accountants raised no objection, but the Institute lodged a petition on the grounds that this proposal was contrary to public policy. It was contended on its behalf that all these functions involved the exercise of personal qualities and the staking of personal reputation and responsibility, and that an unqualified body should not be permitted under the aegis of the legislature to hold itself out as competent to perform audits. Sir Arthur Whinney gave evidence before the Committee of the House of Lords considering the Bill, and it was decided that these powers should not be granted.

Recognition of the necessity for the application of modern accounting techniques and of the Institute as the leading professional organization was shown in a variety of ways. Few inquiries into matters affecting the commercial and financial health of the country were undertaken without the assistance of at least one chartered accountant and generally the evidence of others. The list of appointments to Government and Departmental Committees and to investigate and advise on the reorganization of companies in difficulties grew longer and longer.

The Council showed its appreciation of its debt to Sir William Plender when it elected him for a third term of office as President in order that he might preside over the Jubilee celebrations in 1930.

By that date the membership was approximately 9,000 and the Institute's position had been greatly strengthened in all parts of the country by the growth of the provincial societies and the formation of the London Members' Committee. The Autumnal Meetings, held in every alternate year in one of the large provincial centres, had also become a source of strength, being occasions of the meeting together of leading personalities to join with many other members in discussion of important technical questions and the entertainment of distinguished guests.

The Jubilee celebrations took the form of a week of social gatherings in London and excursions to various places of interest. They afforded an opportunity to repay some of the hospitality that had been offered to the Institute by their professional brethren in other lands, and to entertain members of other professional bodies. The highlight of the week was the Jubilee Banquet in Guildhall, at which 500 members and guests were present, and the toast of the Institute was proposed by the Lord Chancellor, Lord Sankey. In reply to a telegram of loyal greetings, King George V sent a message of congratulation on the eminent position attained by the Institute, and wished it continued success in the interests of the commerce and finance of the British Empire.

To the great pleasure of the whole profession Plender was created a peer in the New Year's Honours list of 1931 and took the title of Baron Plender of Sundridge in the County of Kent.

An instance of the extent to which important financial issues were coming to be decided largely on the basis of the opinions of accountants was the hearing (1934) by the London Passenger Transport Arbitration Tribunal, of which Sir James Martin, F.S.A.A., was a member, of the claim by the private bus companies against the LPT Board, in connection with the transfer of their London undertakings to the Board. Evidence given for the respective sides by Harold Howitt and Sir William McLintock, C.A., was all important to the Tribunal's decision.

In taking steps to safeguard the future of the ownership of their newspapers, the proprietors of *The Times* and the *Spectator* included the President of the Institute for the time being (along with the Lord Chancellor, the Archbishop of Canterbury and other eminent public figures) as one of their trustees. The Economist Newspaper Limited appointed Sir Laurence Halsey in a similar capacity.

The first attempt by Parliament to enforce a particular method of account-keeping on a selected profession was made in 1933 when

Rules having statutory force were drawn up by the Council of the Law Society under the provisions of the Solicitors' Act, 1933. These required, *inter alia*, every solicitor in practice to keep a separate account for clients' monies, and 'to keep such books and accounts as may be necessary to show the receipts and payments on account for each of his clients separately from the receipts and payments on his own account'. The Rules, which came into operation as from January 1, 1935, still left loopholes, and it was not until some years later that conference between solicitors and accountants resulted in the making of new Rules, to which reference is made in the succeeding chapter.

The accountancy profession was gradually perfecting its techniques and expanding its functions. The appearance of new accounting machines reduced the need for much of the routine checking in an audit, and it was prophesied that the time would come when the auditor would arrive with a bag of tools merely to see that the machines were foolproof and working properly – a prophecy that has not yet been fulfilled. In many directions there was fresh scope for the accountant's knowledge and experience. The tremendous rise in the number, and the increase in the size, of joint-stock companies resulted in a growing demand for more scientific management and a greater knowledge of costing, and in addition accountants found that they were called upon to act as consultants and economic advisers, required to consider the individual problems of clients in the light of the general economic situation. In 1921 Sir Josiah Stamp had made a vigorous onslaught on the profession for its alleged failure to make 'a single substantial contribution to economic science over its own field of the analysis of the results of industry, although it has practically a monopoly grip of the required data'.

Though much could be, and was, said in reply to this challenge, it was not forgotten, and it received support from P. D. Leake, who declared in a lecture given in 1926 that the measurement of industrial production known as profit and loss was still an undeveloped science. It was realized that accounting as a science occupied a position midway between economics and business administration, and when an Accounting Research Association was formed in 1936 'to promote research, to discover the effects of economic, social and legal changes on methods of accounting theory and practice', Sir Josiah Stamp addressed the first meeting. It was strongly urged in some quarters that the possibility of the Institute co-operating with the Universities should be investigated, but the time for that had not yet arrived. As far back as 1902 a Faculty of Commerce – the first in England – had been created at the University of Birmingham. The courses had been drawn up in consultation with the committee of the Birmingham and Midland Society of Chartered Accountants and received the approval of the President of the Institute, Walter N. Fisher, and the Council. Lawrence R. Dicksee was appointed to the professorship in accounting. In 1919 he was made Sir Ernest Cassel Professor of Accounting and Business Organization at the University of London and F. R. M. de Paula was appointed to a readership in the same subjects at the London School of Economics five years later. When Dicksee retired from his Chair in 1926, he was succeeded by de Paula. A number of provincial Universities had Chairs of Accounting, generally coupled with Business Methods, and as an experiment the London School of Economics set up a Department of Business Administration (1932) with the co-operation of a number of individuals and firms interested in the development of this branch of education. The accounting courses were placed in the hands of S. W. Rowland, who also became responsible for the teaching of accounting at the London School of Economics on de Paula's retirement. The experiment proved so successful that it was later decided to make the Department an integral part of the School's work.

The interest of the Institute in scientific management was shown when the Sixth International Congress for Scientific Management was held in London in 1935. G. R. Freeman and Sir Mark Webster-Jenkinson were both members of the Executive Committee.

The steadily growing burden of taxation and the ever increasing complications of the taxing laws – 'that ill-digested mass of legislation' as they were described by one learned Judge – continually added to the work of accountants as advisers to and representatives of the taxpayer. When in 1919 a Royal Commission on Income Tax was appointed it included two chartered accountants, Sir John Harmood-Banner, M.P. and William McLintock, C.A. William Cash gave evidence on behalf of the Institute, P. D. Leake for the Institution of Mining and Metallurgy, S. S. Dawson, M.COM., for the Association of Trade Protection Societies of the United Kingdom, and H. Lakin-Smith for the Association of Chambers of Commerce. The report, issued in the following year, made some drastic recommendations, among them the abolition of the three years' average as the basis of assessment of business profits, but the change to the profits of the previous year was not made until 1926. While recommending that assessing authorities should be given power to require the production of accounts 'where books have been regularly kept', the Commission stopped short of requiring that there should be regular book-keeping. The Finance Act of 1922 introduced provisions 'with a view to preventing the avoidance of the payment of super-tax through the withholding from distribution of income of a company, which would otherwise be distributed' and gave the Special Commissioners powers to direct assessment to super-tax of the whole income of a private company where it appeared that the company had not, after the end of its financial year, distributed a reasonable part of its income to the members, regard being had to its requirements for current needs and for future development. Where the Commissioners called for information and accounts the directors might, *inter alia*, furnish a certificate by the auditor that (a) he was satisfied that the information in a declaration by the director was sufficient for him to form an opinion whether the proposed distribution was a reasonable part of the income; (b) a *prima facie* case was made out that the proposed distribution was reasonable. The qualifications of the auditor were not defined beyond the statement that he must be a 'member of an incorporated society of accountants' – a definition that had always been and remained unsatisfactory.

An attempt to meet the constant criticism of the complexities of income tax and super-tax forms was made by a Committee appointed by the Chancellor of the Exchequer, under the chairmanship of Mr Justice Rowlatt, in 1923. Memoranda were submitted by all the leading accountancy bodies, but the impossibility of drawing up simple forms for general use and therefore designed to cover the differing circumstances of many thousands of people, prevented any substantial alterations being made.

The Income Tax Act of 1918 consolidated the legislation on the subject up to that date, but subsequent Finance Acts and a considerable amount of case law seemed to demand a fresh effort to reduce it to more manageable proportions. In 1927 therefore a Committee on the Codification of the Income Tax law was appointed, Sir Gilbert Garnsey being one of the members until his death in 1932, when he was succeeded by David H. Allan, C.A. The task was gigantic, and the draft Bill which was part of the report when it appeared in 1936 consisted of no less than 417 clauses and eight schedules. The Committee's labours did not result in its proposals for codification being completely adopted in legislation.

Another inquiry, in which H. L. H. Hill was one of three members of the committee, was that made in 1932 into the taxation of co-operative societies.

All the events to which reference has been made in this chapter took place against a background of growing international tension and trade depression. The signing of the Peace Treaty in 1919 was followed by a wave of economic nationalism, and tariff barriers were the greatest obstacle to any real and lasting revival of trade. The refusal of France and the United States to accept payment of reparations and war debts in goods meant that a vast amount of gold accumulated and remained frozen in those countries, and the consequent shortage of gold in circulation led to a general fall in prices, reduced production and caused unemployment. In Germany inflation had pushed down the value of the mark till at the beginning of 1924 1,000,000,000 paper marks equalled one gold mark. The services of Sir William Plender were invoked by the Dawes Commission on German reparations.

In this country there was grave industrial unrest fanned by inflation and profiteering. The Profiteering Act of 1919 provided for an Investigation of Prices Committee and a Costings Department (responsible to the Board of Trade), of which the chief officers were a chartered and an incorporated accountant. Also attached to the Costings Department was an Advisory Committee of which Sir Nicholas Waterhouse, Sir Harry Peat, and Sir John Mann, C.A. were members, together with the Presidents of the Institute and the Society.

The position in the coal industry was particularly serious and there was a strike lasting some months in 1926, the year of the general strike which lasted nine days and was due in great part to sympathy with the miners. A National Board for the Coal Industry had been formed, of which Sir William Plender was the first independent chairman from 1921–5, and he later (1937) became Chairman of the Coal Mining Royalties Tribunal.

A committee was set up in 1924 and continued in being until 1927 under the chairmanship of Lord Colwyn to consider and report on the National Debt and on the incidence of existing taxation, with special reference to their effect on trade, industry, employment and national credit. A joint memorandum was submitted by the accountancy bodies.

In 1925, when the pound was approaching pre-war parity, the Chancellor of the Exchequer, Winston Churchill, accepted the advice of some prominent financial and economic personalities and made the decision to return to the gold standard, though many doubted the wisdom of this step. By 1930 there were unmistakable signs of a complete economic collapse and there was little confidence in the pound owing to the unfavourable trade balance and the huge expenditure on unemployment relief.

A Committee on Finance and Industry, with Lord Macmillan as chairman, had been appointed in 1929 and among the fifty-seven witnesses were Sir Mark Webster-Jenkinson and H. Lakin-Smith, the latter representing the Association of British Chambers of Commerce. The committee reported unanimously in favour of Britain adhering to the gold standard, and stated that the currency must on no account be devalued. The necessity for raising prices above their then existing level and for co-operation between the central banks and international discussion on the restoration of trade were strongly emphasized. A National Economy campaign was launched to be carried into every part of the country, and a Friends of Economy Fund was opened, Plender being one of the three trustees. The House of Commons agreed to set up a small independent committee 'to make recommendations to the Chancellor of the Exchequer for effecting forthwith all possible reductions in national expenditure on supply services, having regard especially to the present and prospective position of the revenue'. The chairman was Sir George May and Plender and Webster-Jenkinson were among the members. From the committee's report (1931) it was plain that the country was living far beyond its income, and among the recommendations made were cuts in unemployment insurance payments with increased contributions, reductions in teachers' salaries and grants for higher education, increases in school fees, and the abolition of the Road Fund. The Trades Union Council refused to accept the suggested reductions in unemployment pay and teachers' salaries and, as there was a serious split in the Cabinet over the proposals, a National Government, with Ramsay MacDonald as Prime Minister, was formed to deal with the crisis. The gold standard was once more suspended as a defensive measure in support of British credit. In the House of Lords Plender pointed out that national efforts to reduce public expenditure would be unavailing unless they were supplemented by international co-operation on such matters as the revision of war debts and reparations, the lowering of tariff barriers, and disarmament.

Unfortunately there was little in the international situation to encourage hope of any action of this kind. In 1929 a period of unbridled speculation had ended in the collapse of the stock markets in the United States and, high though unemployment was in this country, it was even worse in Germany and America. In 1933 the gold standard was abandoned by the United States, which adopted a policy of deliberate depreciation of the dollar. Bank failures in that country were almost daily occurrences and had their repercussions in other countries. A World Economic Conference held in London (1933) failed to agree on any measure which might save the world from the disasters that had overtaken it and threatened to plunge it into worse chaos. The rise of the Nazi Party in Germany was spreading the fear of war and by 1936 the system of collective security had collapsed.

The whole period covered by this chapter can, so far as accountants are concerned, be viewed as a series of crises in financial affairs in which they were continually called upon to advise.

There were in this period some important staff changes at the Institute. The Hon. George Colville, who had given thirty-six years of outstanding service as secretary, resigned as from the end of August 1935. When he was appointed in 1899 the members numbered 2,500 and its leaders were striving to build up the Institute on sound foundations, a work in which his assistance was invaluable; a great deal of the early dignity and eminence of the Institute was due to his influence. When he retired, the membership was over 11,500 and it had achieved a standing that was recognized the world over. He was succeeded by R. Wynne Bankes, C.B.E., barrister-at-law, who had been assistant secretary since 1929, and Alan S. MacIver, M.C., barrister-at-law, was appointed assistant secretary.

A portrait of George Colville by Sir William Llewellyn was subscribed for by the Council and hung in the Hall of the Institute. A copy was presented to him and Lady Cynthia Colville for their home.

Four International Congresses of Accountants took place during this period. The Netherlands Society of Accountants were the hosts in 1926, when representatives of nineteen nationalities from the principal countries of the world met in Amsterdam for the Second International Congress. The Institute delegates were led by the President, Sir Arthur Whinney.

For the Third Congress in 1929 the accountants of the United States entertained a gathering of over 1,600 people in New York. The Institute was represented by its President, Sir William Plender, and a number of individual members. Sixty-four papers were discussed in the exceptionally humid atmosphere of a heatwave.

It was this country's turn in 1933 and its eight leading accountancy organizations acted as hosts for the Fourth Congress. A most successful series of meetings took place in London under the presidency of Sir William (by now Lord) Plender. In addressing the Congress he suggested that some means might be devised whereby knowledge of the accountancy practice in various countries could be pooled, so as to bring together in concise and clear form essential material concerning the relevant law and practice affecting matters of common interest to the profession throughout the world. The principal social event was a banquet in Guildhall, at which H.R.H. Prince George, Duke of Kent, was present.

The Fifth International Congress held in Berlin in September, 1938, was in many ways an extraordinary event. A less suitable time and place for such a meeting could hardly be imagined, for it had become quite clear that only a miracle could save the world from another war in which Great Britain and Germany would be involved against each other. So tense was the situation that there was considerable hesitation as to whether the British delegates should travel to Germany, and they decided to do so only in the knowledge that an aeroplane was to be kept standing by, ready for use in an emergency. The Foreign Office preferred that they should go in the interest of good relationship, but suggested that wives should be left behind. The Institute was accordingly represented by its President, Charles Palmour, its secretary, Wynne Bankes, and by Stuart Cooper, Sir Harold Howitt and Tom Walton. The atmosphere was not made any easier by the fact that the whole affair was under the patronage of the National Socialist Government, and fascist salutes between Germans and Italians were continuous. The delegates first called at the British Embassy and asked if the safe conduct pass they had received from the Germans would be valid should war break out. In reply they were told that they had surely heard of 'the scrap of paper'. The President of the Congress was Dr Otto Mönckmeier, President of the Institut der Wirtschaftsprüfer, but the presiding genius was the Government representative, Reichsminister Dr Hans Frank, Reich Leader for Law, who was later to gain an unenviable notoriety as Governor-

General of occupied Poland, and was sentenced to death at the Nuremberg Trials for his appalling war crimes.

On the last day of the Congress the British Prime Minister, Neville Chamberlain, paid his third flying visit to Hitler in a desperate effort to avert the final disaster, and on the same evening a message from London advised the immediate return of the delegates, advice which was followed with relief by those who, in spite of the lavish hospitality and organizing genius displayed, had endured rather than enjoyed the previous few days.

The tragic events of the years which followed the Berlin Congress brought a rude cessation of international co-operation of this kind. It was not until 1947 that on the initiative of the Institute a decision was made to resume the practice of holding Congresses, and out of this decision came the Sixth International Congress on Accounting, held in London in 1952.

The titles of the papers read at the International Congresses by members of the Institute are given in Section 4.

# Chapter Five

# 1938-1957

*Impact of the Second World War and courses for returning members. Change in attitude towards members in industry. Enlargement in the concept of the functions of the Institute. Issue of recommendations on accounting principles. Summer courses and students' training. Co-operation among accounting bodies in parliamentary matters. The Companies Act,* 1948. *Attempts at co-ordination of the profession. Integration with the Incorporated Society.*

THE YEAR 1939 opened in the certainty that war was inevitable. This time there were no illusions about the nature of the coming struggle. Total war had long been foreseen and now it was on the way. It had to be fought with new and terrible weapons, and above all it was a test of the whole nation's grim determination to fight in defence of freedom and the way of life that only freedom made possible. In the words of the Prime Minister, Neville Chamberlain, when he broadcast on September 3, 1939, to tell the people of this country that once again we were at war with Germany, it was to be a fight 'against brute force, bad faith, injustice, oppression, and persecution', and in the later words of his great successor, Winston Churchill, the British people must expect 'blood, toil, tears and sweat', a prophecy that was to be amply fulfilled.

For total war there had to be total organization and measures were soon passed which aimed at conserving the country's material resources and bringing all possible human resources into the mighty effort required to survive and win. In the previous year a Central Register had been established and by the beginning of 1939 over 6,000 members of the Institute out of a total membership of about 13,000 had responded to an invitation from the President, C. J. G. Palmour, to enrol their names as being ready in time of war or other national emergency to offer themselves for appropriate work in their professional capacity, while 3,000 others had indicated that they were prepared to undertake whole-time national service. The establishment of the register took place at the same time as the introduction of a Schedule of Reserved Occupations. A system of deferment was introduced and an accountants' committee was set up with Palmour as chairman, which took an active part in making representations to the Ministry of Labour and National Service to ensure that the profession would not be so denuded of men as to make it impossible for accountants to carry out their duties, a large proportion of which were of an essential public nature. Clearly there was going to be no lack of work requiring an accountant's training, and Palmour represented the accountancy profession on an advisory council formed to deal with the utilization in Government Departments or elsewhere of persons with scientific, technical, professional or high administrative qualifications. Some at least of the lessons of 1914–18 had been learned and a Ministry of Supply with wide powers was created. Here too an accountants' advisory panel was needed to advise in the selection of suitable accountants or accountancy firms to undertake the examination of accounts and other work, mainly in connection with the numerous controls imposed. The chairman of this panel was Sir Nicholas Waterhouse; Sir Herbert Smith of Birmingham was a member, and the secretary of the Institute was secretary. It should be recorded here that Palmour remained President of the Institute for the six years of war which were to follow and bore much of the brunt of the problems which this involved.

Some of the chief public appointments of members in this period are noted in Section 9.

Wartime legislation placed many new burdens on practising accountants, and there was an almost continuous flow of statutes, orders and regulations. The Government attempted from the start to keep profiteering in check. The Prices of Goods Act, 1939, was designed to prevent the prices of certain goods from being raised above the pre-war price by more than the increase in the cost of production and selling. In addition to a Central Price Regulation Committee, regional committees were set up on which a number of members served. The Board of Trade could direct the method of computing prices and require any person carrying on business to keep books of account and other records in a specified form and to produce them for examination when required. The Minister of Supply had power to compel any contractor to produce his accounts and, if they were not kept in a manner that would enable a fair price to be determined, the Minister might specify the form to be adopted; a control of a kind not hitherto known in this country. Home trade supplies had to be limited in order to divert production into export channels and to release productive resources for war purposes. An auditor's report on the businesses concerned was required by the Board of Trade in a form agreed with the accountancy profession. Under the Civil Defence Act air raid shelters had to be provided for employees, and claims for grants for capital expenditure on these had to be certified by a qualified accountant. The House to House Collections Act, 1939, and the War Charities Act, 1940, both contained provisions requiring the keeping and audit of accounts. The Prevention of Fraud (Investments) Act, 1939, which waged vigorous war on share-pushing, was of considerable importance to auditors, particularly Section 12, which provided, *inter alia*, that 'any person who . . . by the reckless making of any statement, promise or forecast which is misleading, false or deceptive, induces . . . another person to enter into . . . any agreement for . . . subscribing for securities . . . shall be guilty of an offence . . .'

The first successful prosecution of an auditor under this Act was the case of Regina v. Wake and Stone, heard in the Central Criminal Court in June 1954. A prospectus issued by a furniture manufacturing company inviting the public to subscribe contained a statement by the auditor that the stock and work-in-progress had been valued by the company's officials at the lower of cost or market value. About a year later, the company was in difficulties and proceedings were taken against the managing director and the auditor. It was not disputed that the timber had been overvalued. The stock sheets had plainly been altered after the original valuations by percentage additions and in this form had been seen by the auditor who, without further inquiry, had accepted the managing director's explanation that the alterations had been made because the original valuations were wrong. The auditor was charged on four counts with fraud and on three with recklessness. He was acquitted on all the charges of fraud and found guilty of one charge only of recklessness, for which he was fined, the Judge remarking that he had been so excessively careless as to be reckless.

The Act also gave the Registrar of Friendly Societies wide powers to require the production of books and accounts and provided for the audit and publication of the accounts of unit trusts and of the managers' remuneration in relation to such trusts.

Wartime taxation vitally affected the work of accountants. The imposition of a new excess profits tax of 60 per cent, which was raised to 100 per cent in 1940, required the establishment of a standard for every business, and the comparison of that standard with the assessable profit of each successive trading period. A purchase tax with differential rates brought a great number of practical difficulties in its train, and the introduction of the P.A.Y.E. (Pay As You Earn) system of collecting income tax in the Finance Act, 1940, threw additional responsibility upon employers and their accountants.

All these and many other demands would have had serious effects at any time, but added to the continual pressure for the release of more men for the fighting forces they made the situation facing practising accountants for a time almost desperate. Overworked themselves, they found it increasingly difficult to obtain staff with the necessary training and experience to perform the normal work of current audits, let alone to cope with the complicated problems produced by the requirements of the Chancellor of the Exchequer and Parliament. It was this, no doubt, that caused the President to make his blunt, but timely, 'no poaching' statement at the annual meeting in 1940. He said that the Council was strongly of opinion that no member should seek to make good any shortage of staff by approaching the employees of another member or encouraging them to leave his employment; 'in other words the duty and obligation in regard to staff is the same as that in regard to professional work – no poaching'. The London Members' Committee did their best to help their professional brethren by keeping a list of those members who would be willing to assist other accountants in the conduct and supervision of their practices. In its second report, issued in 1940, the Select Committee on National Expenditure urged in the most vigorous terms that the greatest possible use should be made of the services of qualified accountants, in order to avoid the difficulties that arose in the First World War when they had to be withdrawn from the Forces to help to prevent or correct financial irregularities. In view of pressing demands on every side for their services, the age of reservation for accountants was accordingly reduced to 25 in 1940, though it was raised again to 30 in the following year.

The intense bombardment from the air, and later the flying and rocket bombs, which in addition to bringing death to many people, brought destruction to much property, faced auditors with an unexpected professional problem. In the interests of the defence of the realm it was essential that nothing should be published in any form that might help the enemy to identify the places where bombs had fallen or reveal the amount of damage suffered. The vulnerable assets of a company might be accurately described as in ruins, but to disclose the true position in the accounts might be highly dangerous. In August 1941 the Council helped to solve the auditor's difficulty by issuing to practising members a letter giving alternative forms of wording which might be appropriate as a note on the balance sheet of a company whose assets had suffered war damage.

The buildings round Moorgate Place suffered very badly during the raids, but the Institute was extremely fortunate and escaped with nothing worse than a few broken windows.

An interesting decision on the question whether books of account were 'goods' insurable under the War Damage Act, 1943, or 'documents' expressly excluded from insurance under that Act, was given by Mr Justice Humphreys in the King's Bench Division on March 1, 1945. He held that a 'document' was something which made something evident, which gave information on something, and he thought that the Board of Trade might say that account books were merely evidence of work done, purely personal to the owner of the business and of no value to anyone else. The word 'documents' must include ordinary books of account.

Sums were made available from Institute funds each year for sending text-books to prisoners of war. Special arrangements were made in co-operation with the British Red Cross Society for the holding of examinations in prisoner of war camps, and with the Service authorities for candidates in the Forces to be examined overseas. Only a handful of students were able to avail themselves of these facilities each year, but they were of great advantage to the few who could do so, and the high proportion of successes was a heartening indication of the morale and faith in the future of those whose liberty had been so rudely interrupted. The opportunities provided in this way were the only occasions on which the examinations of the Institute have been held outside England and Wales.

Some 3,000 members of the Institute – about one-quarter of the total membership – served with H.M. Forces during the 1939–45 war, many of them throughout the whole war; a substantial number had been members of the Territorial Army. Many decorations were awarded. One V.C. was awarded posthumously to G. W. Gunn, and another to the Hon. W. P. Sidney, later Viscount de L'Isle. Several thousand articled clerks also served with the Forces. In 1951 at St Michael's Church, Cornhill, the Bishop of Stepney (the Right Reverend Robert Hamilton Moberly) dedicated a Roll of Honour containing the names of 202 members and 273 articled clerks who lost their lives.

The citations for the awards of the Victoria Cross were as follows:

*G. W. Gunn* (on November 21, 1941)

'The King has been graciously pleased to approve the posthumous award of the Victoria Cross to the undermentioned Second Lieut. George Ward Gunn, M.C., 143906, Royal Horse Artillery, Wirral, Cheshire. On November 21, 1941, at Rezegh, Second Lieut. Gunn was in command of a troop of four anti-tank guns which was part of a battery of twelve guns attached to the Rifle Brigade Column. At 10.00 hours a covering force of enemy tanks was engaged and driven off but an hour later the main attack developed by about sixty enemy tanks. Second Lieut. Gunn drove from gun to gun during this period in an unarmoured vehicle encouraging his men and reorganizing his disposition as first one gun and then another was knocked out. Finally only two guns remained in action and were subjected to very heavy fire. Immediately afterwards one of the guns was destroyed and the portee of another was set on fire; all the crew killed or wounded except the Sergeant though the gun itself remained undamaged. The Battalion Commander then arrived and started to fight the flames. When he saw this Second Lieut. Gunn ran to his aid through intense fire and immediately got the one remaining anti-tank gun into action on the burning portee himself sighting it while the Sergeant acted as loader. He continued to fight the gun firing between forty and fifty rounds regardless alike of the enemy fire, which was by then concentrated on this one vehicle and of the flames, which might at any moment have reached the ammunition with which the portee was loaded. In spite of this Second Lieut. Gunn's shooting was so accurate at a range of about 800 yards that at least two enemy tanks were hit and set on fire and others were damaged before he fell dead, having been shot through the forehead. Second Lieut. Gunn showed the most conspicuous courage in attacking this large number of enemy tanks with a single unarmoured gun and his utter disregard for extreme danger was an example which inspired all who saw it. He remained undismayed by intense firing and overwhelming odds and his gallant resistance only ceased with his death. But for this very gallant action the enemy tanks would undoubtedly have overrun our position.'

*The Hon. W. P. Sidney* (on February 6–10, 1944)

'The King has been graciously pleased to approve the award of the Victoria Cross to Captain (Temporary Major) William Philip Sidney, 42108, Grenadier Guards, for superb courage and utter disregard of danger in the action near Carroceto in the Anzio beachhead in February 1944. The period February 6–10, 1944, was one of critical importance to the whole state of the Anzio beachhead. The Germans attacked the British division with elements of six different divisions and a continuous series of fierce local hand-to-hand battles was fought, each one of which had its immediate reaction on the position of other troops in the neighbourhood and of the action as a whole. It was of supreme importance that every inch of ground should be doggedly, stubbornly and tenaciously fought for. The area Carroceto-Buonriposo ridge was particularly vital. During the night February 7–8, Major Sidney was commanding the support company of a battalion of the Grenadier Guards, company headquarters being on the left of battalion headquarters in a gully south-west of Carroceto ridge. Enemy infantry who had by-passed the forward rifle company north-west of Carroceto heavily attacked in the vicinity of Major Sidney's company headquarters and successfully penetrated into the wadi. Major Sidney collected the crew of a 3-inch mortar firing nearby and personally led an attack with tommy guns and hand grenades, driving the enemy out of the gully. He then sent the detachments back to continue their mortar firing while he with a handful of men took up a position on the edge of the gully in order again to beat off the enemy who were renewing their attack in some strength. Major Sidney and his party succeeded in keeping the majority of the Germans out but a number reached the ditch 20 yards in front from which they could outflank Major Sidney's position. This officer in full view and completely exposed dashed forward without hesitation to a point whence he could engage the enemy with his tommy gun at point-blank range. As a result the enemy withdrew, leaving a number of dead. On returning to his former position on the edge of the gully Major Sidney kept two guardsmen with him and sent the remainder back for more ammunition and grenades. While they were away the enemy vigorously renewed his attack and a grenade struck Major Sidney in the face, bounced off and exploded wounding him and one guardsman and killing the second man. Major Sidney single handed and wounded in the thigh kept the enemy at bay until the ammunition party returned five minutes later when once more they were ejected. Satisfied that no further attack would be made he made his way to a nearby cave to have his wound dressed but before this could be done the enemy attacked again. He returned to his post and continued to engage the enemy for another hour by which time the left of the battalion position was consolidated and the enemy was finally driven off. Only then did Major Sidney, by that time weak from loss of blood and barely able to walk, allow his wound to be attended to. Throughout the next day contact with the enemy was so close that it was impossible to evacuate this officer until after dark. During that time as before although extremely weak he continued to act as a tonic and inspiration to all with whom he came in contact. Throughout the engagement Major Sidney showed a degree of efficiency, coolness, gallantry and complete disregard for his personal safety of a most exceptional order and there is no doubt that as a result of his action taken in the face of great odds the battalion's position was re-established with vitally far-reaching consequences on the battle as a whole.'

The Council did not allow the endless calls on its time, and the many immediate problems requiring attention, to prevent it from looking ahead; indeed during and immediately after the war the Institute developed in directions and at a pace unprecedented in its history. The importance of some of the steps taken while the country was still fighting for its existence can hardly be overestimated.

The severe depression which had marked the 1930s, coupled with the regular annual increase in the number of members during those years, had made it exceedingly difficult for newly-qualified men to find satisfactory appointments; salaries of or less than £3 a week for employees of practitioners outside the London area and £4 10s 0d within that area were not uncommon. At the same time industry and commerce were beginning to appreciate the value of what is now known as management accounting, and also that the full-time service of a qualified accountant could be of direct assistance to them in the day-to-day planning and operation of their businesses. The result of both these factors was that an ever growing number of chartered accountants were taking posts in commercial and industrial concerns, and the two classes of non-practising members – those employed by practising members and those in industry – formed the majority of the Institute membership. But they had no representation on the Council and they felt that their needs and the contribution that they could make were ignored.

It was not, therefore, surprising that at the Annual Meeting in 1941 – during one of the darkest periods of the war – a motion was passed that in the interests of the whole membership it was desirable that the Council should include not less than five Associates, whether practising or not, and that the Council be invited to lay before the next Annual General Meeting proposals to give effect to this policy. Accordingly at the Annual Meeting in 1942 the Council presented a report on its constitution which was approved, though not without several other motions being brought forward and defeated. The really important feature of the Council's report was the recognition that the wide practical experience of members in appointments of responsibility in commerce and industry could clearly make a valuable contribution to the consideration, in association with practising members, of the financial problems of the business community. While the Council still considered and recommended that, having regard to the objects for which the Charter was granted, membership of the Council should 'as a general rule' be confined to practising members, it proposed the establishment of a committee, to be known as the Taxation and Financial Relations Committee, 'to consider matters affecting taxation and the financial relationship of the business community with the Inland Revenue or other Government departments'. The functions of the committee would be of an advisory character with wide terms of reference, it being intended that non-practising members in London and the provinces who held commercial appointments and associates employed in the offices of practising members should be fully represented, and that the committee would have power to appoint sub-committees for regional or specific purposes and to co-opt members of the Institute to such sub-committees. By this means it was hoped to establish an active and effective liaison between the practising and non-practising sides of the profession.

The effect which the adoption of this report was to have on the status of the Institute and on the relationship between the Council and the general body of members would certainly have surprised those who prepared it and thereby 'builded' better than they knew. Although the original proposal was for a change in the constitution of the Council, the results of the establishment of the Taxation and Financial Relations Committee, whose first chairman was Harold Barton, have been infinitely greater and more beneficial than could have been achieved in any other way.

It may be added here that the 'general rule' referred to above was broken in 1943 when for the first time in the Institute's history a Fellow not in practice, F. R. M. de Paula, was elected to the Council.

The establishment of the new committee made possible for the first time the close collaboration of practising and non-practising members; this in itself brought a new spirit into the life of the Institute, and because the members were drawn from all areas of the district societies and because in each of those areas a similar regional committee was established, this new spirit spread throughout the country. Hitherto the attention of the Council, so far as concerned its internal relationship with members, had been mainly concentrated on matters of administration, particularly its primary functions of acting as an examining and disciplinary body. Now it embarked upon a deliberate policy of issuing official guidance on technical matters, a course that came to be welcomed on all sides and enhanced its reputation with its own members, the public and the Press.

Only a few months after the committee had come into being the Council issued (on December 12, 1942) the first of its series of recommendations on accounting principles. These began in a modest way dealing with subjects of topical interest, namely the accounting treatment of the newly-introduced tax reserve certificates, and of war damage contributions, premiums and claims. They soon, however, ventured on to more controversial ground, and much of the substance of the recommendations made up to

1944 found its way into the report of the Committee on Company Law Amendment and eventually into the Companies Act, 1948. The recommendations had a profound influence on accounting practice and immensely strengthened the hands of members of the Institute when advising or persuading company directors who might still wish to present their accounts in the manner permitted by the Companies Act, 1929, though this procedure failed to give shareholders the information which current opinion considered they ought to have. With memories of the Royal Mail Steam Packet case still in mind, many accountants thought that secret reserves and other items that might conceal the true position from shareholders were no longer, if they had ever been, a desirable feature of company accounts.

With the invaluable assistance of the new committee the Council also embarked upon an intensive study of many taxation matters on which they felt that some revision of the law was necessary to remove anomalies or inequities. Memoranda from the Council came to be regularly submitted to the Chancellor of the Exchequer and to the Board of Inland Revenue on proposals made in Finance Bills. This practice has been continued and although the Institute's representations are not always accepted, they meet with a fair measure of success and lead to useful discussions. Moreover, the Institute has established in this way a reputation for putting forward a completely impartial view, based on the experience of a wide cross-section of its members, and uninfluenced by the special interests of any particular section of the tax-paying community.

Some of the more recent recommendations of the Council are referred to later, but it may be said now that all their statements on technical subjects have been authoritative in the highest degree. Invariably there was much detailed groundwork of research and drafting, extending over long periods, by the Taxation and Research Committee (the cumbersome name of Taxation and Financial Relations Committee given to it at its birth was dropped in 1949) with the assistance of the regional committees already mentioned. The subject was then considered by a committee of the Council and finally by the Council itself. By this time some 300 chartered accountants might have contributed to the preparation of the document in one way or another, and even then a statement would only be published if it fulfilled three stringent conditions that the Council imposed. First, the substance of the document must be approved by a substantial majority of the Council members; second, it must be reasonably concise in form; and finally, there must in the opinion of the Council be a real need for a declaration on the subject and the document must make a definite contribution thereto. Sometimes the Council statements were issued in the form of 'Notes' instead of 'Recommendations' where a firm recommendation was not possible or where the subject matter was not a question of accounting principle. These, expressed simply and clearly, helped the reader to make up his own mind.

The increasingly important subject of management accounting was not neglected. In 1952 the Taxation and Research Committee appointed a standing sub-committee to consider and report on the objects, principles and technique of management accounting, and the possibilities for improvement and further development of this service to management, not only by accountants engaged in industry and commerce, but also by accountants in public practice. The Cost Accounting Sub-Committee, which had been in existence for some time, was dissolved and its two drafting sub-committees were transferred to the Management Accounting Sub-Committee. Notes on management accounting, explaining its nature and purpose, were issued in 1954.

During 1944 and 1945 the Council was much concerned with the position of students resuming or commencing their studies after long years of war service. It was recognized that some concessions were necessary but that any modification of normal requirements must still ensure a proper standard of qualification. The modifications therefore applied only to those whose careers had been interrupted by the war. Special rules were made for exemption from the preliminary examination where an ex-serviceman had not been able to obtain the necessary standard for entry into articles; exemption from the intermediate examination was permitted under certain conditions where articles had been interrupted by war service. In normal circumstances the period of training for these ex-servicemen was reduced from five to three years. Several thousand students took advantage of these concessions in the immediate post-war years.

Some important alterations in the examination syllabus were introduced in 1944. The knowledge of law required was made less extensive and confined to matters more directly concerning the profession; a separate paper on taxation was introduced into the final examination, and to conform with modern conditions the subjects of costing and mechanized accounting were given greater prominence.

Because of the large number of articled clerks serving with the Forces the number sitting for the examinations during the war period was very much reduced, and in consequence the number of new admissions to membership dropped to a very low figure. On the other hand the number of those entering into articles was not so seriously affected, though those who did so knew that in all probability their service would soon be interrupted. As soon as the war ended there was an almost overwhelming rush of young men wishing to become chartered accountants, and to complete their examinations.

The Council decided to examine the whole question of the training of articled clerks. The operation of the Tuition Scheme had been a source of embarrassment. There had been serious difficulties over the interpretation of its arrangements, and the number of students enrolling had been disappointing. With the outbreak of war the scheme virtually came to an end, and little was heard of it until 1944 when at the Institute Annual Meeting a resolution proposed by E. Miles Taylor was passed calling for a full report to be prepared and laid before a special meeting. A special committee of the Council had to undertake an arduous task, which was not made any easier by being carried out during the intensive bombardment of London by flying bombs, which frequently interrupted its labours. Nevertheless the work was completed within five months and a full and frank report on 'The work and liabilities of the Union of Chartered Accountant Students' Societies Tuition

Authority' was circulated to members and adopted at a special general meeting on October 31, 1944. The report envisaged the possibility of the Council having to provide students returning from war service with a suitable alternative to the remaining obligations of the Tuition Authority, and the scheme quietly faded out of existence. Students resumed their postal courses with the tutors of their choice, and there was no demand for lecture services on the ambitious scale originally proposed; very few requests for the return of lecture fees were received, and the total expenditure incurred by the Institute on the winding up in the three years to 1948 was no more than £120.

In 1946, the Council issued a statement on training, which contained no proposals fundamentally changing the system that had been in operation since the foundation of the Institute in 1880.

Great efforts were made also to assist members returning from war service. Refresher courses of three weeks' duration were held at Cambridge and Oxford colleges in 1945 and 1946. 'Refresher' was not entirely an apt description since returning members had to familiarize themselves with a mass of new legislation affecting their work, as well as the pronouncements on accounting principles made by the Council through the Taxation and Financial Relations Committee. These courses were extremely successful and it was hoped to acquire suitable premises and teaching staff to enable a continuous series to be held on a residential basis, but this was not found to be possible. The district societies also arranged special lecture programmes. In their place, however, and very largely as a follow-up on them, summer courses were established on a permanent basis – as more fully described in section 6.

Two other steps taken in 1945 may be mentioned as evidence of awareness of the problems ahead. The first was a published statement by the Council that having regard to the increased cost of salaries and other expenses, a substantial increase in fees over those ruling in 1939 was justifiable, and the second was a temporary and very slight relaxation of the unwritten rule against advertising, to permit a returning member to announce in the Press that having returned from national service he had resumed practice at a stated address.

The Institute was ready to make grants from its funds towards the cost of the refresher courses and to help students towards the resumption of their studies. In the event the amount required was negligible. The needs of members were met by the course and lecture arrangements, a great deal of time being willingly given by many members who acted as speakers and otherwise assisted, while the financial needs of students were covered by the Further Education and Training Scheme administered by the Ministry of Labour and National Service.

Financially the war period was a lean time for the Institute. It had been accustomed to substantial annual surpluses on income and expenditure account; now it had the new experience of substantial deficits. The main causes of this change of fortune were the falling off in the number of new members and consequently in the admission fees and annual subscriptions, and the fact that the subscriptions of members serving with the Forces were waived, the total sum forgone in this way being over £16,500 up to March 1945. In spite of this, generous subscriptions were made to charities connected with the war, and from January 1, 1940, the net interest from the Institute's substantial holdings of Government stocks was surrendered as a gift to the Government.

It was evident that serious deficits would be incurred in the years after 1945 on a scale which would make disastrous inroads on the dwindling accumulated fund. Inflation was in full swing and this, combined with the increased activities of the Institute and the arrangements for the resettlement of returning servicemen, meant that its income would fall far short of its necessary expenditure. Since the amount of members' annual subscriptions was fixed by the Royal Charter, there was nothing for it but to appeal to members to increase them voluntarily by 100 per cent, pending a revision of the Charter. Eighty per cent of the members responded to the appeal during the years 1946, 1947 and 1948, and how necessary it was can be judged from the fact that in 1946 there was still a deficit of £8,000 after bringing into account voluntary fees of

£15,000. In December 1948, the Institute obtained a supplemental Royal Charter and new bye-laws. It was therefore no longer necessary to rely on voluntary payments, and a new and increased scale of annual subscriptions came into force on January 1, 1949. But the need to safeguard and strengthen the financial position and permit the Institute to continue to expand its activities and the services rendered to members necessitated further increases as from January 1, 1950.

The general purpose underlying the changes in the Charter and bye-laws was to give the members greater control of affairs, and to facilitate administration and management. The original Charter, containing the incorporation clause and expressing its objects, was retained, but the operative clauses were repealed and more emphasis was put on the bye-laws, thus making administration, and future possible changes therein, more simple. Many of the changes related to service under articles, and were designed to improve the training, by investing the Council with considerable power to supervise the conditions of service and to check any abuses of the system without lessening the basic responsibility of the individual principal. Short periods abroad or in industry, under suitable safeguards, were allowed and a more liberal period of absence for study was permitted, but the major period of training remained to be served in a practising member's office.

The procedure adopted in dealing with disciplinary cases underwent a radical change. Hitherto when a formal complaint against a member had been preferred it had been tried by the whole Council, and there had been no right of appeal. A Disciplinary Committee was now set up to hear and adjudicate, subject to a right of appeal before an Appeal Committee of five set up specifically for the purpose.

The extent to which in recent years members of the Institute had taken full-time employment in industry and commerce was recognized by the use of the words 'the accountancy profession' instead of 'the profession of public accountants' in one place, and in another 'members of the Institute' instead of 'public accountants'. A suggestion that the Supplemental Charter should provide for the possibility, in appropriate cases and under proper safeguards, of granting Fellowship to members not in practice was considered carefully by the Council, but it came to the conclusion that such a change would not be in the best interests of members as a whole. In the year of the Supplemental Charter Basil Smallpeice, a member in industry, became the first Associate to be elected to the Council, and at the annual meeting in 1950, the members approved a proposal that of the forty-five seats on the Council 'up to five should normally be occupied by members not in practice, subject to the availability of sufficient suitable members willing and able to serve'. These five seats were to be regarded as a pool to be filled by the Council from any part of England or Wales.

In 1953, the President, T. B. Robson, represented the Institute at the Coronation and to celebrate the occasion the Council held a reception at the Festival Hall. In the same year an annual religious service was inaugurated, some members of the Council feeling that the decline of religion throughout the world was in great measure responsible for the state of world affairs.

In 1955 the seventy-fifth anniversary of the grant of the original Royal Charter was celebrated with a dinner held in Guildhall, at which the toast of the Institute was proposed by H.R.H. the Duke of Edinburgh. The President, D. V. House, presided.

In the early post-war years the Council had cause for great uneasiness about certain trends in national education plans. Among the proposals for reform in the Education Act, 1944, was one for the establishment of County Colleges, at which attendance would be compulsory. This would clearly have interfered with the system of articles and, in 1947, the Council made strong representations to the Minister of Education that there should be a right of exemption for articled clerks, but no satisfactory conclusion was reached. The Council's apprehensions about this and other developments were clearly evident in a further statement on the training of articled clerks which was issued in 1948 in amplification of that which it had made two years previously.

Even more disturbing to the Institute was the report, which appeared in 1949, of the Committee on Education for Commerce, under the chairmanship of Sir Alexander Carr-Saunders, of which F. R. M. de Paula was a member. The Council submitted detailed evidence both by way of a memorandum and by oral evidence, but its views were not accepted and the recommendations of the committee, made in general terms and covering a field of widely differing activities, included proposals that were wholly inappropriate for persons wishing to become members of the Institute. If put into operation they would have undermined the whole system of training under articles, though the committee did not indicate that it had found any defects in that system. The main object of the committee appeared to be to secure uniformity in the examinations of all accountancy, and many other, bodies and to replace existing methods of tuition by the introduction of standardized courses in technical and commercial colleges, so that students studying for the examination of different accountancy bodies would all take the same course. It further proposed that these standardized courses should be taken in the daytime during the period of practical training. It was small wonder that the Institute offered the strongest resistance to proposals that were entirely contrary to its own tradition and beliefs. When in 1951 there was reason to believe that the Ministry of Education was anxious to implement some of the recommendations, the Council issued in March of that year a comprehensive report entitled 'Education and Training for Membership' which was widely distributed. Discussions were held with Ministry officials, who were fortunately more receptive than the committee had been, and, after reviewing the Institute's method of training articled clerks, made it clear that the Minister had no intention of interfering in any way with the profession and would not consider any move which might affect the interests of the Institute without full prior discussion. A lengthy statement on the place of the students' societies in the education of articled clerks was a specially interesting and important feature of the 1951 report.

An important innovation was introduced in 1950 and has since been continued. Up to that time examination candidates, whether successful or not, had not been informed of the marks they obtained nor of the pass requirements. All unsuccessful candidates were now notified of the standard of their performance in the separate papers. In addition candidates who were regarded by the moderators as 'bad failures' in the examination as a whole were informed of the aggregate mark they obtained. The moderators expressed the opinion that such a candidate 'has little chance of passing the examination at a subsequent attempt unless the bad failure can be attributed to exceptional circumstances such as illness, totally inadequate preparation or complete lack of effort'. This procedure was designed as a deterrent to further wasted effort, and to encourage the principal to talk matters over with his articled clerk.

The large number of students coming from overseas presented a special problem. A person of any colour, creed or nationality may qualify for membership of the Institute, but to do so must have served his articles with a member in the United Kingdom and have passed the Institute's examinations here. The Council has on several occasions urged members, as far as possible, to take under articles suitable students from overseas, but inevitably many of them experience difficulties in securing articles – difficulties which are also very real for the principal, who is not a free agent in deciding the type of staff which will be acceptable to his clients. With the annual report for 1944 the President, H. M. Barton, made an appeal in which he said:

> 'Chartered accountants have built up a great name for themselves beyond the seas. It is only right that they should continue to offer facilities for imparting to young men from other countries the traditions, skill and experience which will enable them to help in due course in building up the profession in their own countries with the same character and competence as our own.'

It is appropriate to refer here to what is now known loosely as 'the universities scheme'. In 1942 a special committee gave earnest consideration to the question of providing improved facilities for the education of prospective members of the profession through liaison with the universities. This attracted the attention of the Council of Vice-Chancellors and Principals of the Universities in

England and Wales, and a joint committee representing the universities and the accountancy profession was appointed in 1944, under the chairmanship of Sir Arnold McNair, K.C., LL.D., Vice-Chancellor of Liverpool University, the Institute representatives being E. Furnival Jones, W. L. Barrows, D. V. House and the Secretary. The outline of a scheme was agreed, and approved by members of the Institute in general meeting, the Council undertaking to contribute a total sum not exceeding £1,500 per annum for three years by way of grant to the universities participating. Special degree courses, with accountancy, economics and law as their main subjects, were started at some universities in October 1945. The main features of the scheme, which covered a total period of five-and-three-quarter years, were the adaptation of courses in the participating universities, so as to include the subjects covered by the scheme; whole time attendance at the university for nine terms during the currency of articles, and a minimum of three years' practical training in an accountant's office. The degree was to be accepted in lieu of the professional intermediate examination, but every candidate was still required to pass the final.

In 1945 the Council joined with the National Institute of Economic and Social Research in the appointment of a Joint Exploratory Committee, to continue discussions 'with a view to a closer understanding between accountants and economists regarding the principles applied in their respective fields of work'. The Committee decided that its first task would have to be an examination of the major accounting concepts and of the more important terms commonly used by both accountants and economists. Its report, entitled *Some Accounting Terms and Concepts*, was published by the Cambridge University Press in August 1951. It made disappointingly little impact, chiefly no doubt because, as it stated unambiguously, 'the objectives of the two groups are not the same. . . . The individual accountant is responsible directly to his clients or employer. Economists . . . normally have no particular client. Their work concerns the nation as a whole and its constituent individuals and institutions.'

The case for continuing these joint discussions was not a strong one in view of the entirely different considerations on which the arguments of each side were based, but in the meantime the will of Percy Dewe Leake, a member of the Institute from 1886 until he died in November 1949, offered some prospect of providing a means of research into matters of common interest to accountants and economists. After Leake's death the Council was surprised to learn that he had appointed the Institute as trustee of his residuary estate amounting, before payment of estate duty, to over a quarter of a million pounds. The will provided that the Institute should pay and apply, as directed by the P. D. Leake Committee (which was to consist of five members of the Council, including the President, if able and willing to act), the income of the trust fund for such purposes falling within the legal definition of charity as are likely to benefit and advance the sciences of accounting and of political economy, including the subject of public finance and taxation. The testator made various suggestions, the first of which was that an annual grant or grants might be made to a selected university or universities to establish and maintain a chair or chairs of accounting. In June 1954 the Council was able to announce the establishment at the University of Cambridge (efforts to induce Oxford to co-operate had not been successful) of the P. D. Leake Professorship of Finance and Accounting, to be financed by an annual grant of £3,000. The primary concern of the professor holding the chair would be the conduct and direction of research, and the University was satisfied that a man with skill in accounting technique could further the development of economic thought and knowledge in several important ways. Later in the same year the University announced the appointment of J. R. N. Stone to be the first P. D. Leake Professor; he was at that time Director of the Department of Applied Economics at the University of Cambridge. Grants have since been made for the establishment of a P. D. Leake Research Fellowship at Balliol College, Oxford, and for other Fellowships tenable at Oxford, London and Birmingham Universities. It is important to note that the P. D. Leake Trust is of a general charitable nature and not for the benefit of the Institute alone. The Institute's direct association with it extends only to carrying the administrative burden, consisting of the financial administration of the Trust by the Council, and the appointment of the P. D. Leake Committee who have to determine the use to which the income is put.

The nationalization programme of the Labour Government of 1945 created new problems for the accountancy profession, among which was the loss of professional work by accountants who had been providing auditing and other services for businesses which were to be nationalized. This was clearly a matter for joint action by the accountancy bodies and in 1945 a joint committee was set up to consider the Coal Industry Nationalization Bill in the interests of practising accountants who might be adversely affected by its proposals. In the following year the committee's terms of reference were extended to comprise all parliamentary matters relating to the qualifications and status of auditors, compensation to accountants detrimentally affected by nationalization proposals and any other matters specifically referred to it by the Council of any participating body. The committee was known as the Accountants' Joint Parliamentary Committee and the bodies represented on it were those which were also concerned with the problem of co-ordination of the profession, namely, the Institute, the Scottish and Irish Chartered bodies, the Society of Incorporated Accountants and Auditors and the Association of Certified and Corporate Accountants.

Initially the committee achieved little success, although it considered all measures that came within its terms of reference. Solicitors and parliamentary agents were retained to watch developments and, when it was necessary, they drafted amendments which, if not accepted by the Government, were moved in Parliament. On several occasions deputations from the committee were received by Government Departments. The National Coal Board appointed one firm as auditors for their whole undertaking, and decided against using the services of other independent professional accountants for the audit of its local units. One effect of this was to cause the subject of coal mine accounting to be removed from the scope of the Institute's training and examinations, and to restrict the field of recruitment for the Board's specialized accounting staff. For the British Transport Commission, on the other hand, the Minister decided that the audit of their units should be carried out by independent professional accountants, as also was decided in the cases of the nationalized electricity and gas undertakings. Even so some firms inevitably suffered a serious loss of business and in March 1950 the Council published a statement in reply to criticisms and complaints. This explained that as the Transport Act involved the consolidation of a number of undertakings, the displacement of a number of auditors was unavoidable, and that the Commission intended to employ professional firms so far as might prove practicable and reasonable and would endeavour to take due account of the position of auditors who had hitherto acted. The joint committee sought to obtain acceptance of the principle of compensation to professional accountants detrimentally affected by nationalization but was not successful.

One of the main preoccupations of the committee has been with the audit clause of Parliamentary Bills and Orders for the creation of new public authorities, in an endeavour to establish the principle of professional audit as distinct from Government audit by District Auditors; and to limit the choice of professional auditors to members of the bodies represented on the committee. It was successful for a year or two in maintaining its stand on these two points, but the Mid-Northamptonshire Water Board Order, 1950, after naming the recognized bodies in the audit clause added the words 'any other body which may for the time being be recognized by the Board of Trade for the purpose of Section 161 (1) of the Companies Act, 1948'. A similar formula has been adopted in many other measures, and much therefore depends on the action taken by the Board of Trade.

A long contest was waged between the Joint Committee and the Ministry of Housing and Local Government on the question of professional as opposed to civil service audit. Many Orders were made creating Joint Boards, composed of local authorities, for the administration of water works and other public utility undertakings and the Ministry repeatedly sought to impose audit by District Auditors. The Joint Committee fought the issue on each Order on the basis that the Joint Boards should have the right to choose either professional or district audit. The matter was brought to a head in connection with the Kent Water Bill, and the right of option was established in 1955 when a Select Committee of the House of Lords endorsed a previous decision of the House of Commons, adding a rider that since several committees of both Houses had decided in favour of professional audit, the Minister was no longer justified in recommending the compulsory imposition of district audit.

A vital piece of legislation affecting accountants was the Companies Act, 1948, which consolidated the Acts of 1929 and the new 1947 Act, the latter based on the recommendations of a Departmental Committee on Company Law Amendment set up in 1943 with Mr Justice Cohen as chairman and Russell Kettle as the sole representative of the accountancy profession. The Institute submitted a memorandum and gave oral evidence.

The working of the 1929 Act had disclosed a number of loopholes, particularly in regard to the form of accounts and the information to be given to shareholders, so that the best practice had outstripped the strict letter of the law. Now the law was brought into line with modern outlook and legislation got down to defining, in essential matters, the minimum of information which published accounts should disclose. Previously it had been felt that this was neither practicable nor desirable.

The new Act gave emphasis, for the first time, to the Profit and Loss account, specifying certain expenses which must be disclosed and requiring that this account, no less than the Balance Sheet, must present a true and fair view. For the Balance Sheet it took pains to define the hitherto somewhat flexible terms 'reserves' and 'provisions' and made compulsory the disclosure of certain movements in them during the period of the accounts. It required the disclosure also of loans, including bank overdrafts, specifying which were secured. In regard to fixed assets, by specifying the basis on which their values were to be stated, it implied quite clearly that these amounts were not necessarily a guide to the value of the business as a whole – an illusion which died hard, if indeed it is dead. Those, and other new requirements, made a pronounced advance in the presentation of accounts. Banks, insurance and certain other companies with important international business such as shipping, were exempted from some of the provisions. The nature of the report required of the auditors was specified as also were the categories of persons entitled to be appointed auditors by all but a defined class of companies. For the first time also group accounts became compulsory, either by consolidation or otherwise, for companies owning subsidiaries, and they were required to be covered by the audit report.

The requirements under the new Companies Act involved many fresh problems, some legal and some accounting. The Council obtained the joint opinion of leading counsel (Cyril Radcliffe, Montagu Gedge and Walker Carter) on matters of difficulty affecting accountants and auditors. A booklet containing this opinion and also the Council's own issued recommendations on a number of accounting matters was sent to every member of the Institute.

The President of the Board of Trade set up a General Consultative Committee to advise him upon the use of his powers under the Act, and Sir Harold Howitt was appointed as one of its members. An Accountancy Advisory Committee – including Sir Russell Kettle as chairman, T. B. Robson (who succeeded Sir Russell as chairman) and E. Cassleton Elliott, F.S.A.A. (W. H. Lawson being added later) – was also appointed in view of the many specialized accountancy questions arising.

The Solicitors Act, 1941, was of importance to accountants. Attempts had been made from time to time to tighten up the rules affecting the keeping of accounts by solicitors and new Rules were made by the Law Society under this Act. They included a form of accountant's certificate, dealing in particular with the handling of clients' monies, to be produced by a solicitor once in each practice year. The terms of a memorandum prepared by the Council of the Law Society on the Solicitors' Accounts Rules 1945, the Solicitors' Trust Accounts Rules 1945 and the Accountant's Certificate Rules 1946, in so far as they related to the examination of accounts to be undertaken and the form of the certificate to be given by the accountants were considered and approved by the Institute and other accountancy bodies in 1946.

A tax problem affecting not only professional men as individuals but also the whole future of professions as associations of independent persons in public practice, was tackled by a Joint Committee representing the Law Society and the Institute in 1947. It arose out of the failure of successive Finance Acts to permit in the determination of the taxable profits of a professional man, any deduction to be made in respect of the amounts which must necessarily be accumulated in order to meet capital requirements and to provide in due course for the settlement of goodwill on retirement. A memorandum prepared by the Joint Committee was submitted to the Chancellor of the Exchequer, but neither he nor his successors took any action. In 1950 two important inquiries into taxation began, both under the chairmanship of Millard Tucker, K.C., and both including W. S. Carrington among their members. The first, which reported in 1951, was on the Taxation of Business Profits and was the forerunner of the Royal Commission to which reference is made below. The second dealt with this vexed question of the taxation treatment of provisions for retirement. The Institute submitted memoranda to both committees, and the report of the second, which appeared in 1954, advocated substantial relief for self-employed persons. The urgency of this matter in its effect on the recruitment for and the standard of the professions, was stressed early in 1955 by a joint deputation to the Chancellor of the Exchequer from the General Council of the Bar, the Law Society, and the Institute, on behalf of some twenty professional bodies.

Practising accountants are indebted to Carrington for his part in this prolonged struggle, and reward came when, during his term of office as President of the Institute, some limited though welcome relief proposals were included in the Finance Act, 1956.

While the Millard Tucker Committees were still deliberating, a Royal Commission was appointed in December 1950 'to inquire into the present system of taxation of profits and income, including its incidence and effects, with particular reference to the taxation of business profits and the taxation of salaries and wages'. The first chairman was Lord Justice Cohen, and again Carrington was a member, others being representatives of the legal profession, the City, the trade unions, and economists. The chairman resigned after little more than a year and was succeeded in April 1952 by Lord Radcliffe who, with Millard Tucker as vice-chairman, carried the Commission to the conclusion of its arduous labours, lasting over four-and-a-half years and including two interim reports. An extensive memorandum was submitted by the Institute. It is interesting to recall that in its final report, published in June 1955, a majority of the Commission rejected proposals for the taxation of capital gains, recommended that depreciation allowances for tax purposes should continue to be on the historical cost basis, and suggested as an alternative to the differential profits tax, a single flat rate tax on total profits.

An interesting case touching upon the rights of auditors was that of Fomento (Sterling Area) Ltd v. The Selsdon Fountain Pen Co. Ltd heard in 1957. It was a civil action for breach of contract, but the issue depended upon the proper interpretation of the audit clause in a royalty agreement. For the plaintiff company the auditor had carried out an inquiry into the defendant's records for the purpose of ascertaining the royalties payable to them by the defendants, but the latter refused to allow him to see certain specimens or specifications on the ground that they were not obliged to give information on their business outside the patents. Mr Justice Harman in the High Court decided in favour of the plaintiffs, but his decision was reversed in the Court of Appeal. The case then went to the House of Lords and the Institute briefed counsel to watch the proceedings, as if the decision of the Court of Appeal were allowed to stand it would impose serious limitations on the rights of auditors to obtain the necessary and relevant information under such a clause, and might well have similar effects on a much wider range of audits. By a majority the House of Lords allowed the appeal, Lord Denning saying in the course of his judgment that the work of an auditor was not to be confined to the mechanics of checking vouchers and making arithmetical calculations. He was not to be written off as a professional adder-up and subtractor.

In 1950 R. Wynne Bankes, C.B.E., retired from the secretaryship of the Institute. The son of a distinguished Judge, he had rendered invaluable service to the Institute as assistant secretary since 1929 and as secretary since 1935. Universally popular, he would probably say that, on his side also, his chief pleasure had been his contacts with members of the Institute and of other bodies, both at home and overseas – and perhaps in particular with succeeding Presidents whom he had helped on their official and other duties. His contribution to the solution of the many problems which arose in the Second World War at a time when the Institute staff was depleted should especially be mentioned.

During the years immediately following his retirement preparations went ahead steadily for the resumption of the series of international congresses which the war had appeared to bring to an end. The sixth International Congress was held in London in 1952, the seven sponsoring bodies being the three Chartered Institutes, the Society, the Association and the Institutes of Municipal Treasurers and of Cost and Works Accountants. Sir Harold Howitt acted as President with C. Percy Barrowcliff, President of the Society, as Vice-President and A. S. MacIver as secretary. The numbers present, including delegates, exceeded 2,500, of whom 196 were from the British Commonwealth and 668 from other accountancy bodies overseas. In all 103 societies from thirty-five different countries accepted invitations to the Congress. The American contingent contained no less than nine representatives who had been President of their Institute, and also G. O. May, a member of both the English and American Institutes, who had read a paper at the first Congress in 1904. Apart from the business sessions in the Royal Festival Hall, the chief events were a service in Westminster Abbey and a banquet in Guildhall. The emphasis of the subjects discussed was on the effect on accountants of the changing value of money, taxation, the raising of capital, and the development of the accountant's usefulness in the industrial field.

In 1957 the seventh International Congress took place in Amsterdam by invitation of the societies of accountants in the Netherlands. The Institute's representatives were led by its President, W. H. Lawson.

It is convenient to close this chapter at 1957 when a most significant event took place, namely integration into the Chartered Institute of the Society of Incorporated Accountants ('and Auditors' had been dropped from the title in 1954). The early chapters have referred to the coming into being of that Society in 1885 and the many attempts that were made over the years to agree some form of association with them, and some method of unification of the profession as a whole.

Though these happenings have been chronologically reviewed in each succeeding chapter, it is felt that on so important an issue it would be well to bring them all together in one historical sequence; this has been attempted in Section 1.

In the result there would be no point in repeating here all that took place at the end of the story which, in fact, covers the period from 1943 to 1957 in one long series of discussions, in an attempt at co-ordination of the whole profession, in the drafting of abortive Bills and in the holding of general meetings, till finally integration with the Society emerged. Section 1 also attempts, as this story proceeds, to summarize the reasons which at each stage led to failure or success.

Leaving, therefore, the details of the events to Section 1, it would perhaps be appropriate to finish this chapter with a brief statement of the effect of this integration on the Institute. Although size as such was not the objective, over 10,000 members of the Society exercised their right under the scheme of integration to become members of the Institute. Much rearrangement and goodwill was necessary in solving the administration problems involved, concerning as they did membership of the Council, fusion of District and Students' Societies, the merging of staff, premises, libraries, pension funds and many other activities. The great majority of practising accountants in the United Kingdom became chartered accountants and the confusion hitherto existing in the public mind on this issue was largely resolved; a cause of friction which had long existed between members of the Institute and of the Society had been dealt with; the facilities for attracting young men into the profession as chartered accountants had been substantially extended.

Finally a grateful tribute should be paid to W. H. Lawson on whose shoulders largely rested the negotiations, and the task of satisfying the Institute members. He was described by A. S. H. Dicker, the President, at the special meeting of members in the Royal Festival Hall on February 19, 1957, as 'the chief architect of the scheme'. Tribute should also be paid to the co-operation at all stages of Sir Richard Yeabsley, who, as a member both of the Institute and of the Society, was clearly fitted to be the last President of the latter body, and one of the protagonists of the integration scheme.

As was inevitable, in neither body did the scheme go through without opposition, some sustained to the final voting, as an examination of the results of the meetings, detailed in Section 1, will show. At the Institute's meeting, five members from London and four from the provinces spoke against the scheme – some quite vehemently.

# Chapter Six

# 1957-1965

*Attempt to form an incomes policy. Management training. New legislation. Company accounts and amendment of Company Law. Student training. Practitioner inquiries. Overseas developments. Designation of 'Incorporated' members. Administration of members' offices. Graduates under articles. The Finance Act* 1965.

DURING RECENT years – indeed dating largely from the First World War and much aggravated by the Second – members of the Institute had been greatly troubled by the impact of inflation, and of the resultant rising costs, on their clients' affairs and on their own circumstances. Brief references to the accounting problems involved and to the recommendations of the Institute are made elsewhere in this history. This final chapter, up to August 1965, covers a period in which the Government itself undertook the attempt to formulate an incomes policy which should apply to profits as well as personal earnings. The objective was to keep increases in incomes within the limits which the national economy could bear without undue inflation.

A collateral requisite of that objective was the increase of national productivity, so far as this could be brought about through the application of modern scientific methods and by insistence on efficiency at all levels. The accountancy profession has a major contribution to make in both of these endeavours and the Taxation and Research Committee brought this home to members in its publication *Business Efficiency; the Contribution which the Accountant can make*, issued in 1958. It was, therefore, natural that during this period the Institute should give a great deal of attention to management accounting, automatic data processing, which includes the use of computers, and all else that comes within this field of activity. The profession has sometimes been criticized for failure to give an early lead in this new sphere with the result that other persons and organizations got in ahead of qualified accountants. Whether or not there is any substance in this criticism, there can be no doubt that, from this time, everything possible was done to encourage and improve training and practice in ways that would assist industry to increase efficiency and competitive power. Courses on EDP (electronic data processing) were instituted by the Council. The National Productivity Year (1962–3) and 'The Next Five Years' Conference, which marked its end, helped to impress these aims on the whole country and were supported by the Institute.

In order that students should keep pace with the growing demand for what is sometimes called 'dynamic' costing and management accounting, the final examination syllabus of the Institute was extended in 1957 to cover these subjects. To encourage qualified accountants to further study arrangements were made for (1) a 'Certificate' to be granted by the Institute (in collaboration it is hoped with the Irish Institute) to members who pass an examination in management techniques and (2) a 'Diploma' to be granted by a Board composed of members of five accountancy bodies, for those passing a separate examination in management service at a higher level. Further details are given in Section 7. 'Management accountancy services' are widely defined and those who wish to possess the post-qualification diploma will be required to show a high standard of academic knowledge and practical experience. The diploma scheme, which will not begin to operate until 1966, must be regarded as being in the nature of an experiment. The five accountancy bodies have undertaken to administer it for the first five years of its existence; thereafter any body wishing to withdraw must give at least two years' notice to the others. It will be exceedingly interesting to see how it develops.

In the meantime the increased responsibilities which accountants were being called upon to assume in modern industry had resulted in a notable increase in the number of practising firms with special departments offering expert advice and service in management techniques. Some created separate firms for the purpose, either individually or jointly with other firms. Some have gone so far as to include engineers in their organizations in order particularly to deal with shop-floor problems which this kind of inquiry occasionally involves. These developments raised difficult ethical problems on which the Council issued a statement for guidance of members. One difficulty arising from this type of work was the natural fear of smaller firms that should they introduce a client to a specialist firm they might risk losing an audit, though in the result this fear does not appear to have been well founded. The number of members taking industrial posts in preference to entering professional practice also continued to increase.

Numerous courses in management training were inaugurated to assist members in dealing with the problems facing both management and auditor in relation to the control of the results produced by the processing of electronic data. A number of residential centres for management study were opened under Government and other auspices, including Ashridge College, where a member of the Institute was appointed to the Council of Governors. The Institute was also represented on the United Kingdom Automation Council (formerly the British Conference on Automation).

The rapid development of mass-production methods, particularly in the United States during the inter-war years, made increasing demands on both practising and industrial accountants. It was during this period that G. Charter Harrison, a member of the Institute, played a leading part in the United States, in developing accountancy techniques based on the principles of standard costing and budgetary control. He wrote and published an important book entitled *Cost Accounting to Aid Production* in 1924, and followed it with a further important work entitled *Standard Costs* which was published by the Ronald Press Company of New York in 1930.

In Great Britain also, it is probably true to say that British business was thoroughly awakened by the need for costing and efficiency in munitions and other war production in 1914–18, and that out of this grew the demand for new techniques. It is, however, only during the past two decades that there has been virtually complete acceptance and wide application of methods of financial control based on financial budgets and pre-determined standard costs. In this period the pioneering work of a number of practising firms of British chartered accountants has radically transformed the whole attitude of the profession to these techniques, developing, as they have since done, into the wider field of the programming and utilization of electronic data.

In a community operating under free enterprise one of the chief incentives to efficiency in the face of competition is the profit motive. Undoubtedly the accountant's training has been to help his client to increase profits, and profits are regarded as a major measure of efficiency. Profit returns and percentage yields on capital employed are, and will no doubt remain, among the principal yardsticks of prosperity. A new concept has, however, been introduced into this picture, namely that in times of full employment – the declared objective of all political parties in the United Kingdom – workers will submit to any form of control on earnings only if other forms of income, in particular profits, rents and dividends, are kept within acceptable limits.

It is no part of this history to engage in controversial or political discussions, but accountants are closely affected by Government fiscal and economic policies; indeed they are often called upon for their collective views or individual assistance. Examples of these services are to be found in the appointment of members of the Institute to important public bodies. The Monopolies Commission included Sir Richard Yeabsley, J. M. A. Smith and P. G. Walker. Lay judges of the Restrictive Practices Court included Sir H. Stanford Cooper, W. G. Campbell and D. V. House. The Council on Prices, Productivity and Incomes, and the Iron and Steel Board, which, together with *ad hoc* committees formed to control the prices of various products of agriculture, were all concerned with national objectives.

The duties of these bodies are well known and speak for themselves, but a word may be added about the Council on Prices, Productivity and Incomes because it was unique in character and because its first membership, dubbed 'The Three Wise Men', was drawn from three professions. Lord Cohen, a Lord of Appeal, was Chairman, Sir Harold Howitt represented accountancy and Sir Dennis Robertson was a distinguished economist. Its terms of reference were:

> 'Having regard to the desirability of full employment and increasing standards of life based on expanding production and reasonable stability of prices, to keep under review changes in prices, productivity and the level of incomes (including salaries, wages and profits) and to report thereon from time to time.'

Though appointed by the Prime Minister in 1957, the Council did not report to him or to any other Minister; it had authority, in its own time, to report directly to the public. It did so four times through the Stationery Office between February 1958 and July 1961. The Council was not popular with the Trades Union Congress which, after the first report, declined to co-operate further. The third report suggested the setting up of a national conference on which employers, trade unions and possibly also the Government should be represented. In 1961, when in line with this suggestion the Council ceased, the National Economic Development Council (NEDDY) was set up, with first the Chancellor of the Exchequer as chairman, and, after the change of Government, the Minister for Economic Affairs, representatives of both employers and employed, and other experts. The TUC agreed to join on the express understanding that they were not expected to urge wage restraint on their affiliated unions. Two members of the Institute (John Davies and H. F. R. Catherwood) joined the Council in 1964. In 1963 the National Incomes Commission (NICKY) was appointed, with the status of a standing Royal Commission, to investigate cases of dispute referred to it, and to this body also a member of the Institute (L. C. Hawkins) was appointed. In 1965 that body in its turn was superseded – this time by the National Board for Prices and Incomes, to which another member, J. F. Knight, was appointed.

Arising in part from the need for employers to speak with one voice on industrial problems, another member (Sir Henry Benson) was appointed, in 1963, a Joint Commissioner (along with Sir Sam Brown, an eminent solicitor) by the British Employers' Confederation, the Federation of British Industries, and the National Association of British Manufacturers (formerly the National Union of Manufacturers) to advise on the constitution of a national industrial organization which should integrate these three bodies. This organization was successfully formed by Royal Charter under the title 'The Confederation of British Industry', its first director-general, John Davis, being a member of the Institute.

A fundamental difficulty in the whole problem of rising prices, whether due to 'cost push' or 'demand pull', is the treatment in annual accounts of the resulting inflation. This issue has divided the profession not only in this country but in many parts of the world, and the Council and its committees devoted much time to trying to find an agreed solution or, more probably, an acceptable compromise. The problem involves in particular the proper treatment of fixed assets and their depreciation. The official view of the Council, as set out in Recommendation XV in 1952, favoured depreciation based on 'historical' cost, whilst drawing attention to the question whether profits so computed should be regarded as entirely free for distribution. There was, however, strong pressure from another group, particularly from accountants in industry, in favour of 'replacement' cost. An example of this other view is to be found in the report of the Rochdale Committee of Inquiry into the Port of London Authority (1962). Among a number of other recommendations relating to the accounts the committee expressed the opinion that ports should prepare their financial accounts on a replacement basis because, under inflationary conditions, a charge for depreciation calculated on historical costs necessitated increased borrowings and interest charges when assets had to be replaced or renewed. The problem is still unresolved – the only real solution no doubt being to find a remedy for inflation itself. Meanwhile the profession continues to search for a solution of the accountancy complications involved.

In addition to the foregoing the views of the Institute were sought, during the period under review, on other matters of national importance. Sir Harold Howitt and Sir Thomas Robson gave evidence in 1959, on behalf of the Council, before the Select Committee on the Control of Nationalized Industries. In 1961 the President, P. F. Granger, was invited to attend the annual meetings in Vienna of the World Bank, the International Finance Corporation Development Association and the Monetary Fund. In 1961 Sir Thomas Robson gave evidence in Paris to assist the French Legislature in its proposals for Company Law Reform. The Council having advocated the introduction of a decimal system was invited in 1962 by Lord Halsbury, the chairman of the Committee on Decimal Currency, to give information as to the nature and magnitude of the difficulties likely to arise within the scope of the work of the profession, in the event of the adoption of the decimal system; the Council made a number of suggestions. In 1963 the Institute submitted a memorandum to the Richardson Committee, of which Sir Henry Benson was a member, stating that there were no apparent advantages to justify the replacement of the purchase tax by a value-added tax (turnover tax) which would require the introduction of extensive new administrative machinery.

The rival claims of professional audit, or Civil Service audit by District Auditors, came up prominently in connection with the London Government Bill (1963). This proposed that district audit should be imposed compulsorily on all London boroughs as reconstituted, notwithstanding that nineteen of the thirty-two new boroughs previously had the right of choice. Strong representations were made by the recognized bodies and a deputation waited on the Minister of Housing and Local Government. The President, P. F. Carpenter, took the unusual step of writing letters of protest on the subject to *The Times* which appeared on March 29 and April 9, 1963. But all these efforts were unfortunately in vain, as although arrangements were made for an amendment to be tabled on the Committee stage of the Bill, the guillotine was in operation and the amendment was not called. The Bill therefore became law with the audit clause unaltered.

When the Nathan Committee on Charitable Trusts reported, in

1952, its recommendations were nearly identical with those made by the Council in a memorandum submitted to it in the previous year. In particular the restricted range of investments permitted to trustees had been criticized and the criticisms were repeated in a further memorandum submitted to the Chancellor of the Exchequer by the Institute in 1959. The Trustee Investments Act, 1961, which followed, allowed a far wider range of investments than formerly, including debentures and stocks and shares of certain public companies in the United Kingdom. The Nathan Committee had recommended the professional audit of the accounts of charities but there was considerable opposition to this proposal, when it was discussed in the House of Lords, and it was not accepted. The Charities Act, 1960, required an annual statement of account to be submitted to the Charity Commissioners (or the Minister of Education as the case might be) and gave the Commissioners power to order an investigation and audit by a member of one of the recognized bodies.

The Building Societies Act passed in the same year incorporated all the major proposals in two memoranda submitted by the Institute to the Treasury. For the first time it placed upon building societies a statutory obligation to prepare accounts showing a true and fair view and required the auditors to state whether in their opinion such a view is shown. As a result of this Act the Council issued a booklet on the audit of building societies and drew the attention of the Chancellor of the Exchequer to the desirability of similar amendment of the legislation governing the accounts and audit of friendly and industrial and provident societies.

The regulations made under the Protection of Depositors Act, 1963, were extremely detailed. The accounting provisions of the Companies Act, 1948, were made to apply, with some minor modifications, to the accounts to be delivered under the 1963 Act, and additional information relating to deposits and depositors was required, as well as a great deal of information about 'instalment credit agreements'.

Memoranda had been submitted in 1955 and 1956 to the Mocatta Committee whose findings resulted in the Cheques Act,

1957, designed primarily to dispense with the necessity for the endorsement of cheques paid into a bank for the credit of the account of the payee. Under the Act an unendorsed cheque which appears to have been credited to the payee is evidence of receipt by the payee of the sum payable, and though this did not in any way alter the law in regard to the statutory requirement to give a stamped receipt for a sum over £2 if asked for, it inevitably led to this requirement being honoured more in the breach than the observance. The Council, taking a practical view, urged upon the Chancellor of the Exchequer the benefit of abolishing the stamp duty on receipts, since the duty was negligible as a source of revenue and the confusion that existed presented difficulties to auditors.

The period under review in this chapter saw great activity in the capital market, not only in mergers and reconstructions of all kinds, but in the raising of further capital from the market. Assistance asked from the profession for these purposes was very considerable, particularly in the giving of reports for prospectus purposes in line with the requirements of the Companies Acts. It had become not unusual for the accountants' report to be signed by the auditors of the company making the issue and also by another member of the profession acting as reporting accountant to the issuing house sponsoring it.

The considerable task of reviewing and reporting on the Companies Act, 1948, to consider in the light of modern conditions and practices, including the practice of take-over bids, the duties of directors and the rights of shareholders, and to recommend desirable changes, was given in 1959 to a committee under the chairmanship of Lord Jenkins, of which Sir William Lawson was a member. The previous few years had seen the development of the take-over bid and this had produced a number of new and disturbing problems. Once again the Institute submitted both written and oral evidence. The committee's report, which appeared in 1962, contained about 350 recommendations and its whole tenor was in favour of greater disclosure in accounts. A sample inquiry by the Board of Trade showed that about 90 per cent of all exempt companies were audited by 'recognized' accountants and the committee, endorsing the view expressed by the Institute, saw no good reason for continuing the distinction made in the 1948 Companies Act between exempt and non-exempt companies. It also accepted the suggestion of the accountancy bodies that the requirements of the Act should be amended so as to allow the wording of auditors' reports to be shorter and simpler.

The Councils of the Institute and of the London Stock Exchange have co-operated on many matters. Attention and interest were directed by the latter Council to the presentation of accounts when it broke new ground in 1964 by issuing recommendations for improving the information given by boards of directors to shareholders of public quoted companies. The four points on which special emphasis was laid were the supply of information as to the composition of a group of companies and as to major interests in associated companies; the disclosure of turnover; the provision of an analysis of trading results where widely differing operations are carried on by a company or group; and the issue of quarterly or half-yearly interim reports giving facts and figures.

The Stock Exchange also introduced more stringent requirements in connection with the accounts of its own members, whose balance sheets were required to be covered by a report by an accountant which defined the scope of his audit. The Stock Transfer Act, 1963, gave effect to recommendations made by a committee convened, four years previously, by the Council of the Stock Exchange; in the introduction to a guide to the changes acknowledgment was made of the assistance given by the English and Scottish Institutes.

In January 1965, the Institute issued to the Board of Trade a very detailed memorandum covering the matters which it hoped the Government would deal with in the anticipated legislation to amend the Companies Acts following the proposals of the Jenkins Committee. In May of that year it also sent to that Department a memorandum on points for consideration in connection with the revision of the Companies Winding-Up Law and Rules.

Reference in this connection should also be made to *The Accountant*, which journal instituted in 1954 annual awards for companies which present their accounts in the best form. The entries for these awards are judged by an expert panel, including several members of the Institute. This competition has contributed greatly to the improvement in the presentation of annual reports and accounts. The awards are normally presented by the Lord Mayor of London at a ceremony at the Mansion House. On two occasions they have been presented by the chairman of the London Stock Exchange, thus indicating further the co-operation between that body and the profession.

The Institute in its original recommendations on accounting principles which commenced in 1942 sought to provide authoritative contributions to criteria of the best practice in accountancy problems and then, when substantial recognition had been accorded to these criteria, both in practice and legislation, it decided to embark upon more detailed and technical matters. Examples of these are to be seen in Section 6 in the notes on the Institute's recommendations, particularly in their reference to the five statements on auditing.

The Council further decided (1964) that, in addition to these technical documents, there was also a need for documents of a high standard to stimulate thought and discussion on subjects not yet sufficiently explored and developed, or which for other reasons were not suitable for a Council Statement. A Research Committee was accordingly appointed to select subjects and authors to write about them, appoint study groups, and arrange for publication where appropriate, it being made clear that the views expressed were not necessarily those of the Council. Sir William Carrington became the first chairman of this committee, and a research foundation was created to finance its activities. To avoid confusion, the Taxation & Research Committee was renamed the Technical Advisory Committee.

A committee, under the chairmanship of W. E. Parker, appointed in 1958 to consider the education and training appropriate for entrants to the profession, reported in 1961. As a result of its recommendations a number of alterations in the system of training were made and are described in Section 6. The broad aim of these was to raise the educational standard of entrants into the profession and to ensure that articled clerks receive adequate training and guidance during their period of articles. The importance attached by the Council to these matters was shown by the appointment of an Education Committee, in 1963, to keep education and training under constant review. This committee took over responsibility for relations with the Universities, for negotiations and arrangements with the Ministry of Education and for discussions with local education authorities and other bodies on educational matters.

In 1963 the Public Relations Committee issued a booklet *See a Chartered Accountant*. This was very widely distributed and did a great deal to spread a better understanding by the public of the nature and range of the services provided by the profession.

In the domestic sphere the seven years under review were a period of great activity for the Institute; important changes were made, some of which necessitated amendment of the Charter and bye-laws. Until 1959 members not in practice were debarred from becoming Fellows, but under a new rule then introduced every Associate automatically becomes a Fellow after the completion of ten years' membership, an Associate in practice still being entitled to apply for Fellowship after practising for five years. Membership of district societies became automatic for all members within their area from the beginning of 1964, when the district society subscription was abolished.

Changes in the staff at headquarters took place in 1962 when Alan S. MacIver, C.B.E., M.C., retired after twenty-seven years' service to the Institute. He became secretary in 1950 after serving as assistant secretary and deputy secretary. He served under thirteen presidents and during his years in office saw the membership increase from a little over 11,000 to over 35,000. F. M. Wilkinson, who had been appointed assistant secretary in 1946 and deputy secretary in 1960, and C. A. Evan-Jones, an under secretary since 1960 who had previously been deputy secretary of the Society of Incorporated Accountants, were appointed joint secretaries on MacIver's retirement. The great increase in the number of members, accentuated by integration with the Society, made the need for increased accommodation an immediate rather than a long-term problem. Temporary offices in Moorgate and London Wall and later in Goswell Road had to be taken to allow the original building in Moorgate Place to be enlarged and reconstructed.

It should here be mentioned that on integration with the Incorporated Society, the Institute took over *Accountancy* as its own journal. *Accountancy* was established in 1889 as the *Incorporated Accountant's Journal* and was renamed *Accountancy* in 1938.

Throughout the life of the Institute there have been numerous complaints from small practitioners, especially in the provinces, that they have to contend with difficulties not fully appreciated by the larger firms. Many of them have referred particularly to the competition which they have to face from 'outside' accountants who are not bound by any code of professional ethics. In 1961, under the presidency of P. F. Granger, the Council, with the assistance of the District Societies, undertook an inquiry into the problems of the small practitioner, and the extent of the interest evoked may be judged from the fact that the submissions received resulted in a report which exceeded 200 pages. The subject of registration figured prominently in the replies to the inquiry, but the same objections that have always defeated attempts to form a register were felt still to exist. Many other proposals arising from the inquiry were, however, followed up.

Another inquiry of particular interest to practising members was undertaken in 1963 when their assistance was sought in obtaining reliable information about current levels of fees, charging rates and remuneration of partners and staff. The information, which was purely factual and based mainly on figures for the year 1962, was collated on a confidential basis by The Economist Intelligence Service and a committee was set up to consider the facts revealed. It was estimated that there was an aggregate working population of 73,000 in firms of chartered accountants in England and Wales, of whom 12,000 were working partners. Qualified staff numbered 9,000 (including members of other accountancy bodies) and unqualified staff 21,000; 15,000 articled clerks and 16,000 other staff made up the total.

Differences of opinion between the auditors and the directors of a company do not often become the subject of public debate and the occurrence of such an incident in 1963 caused considerable comment. When the report and accounts of The City of London Real Property Company Limited were sent to its shareholders in that year they were accompanied by a reference in the following terms to a difference between the board and the auditors: '. . . The auditors were not prepared to give an unqualified certificate unless the balance sheet reflected their view, so it is presented in accordance therewith. As, however, the all important mutual confidence between the board of a company and its auditors no longer exists a change is in the opinion of the board in the interests of the stockholders.' Because of this announcement the Institute felt constrained to issue a statement of the principles involved and pointed out that the fact that the auditors of a company disagree to a material extent with accounts submitted to them by directors is not a justification for displacement of the auditors unless the reasons for the proposal are such that the auditors have ceased to retain the shareholders' confidence. The statement added that in some circumstances the performance of auditors' duties may lead inevitably to differences between the directors and themselves. 'The existence of such a possibility is among the reasons why auditors are appointed. . . . The purpose implicit in the appointment of auditors under the Companies Act would be defeated if there were to grow up a practice of displacing auditors whenever a disagreement between them and the directors of a company occurs on a matter of accounting principle.' The proposal which gave rise to this statement by the Institute was much discussed in the City and was withdrawn without being put to a vote at the general meeting of the company concerned. It was, however, felt that the Institute had performed a useful service by its enunciation of the principles set out in its statement.

A matter of particular importance to holding companies and their auditors was raised towards the end of 1964 in connection with the accounts of Seager Evans & Co. Ltd. The auditors of the parent company were auditors also of some of the subsidiaries, but the major operating subsidiaries were audited by other firms. The parent company's auditors, whose head office is in America, felt that their coverage by direct audit was 'inadequate to furnish a basis for expressing an opinion on the consolidated accounts'. They therefore considered it necessary to review some of the audit work done by the other firms, to obtain further information and explanations from the managements of the subsidiary companies, and to carry out certain independent audit verifications in relation to their accounts. The board of the parent company, having considered the matter, decided that other arrangements should be made, and following a request by the chairman, their auditors resigned, on the ground that they could not express an opinion without the scope they required. Another firm accepted appointment as auditors of the parent company without any change in the existing conditions, and it appeared, therefore, that there was a distinct cleavage of opinion between two highly reputable firms of accountants as to the scope of audit needed to carry out their duties.

In 1948 the Council had taken counsel's opinion on the responsibilities of auditors of holding companies when reporting on group accounts under the provisions of the Companies Act of that year. The advice received was that the auditors must take responsibility for accepting the financial statements of subsidiaries incorporated in group accounts, and that if they felt that they could not rely on the reports of other auditors they must make any inquiries they thought necessary.

During the period covered by this chapter, there has been a noticeable tendency for firms of practising members to merge with each other, either in complete amalgamation or in some other form of association. The reason for this is, no doubt, in line with the similar tendency in industry, and so that the staffs of members' firms may be able to cope with the ever increasing demands of their clients in this country and overseas. Even in the one or two partner firms the wide range of accountancy services required by commerce and industry has made it increasingly difficult for them to solve their problems without recourse to some extent to amalgamations. The tendency has also, no doubt, been due to the advent of management consultancy work in that some firms, feeling unable to support a specialized firm or department supplying this service to their limited number of potential clients, have joined with other firms for the purpose. In the case of some firms the above developments have raised acutely the need to be allowed to have more than twenty partners, a restriction which was imposed by the Companies Act, 1862, and which, as agreed in the Jenkins recommendations for Company Law amendment, is now out of date.

At the end of 1964, F. M. Wilkinson retired from the staff through ill health, after two years as joint secretary. The first chartered accountant to hold that office, his outstanding contribution, for which the Institute will ever be grateful, was in the technical field. His influence was, however, felt also in many domestic matters and in overseas relations. He joined the staff in 1944 primarily to take over on the death of S. W. Rowland the secretaryship of the newly formed Taxation and Financial Relations Committee, and remained largely responsible for its work and for that of its succeeding committees, including in particular the issue of the Council's 'recommendations'.

In the years 1957 to 1964 contacts with accountancy bodies throughout the world were maintained and developed. The Institute played a prominent part in the International Congresses which were held at Amsterdam in 1957 and in New York in 1962. The Amsterdam Congress, which was the seventh of the series, was honoured by the presence of, and by an address from, Prince Bernhard of the Netherlands at its opening session. At the eighth Congress in New York all the subjects discussed related to the theme of 'Auditing and Financial Reporting in the World Economy'. Some details of those taking part at these congresses, and of the papers read by members of the Institute, are given later.

The Institute helped to initiate the First European Accountants' Congress, which was held in Edinburgh in 1963, and also participated in the fifth Congress of the Union Européenne des Experts Comptables Economiques et Financiers (UEC) held in Vienna in 1964, the first UEC Congress to be attended officially by the

Institute since it joined the Union. The principal discussion on this occasion was devoted to a highly controversial proposal for a standardized European presentation of accounts; the British point of view was clearly expressed by W. E. Parker, in agreement with views also expressed by representatives from Scotland and from Holland. The difficulties of introducing standard accounts which would have to present widely varying circumstances, methods and needs are obvious, and Parker stressed particularly the disadvantages of trying to force accounts into a mould that could do no more than produce a superficial uniformity which might be misleading. 'To the British accountant,' he said, 'attempts to standardize on a uniform national scale, let alone on an international scale, the form in which accounting information is recorded and reported seems to be fraught not only with difficulties but with dangers.' He emphasized that it would be wiser first to seek uniformity at the beginning of the process, namely on the principles on which accounts should be prepared.

Plans for the future envisage further international congresses at five-yearly intervals and those of the European accountancy bodies perhaps every three years. If these plans mature they will facilitate an exchange of views and in due course, it is to be hoped, a movement towards uniformity in accounting principles.

In January 1965, when Corporation Tax and Capital Gains Tax were proposed, the Institute submitted a memorandum to the Chancellor of the Exchequer with views concerning them. Later when these proposals were incorporated in the Finance (No. 2) Bill, 1965, a further very detailed memorandum was submitted dealing with the administrative problems involved, though not expressing any political views. Many companies, in preparing their annual or other accounts, were in the position that though they knew a liability for corporation tax was running, they would not know until the Budget Statement of 1966 what the rate of that tax was to be. In this uncertainty, the Council of the Institute took the exceptional course in July 1965 of advising on the range of liability which should be accrued, based on such evidence concerning the possible rates of tax as was available from statements made by the Chancellor.

In July it was announced that, within days after the Finance Bill should have become law, the Council had arranged for there to be available for clients, managements and the professional and business community generally, booklets on these two taxes 'for guidance on the most sweeping fiscal changes in half a century'. The response was tremendous, and by the end of August applications had been received for more than 100,000 booklets. The extra work which this fiscal legislation would impose upon members of the Institute, whether in practice or otherwise, was very much emphasized by the President (W. G. Densem) and by speakers at the annual meeting in May.

At a session, called for the purpose to follow the annual meeting, a series of publications was embarked upon designed to help members in the administration of their offices. It was intimated that the subjects to be covered by this series would include practice development and insurance; the provisions to be made for retirement; office organization and the selection, training and management of staff; control of the use of time, the keeping of time records and the vital problem of fees; mergers and associations and the constitutional arrangements of a practice.

In May 1965 there appeared a report of an inquiry into the training and experience obtained under articles and the subsequent professional progress of university graduates articled to members of the Institute from 1952 to 1963. The report was compiled by three appointments officers, and all but one of the university appointments boards in England and Wales participated in the survey; almost 2,000 graduates supplied information. The Institute co-operated by providing lists of graduates who had entered articles in the years concerned. The publication of the report was evidence of the concern of the Institute to examine its recruitment of graduates and to hear their views on education and training.

The conclusions and recommendations in the report related to matters of fundamental importance to the future of the profession. They showed that one in ten of articled clerks were graduates (including 40 per cent from Oxford and Cambridge and 13 per cent from London), but that as 85 per cent of them eventually qualify as compared with 60–65 per cent of non-graduates, the percentage of graduates entering the profession is 12–16 per cent of the total. The intake of graduates per annum had increased from 132 to 318 during the period of twelve years but despite the greater output from the universities and the much improved salary prospects, recruitment had in fact fallen off since 1960. The success of graduates at the professional examinations was well in evidence; something like 90 per cent of those who qualified for membership did so within a period of 4½ years from commencing articles. Naturally there was criticism of the training and experience during articles. The report showed that more graduates than formerly were being trained in the larger firms and that they had been very satisfied with their experience. There was comment upon the lack of integration between theoretical and practical work and on the absence of guidance as to suitable reading for the Institute's examinations and as to the student's progress in studies and training.

Ever since integration with the Incorporated Society in 1957 there had lingered a sense of grievance that under the Scheme some of its members though becoming members of the Institute were not entitled to be designated 'chartered accountants'. A request for the removal of this restriction was raised at several subsequent annual meetings until in 1965 it was notified that, subject to the due approval of members and of the Privy Council, steps would be taken to amend the Charter and bye-laws. Conditions were still to be maintained requiring that any such member who wished to practise must have had certain defined previous experience of practice, but subject to this all 'Incorporated Accountant' members of the Institute were to be entitled to become 'chartered accountants'.

On the eve of sending this history to press, it was announced that the purchase had been completed of major interests in adjacent properties for the redevelopment of the Institute's Hall in Moorgate Place. This means that, when building permission can be obtained, headquarters will have been secured for members in the heart of the City of London and in a building which, if not historic as buildings go, is admittedly of outstanding historic interest. The extension will no doubt, where possible and desirable, be in keeping with the present fabric and the risk of having to migrate elsewhere to find the further space necessary will have been avoided. A photograph of the model is shown between pp. 146 and 147. It will be noticed that the old style of the building is to be continued for the whole length of Great Swan Alley, and that the modern extension is to be kept quite separate.

# Epilogue

IT CANNOT be expected that a history of this nature will have any wide appeal to the general public. It is, however, hoped that it will be of interest to many members and to an appreciable number of people outside the profession who have close association with it. An attempt has been made, without too much detail or repetition, to deal with the early history of the profession and with the struggles, involving both success and failure, to achieve unity not only in the form of the accountancy bodies which have emerged, but in the accountancy principles and spheres of usefulness to which their members all aspire.

Apart from attempting to review briefly the steps which the Council and members of the Institute have themselves taken to develop, train and discipline a new profession and to codify its aims and principles, reference has also been made to certain Acts of Parliament and legal decisions which have had a direct bearing on these matters. Summaries dealing separately with the administrative issues that have arisen, and notes on a few of the firms and individuals involved, have been attempted in the Sections of Part II which follows.

Over the period of this history – and particularly in recent years – the ever increasing work falling on the Council and its committees has become a major burden on the individuals concerned, particularly those in positions of special responsibility. Criticisms, though not frequent, have from time to time, at annual meetings and otherwise, been levelled at the cost involved, at the need for so much effort with its resultant output of paper and advice, and at what is sometimes called the proof of Parkinson's Law. This no doubt is natural and represents a difficulty inherent in running any large professional body growing both in number of members and in the variety of the work they perform – it being impossible to delegate to the secretariat executive action on many of the problems which arise. To meet this position the procedure for Council, committees and sub-committees has been closely defined, and to an increasing extent help on these committees has been invoked by co-opting members who are not on the Council. In 1965 proposals were put to members to increase the number of members of the Council to sixty.

As to the future, it would seem likely that, whilst the basic training for the profession must take place, as in the past, in the practising firms, greater use will be made also of the opportunities offered by the Universities and other centres of higher education and of the experience available in the industrial accountancy field. It seems that an ever growing proportion of the membership of the Institute will, whether remaining in practice or not, become involved in management in its various forms. This will accentuate the need for the non-practising member to continue to identify himself with and to remain interested in the profession, and for the practising member to train an increasing number of students whose services he knows he will never be able to retain.

The nature of the work in most practising offices will no doubt continue to be based, as it has been for a long time, on the audit of industrial, commercial and financial concerns and the legal and financial consequences entailed by their accounts, such as taxation, the raising of capital, investigations, share valuations and advice. Following the General Election in 1964 the profession is left wondering what action, already much delayed, the Government will take on the Jenkins report on the Companies Act with its wide implications affecting auditors personally and the nature of their work. The Government's search after some form of 'incomes policy' must also have a bearing on the main handiwork of the accountant, namely the presentation of the 'true and fair' view of the results of enterprise, and make further calls on him for assistance in the drive for increased national production from which alone, in the long run, can increased demands for income be met.

Since the grant of the Charter in 1880 the number of members of the Institute has increased from a few hundred to 40,000 and it is no small achievement to be able to claim – as is undoubtedly the case – that during such a period of expansion the standing of a 'chartered accountant' throughout the world, both in the quality of his work and in his accepted standard of integrity, should also have been enhanced. The events in this progress have been recorded in an endeavour to give an impartial review of the problems which this development has involved, including as they have done the overall necessity throughout for all members, in the face of competition from unqualified persons, to maintain high professional ethics; the obligation on those in practice to sign an audit report in a form currently prescribed by statute; the need for a wide basis for the training of students; and the need for provision of subsequent study and examination for those members who wish to specialize in management.

One of the most significant developments has been the change in professional outlook which has taken place in the last quarter of a century. For sixty years after the granting of the Charter the attention of accountants was fixed, almost exclusively, on the past records of those business enterprises which were solvent, or on the patching-up or winding-up of those which were not. The idea that planning for the future would prove to be an inevitable and worthy addition to their activities and an obviously suitable employment for their professional skill and experience was slow to develop. It needed the stresses and responsibilities of the Second World War to give it further momentum; the phenomenal growth and multiplication of companies, followed by amalgamations and group formations, since the war, have produced many problems of management which accountants can help to solve, wholly or partially, with the aid of this forward-looking and vitally important approach, now firmly established.

It is ninety-five years since the foundations of an organized accountancy profession were laid here by the formation of the old Institute and other bodies in 1870. The Institute of Chartered Accountants in England and Wales, into which they merged in 1880, has attained, it is hoped, to a position and to a prestige entitling it to take a prominent part in the maintenance and growth of that economic efficiency which is essential to the progress of mankind. Apart from the growing contribution of its non-practising members, this is a function not only of the big firms, employing staffs of hundreds, auditing great industrial companies and providing management consultancy services and highly sophisticated financial advice, but also of the smaller firms and the sole practitioners, providing the essential accountancy services for farmers and small shopkeepers, writing up their books and working out their tax, just as they have been doing since the founder bodies were brought into being nearly a century ago; and some had been in existence long before that time.

William Quilter, *President* of the *old* Institute of Accountants in 1870.

William Turquand, *President* 1880–2.

*to face page 146*

Frederick Whinney, *President* 1884–8.

William Welch Deloitte, *President* 1888–9.

Edwin Waterhouse,
*President* 1892–4.

George Walter Knox,
*President* 1896–7.

Ernest Cooper, *President* 1899–1901.

Sir John Harmood-Banner, *President* 1904–5.

Sir William Peat, *President* 1906–8.

Lord Plender, *President* 1910–12 and 1929–30.

Sir Charles Palmour, *President* 1938–44.

Sir Harold Howitt, *President* 1945–6.

Model of proposed redevelopment of Hall in Moorgate Place, 1965.

DI CESARE RIPA.

ECONOMIA.

gimento, che deue tenere il padre de i figliuoli, perche nel mare delle delitie giouenili eglino non torcano il corſo delle virtù, nelle quali ſi deuono alleuare con ogni vigilanza, & ſtudio.

La ghirlanda de l'oliuo dimoſtra, che il buono Economo deue neceſſariamente mantenere la pace in caſa ſua.

Il compaſſo inſegna quanto ciaſcuno debba miſurare le ſue forze, & ſecondo quelle gouernarſi tanto nello ſpendere, come nell'altre coſe, per mantenimento della ſua famiglia, & perpetuità di quella, per mezo della miſura, che per ciò ſi dipinge matrona, quaſi che à quella età conuenga il gouerno della caſa, per l'eſperienza, che hà delle coſe del mondo. ciò ſi può vedere nel ſeguente Epigramma fatto da vn belliſſimo ingegno.

H 2 Illa dor-

'Economia' ('The Institute Lady') from *Iconologia*, by Cesare Ripa, Rome, 1603. See page 215.

# Part II
# Special Features

# Section 1: The Structure of the Profession

*(It is recognized that the subject matter of this section has been in part referred to chronologically in Part I. Nonetheless the story of the development of the accountancy bodies concerned is so important that it has been thought well to summarize it here.)*

THE HISTORY of the profession on an organized national basis in the United Kingdom dates from the grant of the Institute's Charter in 1880, for although there were separate local bodies in Scotland from 1854 and in England and Wales from 1870, there was not until 1880 any chartered organization which covered the whole of either area. Ever since that date discussions have continued with a view to codifying and protecting the work of a public accountant and to broadening membership of the profession by some form of closer association between the Institute and other accountancy bodies.

It must be borne in mind that in the United Kingdom there has never been any restriction on the practice of accountancy or anything to prevent people forming themselves into an association of accountants of one kind or another. Apart from the three main bodies of public accountants whose members were designated respectively as Chartered, Incorporated and Certified, there came to be others who dealt primarily in specialized fields, as indicated by their titles, e.g. Cost and Works Accountants, Municipal Treasurers and Accountants and District Auditors. As the profession has developed many members of the Institute have moved from public practice into positions in industry and commerce and, though they are still members of the profession, their separate role as non-practising members has had to be considered.

Attempts at closer association have taken many forms which may conveniently be referred to by the terms adopted in each case, namely merger, registration, co-ordination and integration. In the result however no increase in the Institute's membership due to association with another body took place until integration with the Society of Incorporated Accountants in 1957. It must not be denied that along this stormy path harsh things have been said from time to time both by some Institute members concerning – as they regarded it – the lower standard of qualification for other bodies, and by members of those other bodies about what they no doubt considered the 'pedestal' attitude of the Institute. It is, however, clear from the recorded speeches at annual and other meetings that different views were expressed in each body, and that throughout, although all but the last attempts were abortive, it was the difficulties of the problem, as much as personal considerations, which proved the stumbling block.

These difficulties may broadly be said to have been:

(a) The failure to find any suitable or acceptable definition of a 'public accountant'.

This difficulty stems from the fact that everyone is an accountant from childhood onwards, and that accounting enters into most human relationships. It is not therefore easy to define the nature of the work on which an individual may not hold himself out as willing, for reward, to help another without being duly qualified. Many definitions have been attempted and have found their way into draft Bills but none has been found entirely satisfactory in this country.

(b) The need to decide the standard of qualification by training and examination required of a public accountant in order adequately to protect the public. This raises contentious issues such as the adequacy of the student's training, of his examinations and the marking of his papers, of his relationship to his principal during training and his disciplinary control when qualified. It even raises the question as to whether every member of the public necessarily needs in his accountant for all purposes, the same – presumably the highest – standard of qualification, with its presumed influence on the fees he will be required to pay.

(c) The problem of the 'sitting tenant'. This involves decisions as to how far individuals in practice in a specialized line of accounting, whether as qualified members of an existing body, or even unqualified, are to be allowed to come under the general umbrella as public accountants. In so far as they are not qualified and members of a responsible body, the question of their supervision is also involved.

It is probably true that many of these difficulties became more accentuated as time marched on and accountancy became more diversified. There may be those who feel that our forefathers ought somehow or other to have solved their difficulties before other bodies of accountants were formed, but there is also much to be said for the view that they were wise in their generation and that it is desirable, in so varied a subject as accountancy, that it should be left to Parliament or to custom to decide which type of accountant is best suited for which type of work.

It would be somewhat tiresome to review in detail the comments and speeches that have been made on the vexed problems over the years, but it may at least be of interest to note what the chief milestones have been, and the main obstacles, whether or not surmounted.

1880. The Institute which came into being in this year was itself a merger, or at least a getting together of one London and four provincial bodies which had been formed in the period since 1870. Apart from admission to membership of the Institute as 'chartered accountants' of those who at the date of the Charter had had defined periods of experience in practice or in service in a practising accountant's office (conditions which were somewhat eased for such individuals by amendment to the bye-laws in 1891 and 1893), all subsequent entry had to be on the basis of periods of articled service to members in England and Wales (by amendment of the Charter in 1961 this area was extended to cover the whole of the United Kingdom) and the successful passing of examinations. There were also in the Charter restrictions on the nature of other activities in which members were to be permitted to indulge.

Conversely legal decisions came to be given which protected members against the use of the description 'chartered accountant' by persons who were not so entitled.

1885. In this year the Society of Accountants and Auditors (the forerunner of the Society of Incorporated Accountants) was formed under the then current Companies Act with a licence from the Board of Trade. Its formation was no doubt prompted by a feeling among other accountants that the Institute's terms of entry were too restrictive, particularly in their insistence on experience in public practice or articled service therein. There were accordingly included in the Society's membership, apart from practising accountants and their staffs, municipal and county treasurers and accountants in responsible positions in business and the Government. Examinations for the Society began in 1887 and the system of articled service was introduced, but not made essential, in 1889.

1893. Private Member Bills were presented to Parliament both by the Institute and by the Society but failed to pass into law. Their object was in effect to close the profession and to set up a register of all practising accountants. At the Institute meeting Frederick Whinney expressed the hope that public accountants would be known as chartered accountants. The collateral object of the proposals was to counter the encroachment of the District Audit Department of the Local Government Board in the audit of Local Authorities, and of the Department of Official Receivers in Bankruptcy.

1897. A further attempt was made in this year and a new Bill was drafted, this time as a result of collaboration between representatives of the Institute and the Society. In effect it also was a registration bill requiring the registration of all *bona fide* practising accountants. It went further, however, so far as concerned members of the Institute and Society in that it proposed that members of the Society should become members of the Institute in defined categories. For a limited period other persons who had been continuously in practice for ten years were also to be allowed to apply for membership. Special meetings to consider the proposals were held by both the Institute and the Society but at neither were they approved. They were recommended to members at the Institute meeting by Walter Knox, T. G. Shuttleworth and C. Fitch Kemp and opposed by Ernest Cooper.

It is of interest to note that the definition of a public accountant attempted in the Bill was one whose 'principal business or occupation was the performance of the functions of a public accountant'.

1909. In this year another Bill – the Professional Accountants Bill – drafted during the previous three years by the Councils of the Institute and the Society was presented to special general meetings of their members. This also was a registration measure covering all members of the Institute and Society in practice and any other persons who could prove that they were similarly employed. It differed from the 1897 proposals in that there was to be no merger of the separate memberships of the Institute and the Society. Its definition of a professional accountant was on the same lines as that suggested for a public accountant in 1897.

At the Institute meeting the Bill was recommended to members by W. B. Peat and this time Ernest Cooper gave his support. The meeting approved, as also did that of the Society. The proposals were submitted as a Private Member's Bill to the House of Lords where it did not obtain the necessary majority, opposition coming in part from the Scottish and Irish Chartered Accountants who were apprehensive as to what their rights to practise in England and Wales would be. The Bill was then amended to meet the objections which had been raised and was re-submitted to the House of Lords in 1911. This time it obtained a second reading and was to have been considered by a Joint Committee of both Houses. In the end, however, Parliamentary difficulties were raised and the Bill had to be abandoned.

1930. In this year two events took place which had an important bearing on future negotiations for the organization of the profession:

(a) The Local Legislation Committee of the House of Commons decided, in giving its ruling on the Cardiff Bill, to include the London Association of Accountants Limited in the audit clause, thereby making its members eligible for appointment as auditors to the Cardiff Corporation. This reversed decisions which over many years had been made in similar cases. The Association (which, after merging with other bodies, subsequently became the Association of Certified and Corporate Accountants) had now secured recognition and would need to be considered in future discussions concerning the profession. Although some of its members were in public practice, they were mostly recruited from industry and had received their training there.

(b) A Departmental Committee under Viscount Goschen was set up to report on registration, namely on the desirability of restricting the profession of accountancy to persons whose names would be inscribed on a register established by law. The Institute evidence, given by Sir William Plender, William Cash and its secretary George Colville, was against registration and even asked that, if registration were enforced, the Institute should be excluded from such legislation. The Society made it clear that they had always advocated registration but were conscious of the difficulties of the existing situation. The Association, naturally jubilant at their Cardiff success, were in favour. The committee heard a large volume of evidence and finally reported against registration. They thought there was no public demand for it; no satisfactory definition of a public accountant had been forthcoming; and they were not satisfied that it was desirable from the public point of view to have the same standard of qualification for the whole profession. There were also many individuals, other than practising accountants, who had acquired a vested interest in accountancy work.

1943. Although references to the subject were often made at annual meetings of members, nothing further was heard officially until Charles Palmour announced in his presidential address that members of the Councils of the Chartered bodies, with representatives of the Society and the Association, had been probing the possibilities of closer co-ordination and co-operation within the profession. He said he hoped a Bill would be presented to Parliament with the main object of safeguarding the public by prohibiting anyone practising as an accountant unless he held a certificate or licence permitting him to do so, while safeguarding the identity of chartered accountants then and in the future. The 'probing' to which he referred no doubt had reference, among other matters, to a scheme based on the model of the General Medical Council which in 1942 had been prepared by Thomas Robson.

In the result a Co-ordination Committee was set up in 1942 comprising representatives of the Institute, the three Scottish Chartered bodies, the Society and the Association, the Irish Institute joining in 1943. This body remained in session until 1955 – twelve years of continuous effort – at first under Palmour's chairmanship and thereafter under the chairmanship of Sir Harold Howitt. It did not succeed in its main object but the fact that the Councils and individuals concerned gave so much thought and time over so long a period is proof enough of the genuine desire of all concerned to find a solution if one were possible. It was, no doubt, the close contacts this involved with the Society, and particularly with one of its past Presidents – Richard A. Witty – which helped towards the later integration with that body. Although not the compelling motive, it was known that a leading Labour Minister had said that the Government was embarrassed by the number of accountancy bodies, and hoped the profession would put its own house in order.

1946. By 1946 a draft Bill was agreed upon and was presented to general meetings of the six bodies concerned. It was to be known as the Public Accountants Bill. It was to establish by statute, but under the control of the profession, a Public Accountants Council in England and Wales (and a similar Council in Scotland) which would license an accountant to practise public accountancy, and would register bodies of accountants. There was to be no interference with the autonomous position of the accountancy bodies. In the Bill the following attempts at definition were made:

> 'Public Accountant' means a person who carries on a Public Accountancy practice and who, in connection with that practice, offers his service for reward to members of the public, except that it does not include a person who carries on such a practice as part of and as subsidiary to his principal business or practice. 'Public Accountancy' means the 'preparation, investigation, audit and certification of balance sheets, profit and loss accounts and statements of income and expenditure or other similar accounts, or any one or more of those functions'.

All the sponsor bodies approved the draft Bill and entrusted its future progress to the Co-ordinating Committee (now so named) with power to amend. In June 1947 an amended draft was presented to the Board of Trade with a request for early submission to Parliament. Progress was inevitably delayed, in particular by criticism made in discussions between the Board of Trade, other interested Government Departments and specialized accountancy bodies.

Difficulties also arose in considering the best method of dealing, by absorption or otherwise, with the whole, or part, of three other accountancy bodies who claimed recognition, namely the British Association of Accountants & Auditors Ltd, the Association of International Accountants Ltd and the Faculty of Auditors Ltd, as well as the Institute of Municipal Treasurers and the Institute of Cost and Works Accountants. In the meanwhile the Companies Act 1948 became law and discussion had to take place with the Board of Trade to ascertain whether the audit clauses of that Act could be extended to apply to all companies (including exempt private companies), and whether auditors to be authorized under the Act should be required to have had a defined amount of professional experience.

1950. Nonetheless, efforts to find a solution continued and a further Bill entitled 'Accountants (Public Practice) Bill' was drafted in 1950. It never, in fact, saw the light of day, but it may perhaps be mentioned that its main object was to protect the qualified from the unqualified accountant and to prohibit advertising. It again dealt with claims for recognition by the Institutes of Municipal Treasurers and Accountants and of Cost and Works Accountants. It invoked the help of the Board of Trade under the Companies Act, in the recognition of auditors, and handed to that Department functions which under the previous Bill were to have been performed by the Council, including in particular the recognition of other bodies of accountants. It attempted to safeguard further the position of lawyers and others who are naturally involved in accountancy work, by defining a practising accountant as 'a person who is entitled to describe himself as an accountant in public practice and who carries on an accountancy business or practice not being an accountancy business or practice which is carried on as part of and subsidiary to some other business or practice'.

It attempted to specify the nature of work that unauthorized accountants could not hold themselves out as competent to undertake by defining 'a person carrying on an accountancy business or practice' as a person who 'offers his services for reward to members of the public in connection with the preparation, audit or certification of any one or more of the following documents:

(a) balance sheets;
(b) profit and loss accounts;
(c) income and expenditure accounts;
(d) statements of income and expenditure;
(e) any other account or statement of a similar nature.'

The difficulties and dangers involved (detailed later) were, however, so great that in 1951 the Council decided to withdraw its support.

1955. The Co-ordinating Committee remained in being, primarily to explore the possibility of getting the Companies Act improved on the lines indicated above, and it was not until 1955 that the concept of co-ordination was abandoned. The final blow came when a General Meeting of the Association turned down a proposal to absorb selected members of the three bodies mentioned above which had not obtained recognition, a proposal which was fundamental to the amendments of the Companies Act which the Board of Trade was contemplating.

It is interesting perhaps to consider what were the causes that led to this failure. They may perhaps be summarized as follows:

(a) The continuing difficulty of defining a public accountant.

(b) Claims made for the inclusion of other bodies as negotiations continued. These were resisted except in the case of the Institute of Municipal Treasurers and Accountants and the Institute of Cost and Works Accountants; both of which bodies were accepted but only to the extent of work involved in their particular fields.

(c) Pressure was also brought to bear by the District Auditors.

(d) The special position of banks, solicitors, former tax inspectors and others who did trust and taxation accountancy work as part of their established business.

(e) The Companies Act 1948, which became law in the middle of the discussions, substantially undermined the efforts which were being made to introduce some period of training in a public accountant's office into the requirements for public practice by members of any recognized body. This applied particularly to the Association, which would have been required to provide for a period of two-and-a-half years of such training – known as the thirty months rule. When, under the Companies Act, the Association was included among the bodies recognized by the Board of Trade whose members were to be authorized to become auditors of public companies and private companies (other than exempt private companies), this meant in effect that in future there was no statutory need for the Association to introduce this rule, though they have since done so.

(f) It came to be felt that, although the intention was to allow each recognized body to control its own examinations and its own discipline, by degrees pressure would be brought to bear to have these subjects controlled by some combined body and this the Institute was not prepared to contemplate.

(g) There was no doubt disappointment that no satisfactory means had been found to protect members from the activities and advertising of the unqualified accountant, nor to limit the acceptance of his accounts for tax purposes by the Inland Revenue.

1957. This year must be regarded as a particularly notable one. After many abortive attempts, at varying intervals, since the formation of the Society the integration of the two bodies was finally achieved. Following on the failure of the co-ordination proposals it was perhaps natural that negotiations for some form of getting together with the Society should be viewed in a different light. In November 1954 the then President of the Institute, D. V. House, the President of the Society, Bertram Nelson, and the Scottish President, Sir John Somerville, visited New York to attend, in their official capacities, the annual meeting of the American Institute. They then travelled to Canada where, in the lounge of the Royal York Hotel in Toronto, a discussion arose between House and Nelson on the advantages or disadvantages of integration of the two bodies which they represented. In the result they both agreed to raise the matter with their respective Councils on their return to England. This they did and both Councils agreed that the two presidents with Alan MacIver, secretary of the Institute, and Ian Craig, secretary of the Society, should, in the first instance, draft a memorandum of reasons why integration could be beneficial.

These reasons may be stated as follows:

(a) Over a long period of years, dating in fact back to the previous century, negotiations had taken place between the Institute and the Society for some form of association. Although in the early days the entry qualifications of the Institute were more stringent than those of the Society, the latter had for many years for the most part adopted the requirements of training in a practising office, partly under articles to their own members and partly as 'bye-law candidates' in service in the offices of chartered accountants.

(b) In recent years the majority of the Society's new membership had been trained in the offices of chartered accountants, or of firms which included chartered accountants among their partners, so that clearly the training of that element must be held to have been adequate.

(c) The examinations of the Society also were of a fully adequate standard.

(d) The integration of Institute and Society would mean that the great bulk of practising accountants became members of the same body, so that any confusion in the public mind on that issue was largely removed.

(e) Numerous members of the Institute were in partnership with members of the Society, and accordingly their firms were not allowed to practise either as chartered or incorporated accountants unless all became members of one or the other body.

(f) Institute and Society members in practice were competing for the limited number of students available. If the Institute had been compelled to increase the number of articled clerks permitted to each practising member this would have encroached on the number available to the Society as articled or bye-law candidates, and might have compelled the Society to accept training in nationalized and other forms of public or big business – pressure in which directions was already present. An alternative was for the Society to link with the Association.

(g) Some of the difficulties in running separate District and Student Societies – particularly in the Provinces – would be eliminated.

The draft memorandum received the blessing of the Institute

Council early in 1955 with the result that a special committee, under the chairmanship of W. H. Lawson, was formed to negotiate with the Society, which set up a similar committee, and to iron out the many problems. It was a substantial task and reference has been made earlier to the toil and effort which Lawson put in to bring about a successful conclusion. Once the proposals had been made known to members, he travelled the country explaining them to the various District Societies. Strict secrecy had been maintained throughout the whole of the negotiations. Although many people on both sides had been involved no leak of any kind occurred and the first news of the scheme only reached the general body of members when they received the documents at Christmas 1955. The proposals were later approved by separate meetings and polls of the bodies concerned. The voting is shown by the following table (adopted by permission from A. A. Garrett's *History of the Society of Incorporated Accountants* 1885–1957):

| | *Majority required by constitutions* % | Votes at meetings | | | Postal votes | | |
|---|---|---|---|---|---|---|---|
| | | *In favour* | *Against* | *Majority in favour* % | *In favour* | *Against* | *Majority in favour* % |
| Institute of Chartered Accountants in England and Wales | 66⅔ | 1,097 | 278 | 80 | 10,242 | 4,340 | 70.2 |
| Institute of Chartered Accountants of Scotland | 66⅔ | 163 | 25 | 86.7 | 1,822 | 323 | 84.9 |
| Institute of Chartered Accountants in Ireland | 51 | 48 | 17 | 73.8 | 456 | 93 | 83.1 |
| Society of Incorporated Accountants | 75 | 972 | 111 | 89.8 | 8,747 | 1,327 | 86.8 |

The Society was accordingly dissolved, and the bulk of its members became members of the Institute. The Institute had, however, insisted throughout the negotiations that those members of the Society who had not been trained in, or had not as principals had experience in, a practising accountant's office would need to be designated 'Incorporated Accountant Members of the Institute' and not 'Chartered Accountants'. This provision caused a considerable amount of heart-burning among the Society members concerned, both at home and overseas, but it was deemed necessary – partly to uphold the fundamental principle as to training and experience which the Institute had throughout its history maintained, and also because to give way on this point might have opened the door to a flood of other applications for merger and admission.

As part of the arrangements for integration, it was decided to set up a Joint Standing Committee of the chartered bodies to deal with matters arising in connection with the administration of the scheme and to continue in being to consider matters of common interest referred to it.

1965. At the annual meeting in May it was intimated that proposals would be submitted for amending the position of the 'Incorporated Accountant' members of the Institute so that they might be re-designated 'Chartered Accountants' subject to the condition that if wishing to practise in the United Kingdom they must have had certain defined experience of practice there.

## Section 2: District Societies, Branches, Groups and Autumnal Meetings

AS DETAILED earlier, societies of accountants under differing titles existed before 1880 in London and in some of the leading cities, the earliest having been founded in 1870 in Liverpool. It was primarily due to them and to their determination to have a national body for the profession that success eventually crowned the efforts to secure a Charter.

This getting together involved decisions as to the number of members from the different areas to be elected to the Council of the Institute which the Charter declared should consist of not more than forty-five persons, specifying them by name. The numbers to be elected from each area remained, however, a burning question for several years and the records of the early annual meetings of the Institute contain much heated discussion on this issue. Members were elected from each district society as it was formed. The dates of formation of these societies and the numbers now elected from them are given in the notes about each at the end of this section.

In 1942 a 'Report of the Council on the constitution of the Council', approved and adopted by the annual meeting of members, advocated among other matters 'that, having regard to the objects for which the Charter was granted, membership of the Council should as a general rule be confined to practising members'. In recent years this principle has been modified and some non-practising members have been elected to the Council. The district societies have assisted materially in suggesting, for these appointments, distinguished members in their areas engaged in industry and commerce, who were willing to serve and able to afford the time involved.

Of the forty-five seats on the Council referred to in the Charter, five were later allotted to non-practising members, so that the representatives of the district societies numbered forty. On integration with the Society, life membership of the Council was additionally granted to ten existing members of that body, bringing the total membership of the Council at that date to fifty-five; of these ten members two were non-practising.

The district societies have for long been autonomous in running their own affairs, their meetings and their libraries. In varying degrees they have undertaken an overall responsibility for their local students' societies, and have maintained liaison with educational establishments with a view to recruitment and training. They have helped the Council in any necessary inquiries and activities in their areas and in advice on technical matters with which the Council has been engaged. They have endeavoured to keep members of the Institute, scattered over the country, in touch with the views of the Council and *vice versa*. Their main objects may be said to have been to maintain the standards of the profession and its interests in their districts, to arrange lectures and other functions and to establish libraries.

Originally, it was left to each society to attract its own local members, and to arrange its own finances, with help from the Institute. To assist members in distant areas, and in particular to give them the opportunity of being in touch with each other locally, branches were set up affiliated to the parent society of the district. In certain towns also groups were formed affiliated in the same way. This did not, however, produce a satisfactory volume of membership, and in order to encourage all members to operate through a district society, branch or group, and to have a local forum for the expression of their views, it was decided in 1964 that the Institute dues should entitle all members to membership also of their local societies, without further subscription.

In 1938 a committee of the Council was formed to deal with district society affairs and it has since been the custom of the President and senior committee chairmen to hold a conference annually with the Presidents and Honorary Secretaries from the district societies, on Institute matters generally. Similar conferences are held at any time when there is any special problem to discuss. The President further keeps in touch with the district societies by attending their annual dinners.

An interesting feature in the functions of the district societies was the holding, at intervals of two or three years, of an autumnal conference of the Institute in the area of a selected society. These conferences from the earliest years were an important feature of the Institute's calendar, affording opportunities for local gatherings and hospitality, for papers and discussions, for addresses by the President, and as an available meeting ground for members of the Institute who could attend. Attendances, however, tended to fall away, partly owing to costs but more particularly, perhaps, through the difficulty in finding an acceptable balance between serious and social events, which would encourage sufficient members to give up the time involved. The advent of summer courses may, too, have had an effect. In the result these autumnal conferences were abandoned as from 1958 with intent to replace them by foregatherings and interesting discussions at the time of the Annual General Meeting of the Institute. They had been held at the following places in the years stated:

| | | | | | |
|---|---|---|---|---|---|
| 1886 | Manchester | 1907 | Newcastle upon Tyne | 1937 | Liverpool |
| 1888 | Birmingham | 1910 | Sheffield | 1947 | Brighton |
| 1890 | Newcastle upon Tyne | 1913 | Leeds | 1949 | Harrogate |
| 1894 | Liverpool | 1921 | London | 1951 | Torquay |
| 1896 | Sheffield | 1923 | Nottingham | 1953 | Scarborough |
| 1898 | Manchester | 1926 | Bristol | 1955 | Southport |
| 1901 | Birmingham | 1928 | Birmingham | 1958 | London |
| 1904 | Liverpool | 1934 | Manchester | | |

The following brief historical details of the district societies, all founded by local initiative; of their branches and groups; of their total membership at December 31, 1964, and of their representation on the Council may be of interest:

*Birmingham and District Society of Chartered Accountants*

In 1880, a local meeting of former members of 'The Institute of

Accountants' and of 'The Society of Accountants of England and Wales' was held, and the Society was established in 1882. The Wolverhampton Branch was inaugurated in 1946; the Coventry Branch in 1948; the Stoke-on-Trent Branch in 1956; the Worcester Group in 1958 and the Hereford Group in 1964. The president's badge was donated by subscriptions from past presidents in 1923. Membership 2,248. Council members three.

*Bristol and West of England Society of Chartered Accountants*

The Society was formed in March 1903 with a membership of thirty-nine. The Exeter and District Branch was founded in 1947, the Cornwall and Plymouth Branch in 1956 and the Gloucestershire Branch in 1959. There is a separate branch for the Bristol area so that this Society now has a federal constitution. The president's badge was donated in 1937 by subscriptions given by past presidents and members of the committee. The Bristol Area Branch chairman now has a badge of office which was formerly the Incorporated Society's jewel. Membership 1,210. Council member one.

*East Anglian Society of Chartered Accountants*

Founded 1933. The Society operates over a very wide area making the formation of official groups or branches difficult though active meetings are held in them. Committee meetings and meetings of members are held in the four main centres of the area – Norwich, Ipswich, Cambridge, and Colchester, although the headquarters are in Norwich, the largest centre of the Society. The president's badge was presented to the Society in 1938 by A. E. Lark, a founder member and first president of the society. Membership 523. Council member one.

*Hull, East Yorkshire and Lincolnshire Society of Chartered Accountants*

Founded 1927 as the Hull, East Yorkshire and North Lincolnshire Society of Chartered Accountants. In 1939 the area was extended to include the whole of Lincolnshire and the name altered to the present form. The Grimsby and North Lincolnshire Branch was formed in 1948; the Lincoln and District Group in 1951; and the Scarborough and District Group in 1952. The president's badge, acquired in 1930, incorporates the White Rose of York. Membership 567. Council member one.

*Leeds, Bradford and District Society of Chartered Accountants*
The Leeds and District Society of Chartered Accountants was formed about 1900; the name changed to its present form in 1934. Halifax Group, Huddersfield Group and York Group were all formed about 1950; Huddersfield and York Groups have since become branches each with a chairman's badge. The president's badge was presented to the Society by William Adgie, a former president of the Society, in 1929, to commemorate his fifty years' connection with the profession; it incorporates the White Rose of York. Membership 1,548. Council members two.

*Leicestershire and Northamptonshire Society of Chartered Accountants*
Formed in 1901 as 'The Leicester Society of Chartered Accountants', its area being extended in 1939 to include the counties of Northampton and Rutland. No branches or groups. The president's badge was acquired in 1926. Membership 662. Council member one.

*Liverpool Society of Chartered Accountants*
A certificate of incorporation as a limited company was issued in 1870. The Chester and North Wales Branch was formed in 1948; the South Lancashire Branch in 1954; and the Isle of Man Branch in 1958. The Society, the oldest in England and Wales, was one of the petitioners for the grant of the Institute's Charter in 1880. The president's badge, donated in 1911, was subscribed by the committee and members, and incorporates the Lancaster rose in gold. On the reverse are the names of the past presidents since 1911 engraved inside a compartment with double doors. Membership 1,366. Council members two.

*London and District Society of Chartered Accountants*

With the Institute centred on London, it was not until 1921 that a London Members Committee was formed. In 1942 a new constitution was adopted to bring London into line with the other district societies. The Society has a chairman, for whom a badge of office was donated in 1956 by present and past members of the committee and London members of the Council. There is one Branch, for Bedfordshire, Buckinghamshire and Hertfordshire, and District Groups at Jersey (for the Channel Islands), Oxford, Reading and Southend. Besides these, in London there are four general discussion groups and four specialist groups, two concerned with taxation and two with management. Membership 10,200 (March 1965). Council members twenty-one.

*Manchester Society of Chartered Accountants*

A society of accountants established in 1871 at Manchester was the forerunner of the Society which came into being in 1881, following the formation of the Institute in 1880. The North Lancashire Branch, which has seven sub-branches, was inaugurated in 1948 and in 1965 became a separate society as noted below; Bolton Branch was formed in 1951. The president's badge was presented by a member of the Society in 1923. Membership 2,550. Council members three.

*Northern Society of Chartered Accountants*

Founded in 1883 as 'The Northern Institute of Chartered Accountants'. The Cumberland Branch was formed in 1950 with headquarters at Carlisle. The North Yorkshire and South Durham Branch was transferred from the Leeds Society in 1958. The president's badge was purchased out of Society funds in 1935. Membership 1,056. Council member one.

*Nottingham Society of Chartered Accountants*

Formed in 1901. The Derby Branch was formed in 1951. The president's badge was donated by the president and past presidents in 1924. A Lincoln and South Lincolnshire branch was taken over from the Hull Society in 1965. Membership 658. Council member one.

*Sheffield and District Society of Chartered Accountants*

The Sheffield Society was incorporated in 1882 under the Companies Acts, 1862–80, with Board of Trade licence to omit the word 'limited', though there was a society of accountants in Sheffield for five years before that. In 1907, the name changed from 'Sheffield Incorporated Society of Chartered Accountants' to 'Sheffield Society of Chartered Accountants'. In 1937, it was again changed to its present form. The Doncaster Group was formed in 1964. The president's badge was presented by Douglas Howell, President of the Society, in 1936. An original larger badge, still in existence, had been presented in 1923 by Horace Cawood, then immediate past president. Membership 601. Council member one.

*South Eastern Society of Chartered Accountants*

Formed in 1932. Groups at Bournemouth, Southampton, Portsmouth, Brighton, Hastings, Tunbridge Wells and Canterbury meet regularly through the year, the first three named having in 1965 become a separate society as noted below. The president's badge was presented to the Society in 1935 and bears on the reverse the inscription: 'Presented to the Society by H. B. Chaplin Baldwin, M.A., in memory of his father the first President, Edmund Chaplin Baldwin, C.B.E.' In 1960 badges were purchased for the vice-presidents who are respectively chairmen of Branches for 'Kent and Sussex' and 'Hants and Dorset'. Membership 1,230. Council member one.

*South Wales and Monmouthshire Society of Chartered Accountants*

Chartered Accountants in South Wales met at dinner in Cardiff in November 1913, for the twofold purpose of forming a District Society and of honouring R. H. March upon his being appointed a member of the Council of the Institute. The presidential badge acquired in 1928 incorporates the Red Dragon of Wales and was the gift of March during the year in which he was President of the

Institute. In 1964, T. H. Trump, who was the President of the Incorporated District Society at the time of integration, presented to the District Society the badge which he had been invited to retain and which is now, after some amendment of inscription, held for use by the Vice-President of the District Society. Membership 875. Council member one.

In 1965 two further societies were formed of which no details are at present available as to membership, presidential badges, etc.

(a) *The North West Society of Chartered Accountants* – taking over from the Manchester Society an area north of and including the towns of Burnley, Accrington, Darwen and Chorley; and thence to the estuary of the Ribble.

(b) *The Southern Society of Chartered Accountants* – taking over from the South Eastern Society an area which includes the west parts of Sussex and the counties west thereof, including the Groups at Bournemouth, Southampton and Portsmouth.

It is worthy of note that following the introduction of 'automatic' membership on January 1, 1964, the total membership in the next few months, namely, by the end of April of that year, had increased by about 40 per cent overall.

The presidents' (or chairman's) badges of the district societies normally include, in one form or another, the arms and motto of the Institute along with those of their principal cities. A reproduction of each is shown on the plates following.

The Badge of the President of the Institute

# BADGES OF PRESIDENTS (AND CHAIRMAN) OF DISTRICT SOCIETIES

Northern Society of Chartered Accountants

Sheffield and District Society of Chartered Accountants

Leeds, Bradford and District Society of Chartered Accountants

East Anglian Society of Chartered Accountants

Liverpool Society of Chartered Accountants

South Wales and Monmouthshire
Society of Chartered Accountants

Chairman's badge, London and District Society
of Chartered Accountants

eicestershire and Northamptonshire
Society of Chartered Accountants

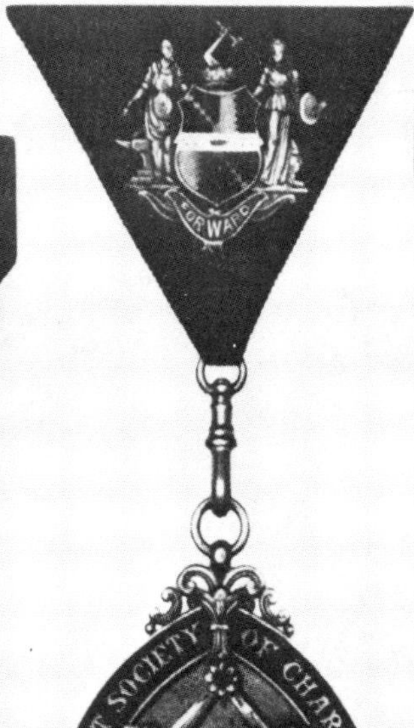


Birmingham and District
Society of Chartered Accountants

Hull, East Yorkshire and Lincolnshire
Society of Chartered Accountants

Bristol and West of England
Society of Chartered Accountants

South-Eastern Society
of Chartered Accountants

Nottingham Society
of Chartered Accountants

Manchester Society
of Chartered Accountants

## Section 3: Students' Societies

THE BROAD principle underlying the running of the students' societies is that they shall be left to look after their own affairs, with parental interest and help from the district society of their area. They have also since 1903 been affiliated in the Union of Chartered Accountants Students' Societies through which body they have contact, and periodical conferences, with the Institute.

In 1935 the Council decided narrowly – indeed by the casting vote of the President – to give financial support to a scheme for the training of students which was to be run by the Tuition Authority, a body set up for this purpose by the Union. Two fundamental features of this scheme were violently opposed by some of the tutorial establishments, namely, a decision by the Authority to appoint one particular firm as the official tutor, and a decision that the names of newly enrolled articled clerks should be handed to that tutor. As the dispute developed, certain amendments were made but they were not satisfactory, and it was only the advent of war that temporarily kept the troubles quiet. They flared up again, at the annual meeting of the Institute in 1943, when a full report was called for by the members.

This report was prepared under serious difficulties during the height of the flying bomb attacks on London, and was duly presented to a special general meeting of the Institute on October 31, 1944. Comments on both sides were quite heated, but in the end Council recommendations were adopted which in effect decided on the liquidation of the Tuition Authority, with an undertaking to give special care to students returning from the war, particularly those who had previously enrolled with the Authority. The Vice-President of the Institute, Sir Harold Howitt, who presided, remarked at the close of the meeting that he hoped, in the language of fairy tale, that the Council and the aggrieved tutors would live together happily ever after.

In retrospect, it is perhaps fair to say that the difficulty arose in deciding how far the Council, as the examining body, could properly go in interesting itself also on the tutorial side. Up till that time its policy was to take no hand in tuition, but following the Parker Report of 1961 this view came to be modified.

Each society has its own technique in the running of its affairs, and in the emphasis which it chooses to give to tuition for the examinations, to more general education, to residential courses, to debates and sports, and indeed to any activity aimed at developing the right sort of mentality and character for a future member of the Institute. This naturally involves the decision, difficult in these days, as to how far to go in letting young people blow off steam.

It may be said that the role of the students' societies is to fit into the general pattern of the training of an articled clerk which, in effect, is a fourfold responsibility undertaken by his principal, by his tutors of various kinds, by himself, and by his society. In particular the students' societies take a special interest in the student in his early days, and when his probationary period is finished, in the sometimes difficult task of developing his wider interests in professional responsibilities and citizenship, at a time when his main objective in life is naturally to get through his examinations.

Since 1948 it has been obligatory for every articled clerk to join his local students' society, and for his subscription to it to be paid by his principal. In the result, the student membership of students' societies is an indication of the numbers of young people seeking to enter the profession. The total of such membership in 1964 was over 16,000.

Integration with the Incorporated Society did not involve so many problems for the students' societies as for the Institute since, for some time previously, the training of students had in some areas already been integrated.

There are now thirty different students' societies in the principal towns or districts.

## Section 4: Overseas Activities

IT IS no part of this history to attempt to deal fully with the developments of accountancy, and of bodies of chartered accountants, outside England and Wales. Nevertheless it would be wrong to omit mention of the part which the Institute has played in assisting the establishment of accountancy bodies overseas on a sound footing.

It has long been the established policy of the Institute to encourage the formation, and to foster the development, of an accountancy body in any country which needs such a body, and where this can be used, under good auspices, as a means of assisting the establishment and maintenance of a vigorous accountancy profession on an organized basis. The Institute has, however, always discouraged the formation of any body which aims at controlling the profession in more than one country and at establishing a permanent international secretariat for this purpose. The wide differences in laws, practice rights, languages and other matters which exist between countries make impracticable the establishment of effective administration, the unity of outlook among the members of such a body, and the holding of examinations for more than one country.

Applying this principle the Institute has favoured the establishment of an overseas accountancy body where there has been reasonable evidence that the body concerned was led by accountants of standing and character, who were inspired by a genuine desire to raise the standards in the profession; that the body could be operated on a sound financial basis; and that it would be ready to accept the co-operation of members of the Institute who carried on their profession in the country. Members of the Institute resident in the country have been encouraged to lend their support and if possible to display leadership in the formative years of the body. Any other advice required has been readily proffered from London.

Contacts with overseas bodies became so constant and complex that in 1954 the Institute set up a separate committee to look after these overseas relationships. This committee has endeavoured to reach some measures of agreement with overseas bodies and governments on the subject of reciprocity of practising rights among their members. The Institute has pleaded, without a great deal of success, that any of its members should be free to practise in any part of the world without necessarily being resident there, provided he declares the origin of his qualification, and that if so described he should be free to choose his own partners as, indeed, he is in England and Wales. Other countries, including some who are or have been members of the Commonwealth, have taken different lines and restrict practice rights in their territories, some forbidding the use there of the names of British firms, some forbidding a member of the Institute to be in partnership there with their own members and some insisting on residence as a condition precedent to the right to practise.

Suggestions have been made by overseas bodies that reciprocity should be interpreted as the right of any chartered accountant practising outside the territory in which he gained his qualification, to be accepted as a member of the chartered body of the territory where he is practising. The Institute has had to resist this interpretation as it would be a departure from its fundamental requirement that its members shall have been trained in the office of a practising member in the United Kingdom.

Several accountancy bodies have been formed outside the United Kingdom and their members have become entitled to call themselves 'Chartered Accountants' as from the date shown below:

| | | |
|---|---|---|
| Canada | 1902 | (Some of the separate provinces using the designation go back earlier, e.g. Quebec 1880, Ontario 1883, Manitoba 1886 and Nova Scotia 1900.) |
| Australia | 1928 | |
| Rhodesia | 1928 | |
| South Africa | 1946 | (The Joint Council of the South African Societies was formed in 1946 but societies |

of accountants in the provinces had been formed earlier and became entitled to use the designation in 1927.)

| | |
|---|---|
| India | 1949 |
| Ceylon | 1959 |
| Pakistan | 1961 |
| Ghana | 1963 |
| Jamaica | 1965 |
| Nigeria | 1965 |

The only one of the above which was itself founded on a Royal Charter was the Institute of Chartered Accountants in Australia. In New Zealand, the New Zealand Society of Accountants was incorporated in 1908 by statute; its practising members are described as 'Public Accountants'.

The Institute has always maintained the closest association with accountants (and accountancy) throughout the world. It has had many conferences with them, formal and otherwise, but until it joined the European Union (UEC) in 1963, no closer formal relationship had ever been formed with accountancy bodies overseas.

The Society of Incorporated Accountants through its South African branches had special relations with the South African societies, to which most of its members in South Africa also belonged. It was regretted that on integration the Institute, by the terms of its Charter and of the scheme, could admit these members only as incorporated accountant members of the Institute. When the Society ceased to exist on that happening, the Institute continued to help Rhodesia with its examination problems, which had previously been supervised by the South African bodies with the help of the Society.

This would seem to be a suitable point at which to mention the activities of the Overseas Accountancy Examinations Advisory Board. The Board is administered by the Chartered Accountants Joint Standing Committee and was formed to advise overseas bodies of good standing, which asked for advice on the scope and conduct of examinations. Although the Board does not conduct the examinations for overseas bodies, it co-operates with local accountants to assist them in establishing a system of examination of high standard. As well as in Rhodesia, the Board has also given help to bodies in Ceylon, Ghana, Malaysia and Nigeria and it is possible in the near future that its activities will spread to further countries.

The numbers of members of the Institute residing overseas over the years are shown in the graph opposite. It may be said broadly that from 1910 to 1950 they were 10 per cent of the total membership and somewhat more from the date of integration with the Society. Of the 4,500-odd members of the Institute overseas in 1964, nearly 1,000 were in practice; a topographical distribution at that date is shown at the end of this section.

Although no formal world-wide association has ever been formed among the accountancy bodies, several very successful international congresses have been held, at which matters of common interest have been discussed.

These have been at the places and on the dates shown below:

| | | | *President* |
|---|---|---|---|
| First Congress | 1904 | St Louis, USA | *A. Lowes Dickinson |
| Second Congress | 1926 | Amsterdam | Emanuel van Dien |
| Third Congress | 1929 | New York | R. H. Montgomery |
| Fourth Congress | 1933 | London | *Lord Plender |
| Fifth Congress | 1938 | Berlin | Dr Otto Monckmeier |
| Sixth Congress | 1952 | London | *Sir Harold Howitt |
| Seventh Congress | 1957 | Amsterdam | J. Kraayenhof |
| Eighth Congress | 1962 | New York | Arthur B. Foye |

**Members of the Institute*

The Institute has been represented at every one of these congresses and its members have played a prominent part in the presentation of papers and in the discussion of the subjects chosen for consideration. It was largely responsible for the initiative which led to the resumption of the congresses after the 1939–45 War. At the London congresses in 1933 and 1952 the Institute's official delegations were led by its Presidents, Lancelot Hill and Thomas

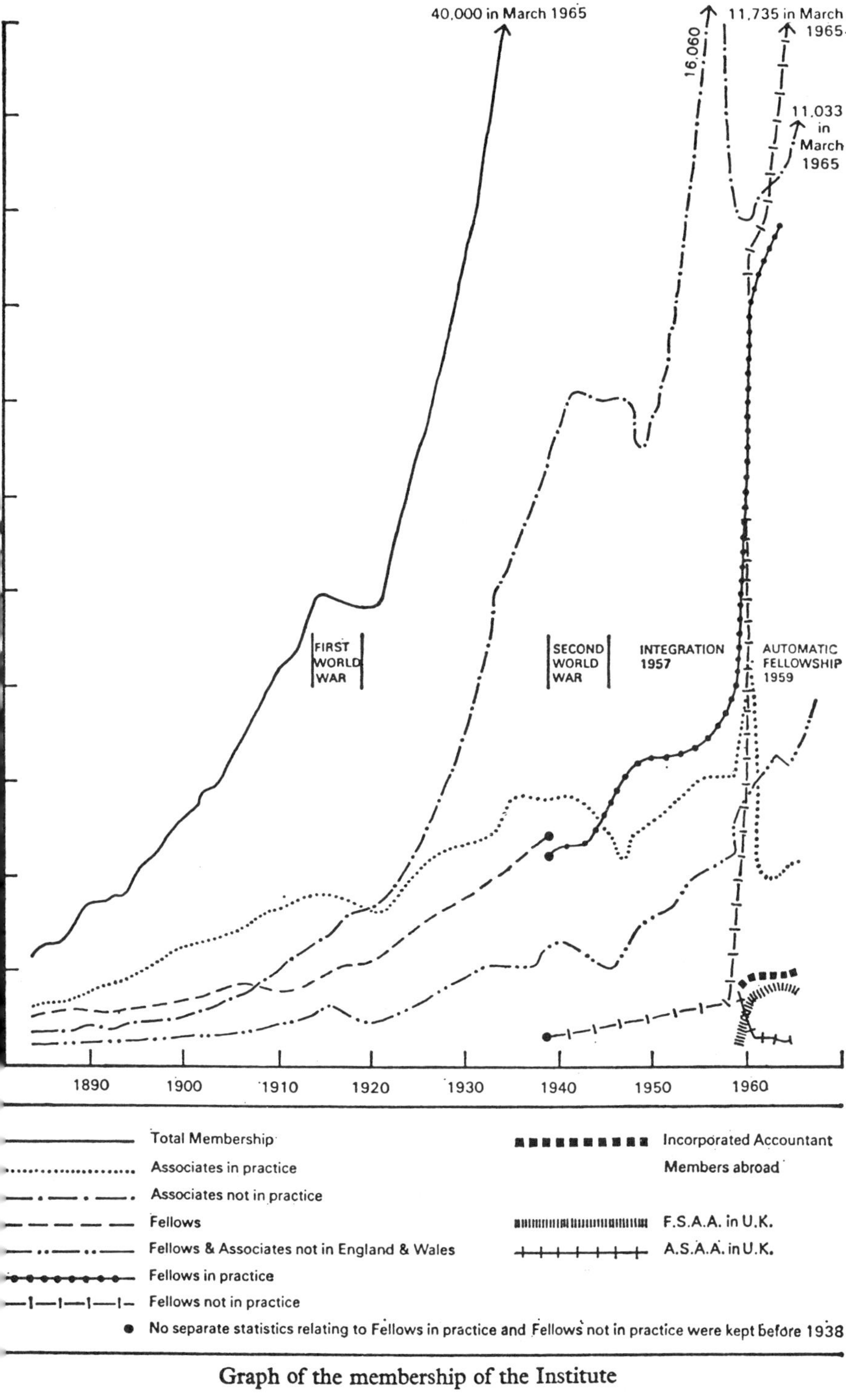


Graph of the membership of the Institute

Robson respectively. In his capacity as President of the 1952 congress Sir Harold Howitt was asked to give one of the opening addresses at the Amsterdam (1957) and New York (1962) congresses. The secretaries of the Institute acted as secretaries for both the London congresses. A list of papers read by members of the Institute at these congresses is given at the end of this section.

A form of international co-operation, in which the Institute did not at first participate, was inaugurated under French initiative after the Second World War. This was to endeavour to form a European body of accountants and resulted in 1951 in the formation of the UEC (the Union Européenne des Experts Comptables Economiques et Financiers) as a federation of European accountancy bodies. The support for this endeavour was of a limited character and the Institute, along with the other recognized United Kingdom bodies and the principal bodies in the Netherlands and Scandinavia, did not find itself able to participate – largely because by the terms of its statutes the UEC aimed at the unification, and possibly the control, of the profession throughout Europe, and wished to make pronouncements on behalf of the profession there. In 1963, however, following discussions which led to changes in the constitution of UEC, the bodies, including the Institute, which had previously abstained, decided to join UEC and Sir Thomas Robson became one of the vice-presidents of that body.

Before the Institute joined the UEC, this latter body had from time to time held four congresses. At its fifth congress in Vienna, in 1964 under the presidency of Herr Ziegler, the Institute participated for the first time, being represented by its President, W. G. Densem, and a large number of its members. W. E. Parker acted as a debater in the discussion 'Possibility, Usefulness and Purpose of a Standardized European Plan of Accounts'.

A European Congress of Accountants, organized by the Institute of Chartered Accountants of Scotland, with the advice and collaboration of an international committee, had previously been held in Edinburgh in 1963 under the presidency of Alexander McKellar, C.A. The Institute had a major responsibility for the initiative which led to this congress being convened; it was well represented by its members headed by the President, Robert P. Winter. A paper *Auditing in Great Britain* was read by S. M. Duncan.

In the long course of years since the founder bodies were established in 1870 and the Royal Charter was obtained for the Institute ten years later, the overseas activities of members have been unceasing and have been a vital element in the growth and progress of the world-wide profession. Particularly in the years which followed the Second World War the Institute itself has participated in these activities in a variety of ways, and in the establishment and maintenance of relations with overseas bodies whose aims and objects were similar to its own. It has sought to reach with them a common understanding that the activities of the accountant's profession are world-wide and that the principles which should govern its actions are universal. In its overseas relations it has been imbued with the belief that the greater the impact of accounting thought in one country upon the thought of accountants in other countries the closer will the profession as a whole come to universal understanding and application of fundamental accounting principles.

Papers read at International Congresses by members of the Institute:

St Louis 1904

*The Municipal Balance Sheet.* H. W. Wilmot.

*The Duties of Professional Accountants in connection with Invested Capital both prior to and subsequent to the Investment.* F. W. Pixley.

*The Profits of a Corporation.* A. L. Dickinson. (In his absence the paper was read by G. O. May.)

Amsterdam 1926

*The Accountant's Certificate in connection with the Accountant's responsibility.* Sir William Plender.

*Education for the Accountancy Profession.* E. E. Spicer.

*The Organization of a large Accountant's Offices in connection with the Accountant's responsibility.* Sir Albert Wyon.

New York 1929

*Problems of Depreciation and Obsolescence – from the standpoint of the Investor in Securities.* Sir William Plender.

*Principles of Valuation – Capital Assets – Historical versus present day costs including Post-War revaluation and exchange and currency problems.* Sir H. Woodburn Kirby.

*Principles of Valuation – External influences affecting Accounting Practice.* G. O. May.

London 1933

*Exchange fluctuations in relation to Accounting as regards operating results and assets values.* A. E. Cutforth.

*Holding and Subsidiary Companies: Accounting principles involved in the treatment of earnings and valuation of holdings.* Sir Albert Wyon.

*The control of charges and profits of statutory undertakings in* (1) *Private or* (2) *Public Ownership and the accounts relating thereto, e.g.* (a) *Railways;* (b) *Docks and Harbours;* (c) *Water;* (d) *Electricity;* (e) *Tramways.* W. Cash.

*Mechanical Accounting.* R. Ashworth.

*Depreciation and Obsolescence; Methods of dealing with these matters, including annual appraisals.* H. G. Howitt.

Berlin 1938

*The auditing of concerns.* C. J. G. Palmour and Stuart R. Cooper.

*Methods of computing cost, and control of prices, by public authorities.* Sir Harold Howitt.

London 1952

*The Accountant in Industry.* F. R. M. de Paula.

*The Accountant in practice and public service.* G. F. Saunders.

Amsterdam 1957

*Principles for the Accountant's Profession.* Sir Thomas Robson.

*The verification of the existence of assets.* Sir Richard Yeabsley as President of the Incorporated Society.

New York 1962
*Accounting and the World Economy*. W. E. Parker.
*Auditing and the World Economy*. Henry Benson.
*Financial reporting and the World Economy*. R. O. A. Keel.

# Members Overseas in 1964

| | IN PRACTICE | NOT IN PRACTICE | TOTAL |
|---|---|---|---|
| *South Africa* | 249 | 476 | 725 |
| *Other African Territories* | | | |
| Cameroons | | 3 | 3 |
| Congo | | 2 | 2 |
| Ethiopia | 2 | 9 | 11 |
| Ghana | 10 | 44 | 54 |
| Ivory Coast | | 1 | 1 |
| Kenya | 43 | 112 | 155 |
| Liberia | 1 | 2 | 3 |
| Libya | 2 | 9 | 11 |
| Morocco | 1 | 2 | 3 |
| Nigeria | 22 | 130 | 152 |
| N. Rhodesia (Zambia) | 12 | 41 | 53 |
| Nyasaland (Malawi) | 4 | 7 | 11 |
| Sierra Leone | 2 | 13 | 15 |
| Somalia | | 1 | 1 |
| S. Rhodesia (Rhodesia) | 65 | 142 | 207 |
| Sudan | 1 | 10 | 11 |
| Swaziland | | 5 | 5 |
| Tanganyika (Tanzania) | 7 | 24 | 31 |
| Tunisia | | 1 | 1 |
| Uganda | 5 | 35 | 40 |
| United Arab Republic | 8 | 23 | 31 |
| Zanzibar (Tanzania) | | 5 | 5 |
| | 185 | 621 | 806 |
| *Australasia* | | | |
| Australia | 30 | 148 | 178 |
| New Zealand | 6 | 41 | 47 |
| Tasmania | 2 | 4 | 6 |
| Norfolk Islands | | 1 | 1 |
| | 38 | 194 | 232 |

| | IN PRACTICE | NOT IN PRACTICE | TOTAL |
|---|---|---|---|
| *Far East* | | | |
| Borneo | 2 | 7 | 9 |
| Burma | 2 | 12 | 14 |
| Ceylon | 28 | 50 | 78 |
| India | 131 | 297 | 428 |
| Japan | 3 | 4 | 7 |
| Malaysia | 37 | 187 | 224 |
| Mauritius | 5 | 14 | 19 |
| Nepal | | 1 | 1 |
| Pakistan | 23 | 68 | 91 |
| Philippines | | 3 | 3 |
| Singapore | 13 | 59 | 72 |
| Thailand | 2 | 14 | 16 |
| | 246 | 716 | 962 |
| *Europe* | | | |
| Belgium | 7 | 24 | 31 |
| Canary Islands | | 6 | 6 |
| Cyprus | 7 | 10 | 17 |
| Denmark | | 6 | 6 |
| Eire | 6 | 37 | 43 |
| Finland | | 2 | 2 |
| France | 12 | 127 | 139 |
| Germany | 2 | 39 | 41 |
| Gibraltar | | 3 | 3 |
| Greece | | 3 | 3 |
| Holland | 2 | 12 | 14 |
| Italy | 5 | 73 | 78 |
| Malta | | 1 | 1 |
| Norway | | 3 | 3 |
| Portugal | 5 | 27 | 32 |
| Scotland | – | – | – |
| Spain | 3 | 14 | 17 |
| Sweden | 1 | 11 | 12 |
| Switzerland | 3 | 70 | 73 |
| Turkey | 1 | 4 | 5 |
| | 54 | 472 | 526 |

| | IN PRACTICE | NOT IN PRACTICE | TOTAL |
|---|---|---|---|
| *Near East* | | | |
| Aden | | 16 | 16 |
| Bahrein | | 6 | 6 |
| Iraq | 3 | 19 | 22 |
| Israel | 6 | 16 | 22 |
| Jordan | | 1 | 1 |
| Kuwait | 1 | 14 | 15 |
| Lebanon | 3 | 8 | 11 |
| Persia (Iran) | 3 | 31 | 34 |
| | 16 | 111 | 127 |
| *South America* | | | |
| Argentina | 5 | 32 | 37 |
| Bolivia | 4 | 4 | 8 |
| Brazil | 10 | 66 | 76 |
| Chile | 2 | 17 | 19 |
| Colombia | | 4 | 4 |
| Peru | 1 | 43 | 44 |
| Venezuela | 3 | 12 | 15 |
| | 25 | 178 | 203 |

| | IN PRACTICE | NOT IN PRACTICE | TOTAL |
|---|---|---|---|
| *Canada* | 46 | 387 | 433 |
| *United States of America* | 19 | 162 | 181 |
| *Central America and Caribbean* | | | |
| Bahamas | 9 | 27 | 36 |
| Bermuda | 1 | 26 | 27 |
| British Guiana | | 16 | 16 |
| British Honduras | 1 | 1 | 2 |
| Guatemala | 1 | 1 | 2 |
| Jamaica | 21 | 55 | 76 |
| Mexico | 2 | 7 | 9 |
| Netherlands Antilles | | 2 | 2 |
| Trinidad | 6 | 54 | 60 |
| West Indies | 20 | 48 | 68 |
| | 61 | 237 | 298 |

In Practice: 939. Not in Practice: 3,554. TOTAL: 4,493

## Section 5: Discipline and Public Relations

*Discipline*

As with all professions, a major task of the governing body is to maintain a high standard for its members in ethical as well as technical matters. This must at times involve the Council in criticism by those who may feel it is setting too strict a standard. The duty imposes the difficult task of holding the balance fairly between the need, on behalf of all members and the public, to uphold the dignity and reputation of the profession, and the natural desire of members to develop their practices in the face of competition – not only from other members but also from unqualified persons. The failure to find a satisfactory formula which could be a basis for the registration of the profession has added to these difficulties.

The Charter of 1880 laid down certain 'fundamental rules' which members were not to violate. They purported to define the limits permitted to members for their association with others in business, namely as to the category of person with whom they were allowed to practise as public accountants, and to forbid participation in profits, commissions or bonuses with any solicitor, or with any auctioneer, broker or other agent employed by them. It was also a fundamental rule that a member not in practice at the date of the Charter should not follow any business or occupation other than that of a public accountant or some business which in the opinion of the Council was incidental thereto or consistent therewith. When the Charter was revised in 1948 this restriction was made to apply only to members in practice.

Violation of these rules rendered the member liable to exclusion or suspension from membership of the Institute, as also did a list of other happenings such as certain convictions in court, action held by the Council to be discreditable to a public accountant, bankruptcy, and failure to pay Institute dues. The 1948 Charter extended the above by making it apply not only to 'a public accountant' but to all members.

There was a proviso in the original Charter whereby the rule forbidding the carrying on of the business of a public accountant in combination with some other business was relaxed in favour of members who were so practising at the date of the Charter. This relaxation was amended in 1948 so that the saying should not attach indefinitely to the firms of such members. It was accordingly made to cease at the end of ten years after the death or retirement of all who were partners in such firms in 1948. It is believed that in 1964 there were only seventeen members (representing twelve such firms) who were still entitled to the exemption.

Neither in the above nor in other respects was the Charter of 1880 amended until 1948 when, in order to facilitate administration and management, many of the provisions of the Charter were relegated to the bye-laws, as was the case also with certain matters concerning discipline. It is, however, worthy of note that the broad principles covering the conduct of members – although naturally elaborated in certain details – remain unaltered. This speaks well for the foresight of the original founders of the Institute.

The main changes in the field of discipline introduced by the new Charter and bye-laws were as follows:

(a) Whereas formerly disciplinary cases were finally heard by the whole Council – a procedure which was cumbersome and difficult to administer – there was set up a Disciplinary Committee as well as the existing Investigation Committee.

(b) It became permissible for a member to be reprimanded or admonished if the offence proved against him was not serious enough to be visited with exclusion or suspension.

(c) The Investigation Committee remained in effect a form of Grand Jury with the duty to consider the facts of any complaint laid against a member, and if satisfied that a *prima facie* case existed, to prefer a formal complaint, not to the Council as heretofore, but to the Disciplinary Committee. That committee was empowered, if satisfied that the complaint was proved, to exclude, suspend, reprimand or admonish the member.

(d) The member was within a defined period to have the right to appeal against any adverse decision, and in that event the Council was under obligation to set up an Appeal Committee to determine the appeal. The decision of the Appeal Committee was to be final and to be reported to the Council, who thereupon merely decided on the publicity, if any, to be given to the finding and decision.

(e) The same procedure was to be followed in respect of certain defined complaints made against an articled clerk. The punishment, if the complaint was substantiated, was to be that in serious cases the clerk might be found not fit to become a member of the Institute, or, if the case was less serious, that he should be reprimanded or admonished.

(f) The Investigation Committee took on the role of adviser, on the request from any member or articled clerk, in regard to any matter of professional conduct. It also advised the Council from time to time as to pronouncements which it considered to be desirable on such matters.

Within the formal list of acts or faults discreditable to a public accountant referred to in the Charter and bye-laws certain more detailed rules of conduct have grown up. The following may be mentioned:

(a) Any member approached with a view to becoming auditor to a company which already has an auditor is put on obligation, before accepting nomination, to inquire if there is any professional reason why he should not accept.

(b) In the circumstances of the Second World War a gentleman's agreement grew up under which members were to respect the difficulties which others were having in completing work and in obtaining staff, and were not without due cause to take either work or staff from each other.

(c) Members have been advised that they should not describe themselves in any way other than as chartered accountants. Descriptions such as 'accountants and auditors', 'taxation advisers', 'insolvency specialists' are considered to be undesirable.

(d) While a member is permitted to have his name shown in directories which have special sections for accountants, it is considered undesirable (except in the case of telephone directories) that an entry should be printed in heavy type or in some other manner which would make the entry stand out from the other entries in the list.

(e) Members have been advised that it may be undesirable to undertake work related to payment by results, and in particular that a member should not be remunerated by a percentage of an amount which he might obtain for his client by way of remission of tax.

(f) Members connected with trade associations have been advised that they must not use their positions as such to acquire professional work which would otherwise not come to them.

In general it may be said that the following examples are typical of the modern kind of case which has come before Council and Committees and of the obvious difficulties which have had to be considered in connection with them:

(a) The problem of advertising whether direct or indirect, e.g. the holding out of members or firms to be specialists in any line of accountancy work, or even the advertising for staff on behalf of clients whereby the name of the member comes into undue publicity.

(b) The description which may be attached to any member in writing a book or letter or in delivering an address. These matters come within the problem of personal publicity.

(c) Complaints by small practitioners who lose appointments on the amalgamation of their clients with large businesses.

(d) Methods adopted in standing up to the competition of unqualified practitioners in the fields, for example, of taxation, and of management consultancy.

(e) The need not to prejudice, if this can be avoided, the position of any member in any proceedings which may be brought against him elsewhere in connection with the complaint.

(f) The position of members who are directors of, or may be employed by, concerns which perform certain of the functions of a public accountant and advertise such services.

(g) The issue by members in practice of booklets which describe the services which they can render to clients.

The following table shows, in the years since the amendment of the Charter in 1948, the number of members tried, the number of them found guilty and the nature of the punishment given:

| | | | Decision | | | | | |
|---|---|---|---|---|---|---|---|---|
| *Year* | *Number tried* | *Found guilty* | *Exclusion* | *Suspension* | *Reprimand* | *Admonishment* | *No action* | *Number of Members of Institute* |
| 1949 | 7 | 7 | 4 | – | 1 | 1 | 1 | 14,632 |
| 1950 | 11 | 9 | 3 | – | 1 | 5 | – | 15,260 |
| 1951 | 12 | 6 | 2 | 1 | 1 | 2 | – | 16,079 |
| 1952 | 20 | 14 | 6 | – | 7 | 1 | – | 16,856 |
| 1953 | 18 | 18 | 10 | 3 | 4 | – | 1 | 17,561 |
| 1954 | 14 | 13 | 9 | 1 | 3 | – | – | 18,151 |
| 1955 | 20 | 20 | 13 | 1 | 5 | 1 | – | 18,772 |
| 1956 | 12 | 12 | 6 | – | 5 | – | 1 | 19,414 |
| 1957 | 26 | 21 | 11 | – | 5 | 4 | 1 | 20,124 |
| 1958 | 21 | 14 | 5 | – | 7 | 2 | – | 31,381 |
| 1959 | 24 | 24 | 16 | – | 6 | 1 | 1 | 32,579 |
| 1960 | 21 | 18 | 5 | 1 | 8 | 3 | 1 | 33,867 |
| 1961 | 27 | 23 | 9 | – | 9 | 5 | – | 35,228 |
| 1962 | 33 | 32 | 13 | 3 | 13 | 2 | 1 | 36,581 |
| 1963 | 33 | 27 | 12 | 2 | 9 | 4 | – | 37,880 |
| 1964 | 10 | 9 | 2 | 2 | 4 | 1 | – | 39,293 |

The above table does not include complaints relating to non-payment or late payment of annual subscriptions.

It is hoped the summary shows that members as a whole are reasonably law-abiding!

### *Public Relations*

Arising in particular out of the restrictions which professional ethics and disciplinary rules imposed on members as against the competition of unqualified practitioners, banks, former inspectors of taxes, etc., the Council in 1960 set up a Public Relations Committee in order, in effect, to present the Institute and the capability of its members to the public in all walks of life, both public and private, in ways which were not permissible to the individual member. In addition it was to make more widely known the special types of service which the chartered accountant can offer, whether he remains in practice or goes out into commerce and industry, beyond services connected with audit, taxation and bankruptcy, on which the profession was no doubt largely founded.

The committee also extended its activities into fields such as publicity given in universities and schools concerning the advantages of a qualified accountant's career; publicity concerning meetings of the Institute and District Societies, with speeches, achievements and appointments of members; and the building up between Institute and members of a sound understanding of the problems confronting the profession and the steps being taken to solve them.

In 1963 the committee was primarily responsible for the issue of the booklet *See a Chartered Accountant*, and in 1965 for inaugurating the series of publications to assist members in the administration of their offices.

# Section 6: Tuition, Refresher Courses and Recommendations

*Students*

Admission to membership in the early days of the Institute was, of necessity, based on defined periods of experience in practice. All subsequent admissions (apart from certain 'Bye-law' candidates of the Society of Incorporated Accountants admitted in 1957 on integration with that body) have been on the basis of articled service in the office of a practising member, in the United Kingdom, followed by examination. This fundamental requirement of articled service has been challenged from time to time by those who think that too much emphasis is put upon the value of practical, as compared with theoretical experience, but without belittling the importance of the latter, the former has remained the sheet anchor of the student's training. This procedure is based on the determination as far as possible to turn out young chartered accountants who not only are well equipped technically, but who will be able to apply judgment to the varied problems, human and professional, which they will meet, and will do so with greater confidence if they have come up against such problems in real life.

In 1946 a committee, presided over by Sir Alexander Carr-Saunders, was appointed by the Government with the following terms of reference:

> 'To consider the provision which should be made for education for commerce and for the professions relating to it, and the respective contributions to be made thereto by universities and by colleges and departments of commerce in England and Wales.'

The Carr-Saunders Report, published in 1949, rejected entirely the Council's views on the training of future members of the profession submitted to it by W. L. Barrows, Sir Harold Barton, Sir Harold Howitt and F. M. Wilkinson. It advocated, instead, raising the age at which articles might be entered into, to at least eighteen years, restricting vocational education up to that age to general commercial subjects by means of courses taken at technical and commercial colleges, streamlining the intermediate and final syllabuses to conform with other accountancy examinations, the eventual elimination of the intermediate by exemption of those who had taken certain courses at technical and commercial colleges, partial exemption from the final for those who held higher certificates for commerce at those colleges, and the adoption of a 'sandwich' principle of articles under which training at those colleges would be given in the daytime concurrently with practical training. The whole purpose seemed designed to standardize the training of accountants and to undermine very much the emphasis placed on the value of practical experience. There appeared even to be the risk of eventual nationalization. The report overlooked the practical point that, if students were not available during the daytime to take their part in audit and other work, their seniors on those jobs working under pressure would tend to lose interest in them and they would not, therefore, get the experience otherwise available. The Council had to take these proposals most seriously (especially as one of their number, F. R. M. de Paula, a non-practising member of the Institute with a wide academic outlook, was a member of the committee), and in 1951 issued a comprehensive report entitled *Education and Training for Membership* in which strong objection was taken to the Carr-Saunders Report. In the end understanding was reached with the Ministry of Education that they had no intention of interfering in any way with the profession, and would make no move without full prior discussion with the Institute.

All the same, the Institute's system of training has been, and will no doubt continue to be, adjusted to current requirements and schools of thought, and in particular collaboration is now encouraged with Colleges of Further Education. The whole problem of tuition and of the articled clerk was reviewed by a committee set up in 1958 under the chairmanship of W. E. Parker. It reported in 1961 and many of the subsequent developments can be traced to its recommendations. In January 1963 the Council appointed an

Education Committee and within eighteen months arrangements had been made for the setting up of education committees of each District Society and for introductory courses for articled clerks, to be followed by later courses designed to introduce students to the problems of their final examinations. The Education Committee also established new links with universities (including the new universities), and commenced work on such themes as text books, teaching methods and management studies.

Along with other schemes for assisting students returning from war service, the 'Universities Scheme' was inaugurated in 1945 in conjunction with a number of universities (though not Oxford or Cambridge) to provide improved facilities for the education of prospective members of the profession. Under this scheme, during a period of 5¾–6 years, an articled clerk was able to obtain both a degree and membership of the Institute. To give exemption from the Institute intermediate examination, the course had to include economics and law as well as accountancy and was normally taken as an internal degree course within the faculty or department of Economics or Commerce.

The time to be spent by the articled clerk on practical work, under the supervision of his principal, was not to be less than three years, and could be in the main so spent either before or after the period of university study – a complete 'sandwich' principle not being allowed. The scheme, when inaugurated, estimated 200 entries per annum at the universities, a figure which, after a slow start in the early years, was exceeded as from 1956–7. As part of the scheme, a Joint Standing Committee of the accountant bodies (now the Institute and the Association) and the participating universities (including for this purpose Oxford and Cambridge) was formed to supervise the scheme and generally to interpret the difficulties of each side to the other. The first Chairman was Sir Arnold McNair (later Lord McNair), then Vice-Chancellor of Liverpool University.

The Charter and the original bye-laws laid down a requirement of five years' service under articles (or three years in the case of graduates of certain universities in the United Kingdom) and over the years since 1880 only the following amendments, all recent, may be noted:

(a) The Universities Scheme, referred to above.
(b) A reduction of articled service to four years was granted in 1963 to graduates from approved universities outside the United Kingdom and to 'sixth formers' in the United Kingdom with a defined standard of education.
(c) Permission was given for six months of articled service to be spent in approved situations in industry and on the principal's business abroad.
(d) A reduction of up to two years of articles and possible exemption from preliminary and intermediate examinations was given to existing clerks of long standing.
(e) Concessions of a similar nature to certain officers in H.M. Forces.

So far as concerns principals it is obvious that some will be better than others, and it must be admitted that in the past there were those who could neither offer adequate personal assistance in training, nor the background of a suitable practice in which the student might gain experience. Principals are, however, now required to satisfy the Council on taking their first articled clerk that they are aware of their obligations. It is also now required that, on passing his final, the articled clerk shall obtain from his principal a certificate to show that the practical work on which he had been engaged has provided proper experience. Further, a probationary period has been introduced into articles, and provision made for the possibility of secondment of a clerk to another practising member for a maximum of six months for wider experience.

The ability of the principal to offer adequate training also had a bearing on the question of the number of articled clerks he should be permitted to employ at any one time. The standard number laid down in the original bye-law, namely two per principal, continued unchanged up to the date of integration with the Society of Incorporated Accountants. On that happening it became clear that, in order to keep up membership to meet the requirements of the profession both in practice and in industry and commerce and, in particular, to fill the gap caused by the cessation of the Society's bye-law candidates trained largely by members of the Institute, the number allowed to each principal should be increased. Accordingly, the bye-laws were altered to allow up to four articled clerks in normal circumstances to each practising member.

The terms of employment have also undergone considerable change, particularly in the following respects:

(a) In the early days – indeed in many cases, and in certain areas up to the time of the Second World War and afterwards – it was the custom for the principal to charge a premium for granting articles varying from a nominal amount up to 500 guineas, or in certain cases even more. Also if any salary was paid it was often in the nature of pocket money, and in some cases represented the return to the student of the premium over the period of his articles. With changed social and economic conditions these terms came to be altered and from about 1950 it may be said that premiums were almost entirely discarded and salaries were paid.

(b) The amount of time to be allowed off for study for examinations has always been a bone of contention, some clerks naturally urging the hardship of studying in the evenings after their day's work at the office, and some principals stoutly maintaining that the minimum of time off from practical work was best in the clerk's interest. Memories of 'the good old days' no doubt played their part. Limits of time off for examinations and other purposes have now been specified.

(c) Power was taken in 1963 for a principal or an articled clerk in certain cases to raise disputed matters with the Council for a ruling or to ask for cancellation of articles.

*Members*

After the Second World War, when members were returning rusty after several years of absence, particularly on matters such as wartime taxation, refresher courses were held at Cambridge and Oxford to bring them up to date. The first refresher course was held at Emmanuel College, Cambridge, in August 1945, and similar courses were established in 1946 at Downing, Jesus and Pembroke Colleges, Cambridge, and at Queen's College, St Edmund Hall, Christ Church and Keble Colleges, Oxford. These refresher courses were attended by a total of 289 members.

They were so successful that they gave rise to a demand for their continuation in peace time and so the summer courses came into being.

The first of these was held at Christ Church, Oxford, in September 1947. The object of this course was, as stated in the report of the Council for 1946, 'to afford members from all parts of the country an opportunity of meeting one another in the manner which proved so successful on the residential refresher courses; and to further the study of accounting concepts by means of addresses followed by group discussions and free exchange of view'. This first summer course was attended by 170 members and was the forerunner of summer courses which have continued to the present day. Up to 1957 each year's course was held at Christ Church, Oxford, and was attended by between 160 and 200 members. In 1958 following the increased membership resulting from the Scheme of Integration, arrangements were made to accommodate the course members in two colleges, Christ Church and Merton College, so that the number attending could be increased to 280, and beginning in 1961 two separate summer courses were held each year, one in Oxford and one in Cambridge.

In 1964 the Council initiated a series of courses on Electronic Data Processing, the object being to give members an appreciation of this subject generally and of the control and audit aspects in particular. A pilot course for potential instructing staff for subsequent courses was held at Hastings in January 1964 and the first members' course, attended by 108, was held at Brighton in May 1964.

### *Recommendations*

Mention should also be made of the recommendations on accounting principles and other practical and technical statements, including a series of statements on auditing, issued by the Council for the guidance of members beginning with the issue on December 12, 1942, of 'Tax Reserve Certificates' and 'War Damage Contribution Premiums and Claims'. Up till that date the Council had hesitated to issue views on technical subjects lest they should be resented by members – and lest standards might come to be set which might on occasion be embarrassing to individuals. These feelings were, however, soon lived down and members over a wide field, particularly through the district societies and technical and research committees, have co-operated in a remarkable way. The original Taxation and Financial Relations Committee, later renamed the Taxation and Research Committee and more recently the Technical Advisory Committee, was established 'to consider matters affecting taxation and financial relationship of the business community with the Inland Revenue or other Government departments'. In making this proposal the Council stated that it was intended that non-practising members, in London and the provinces, who hold commercial appointments, and associates employed within the profession, should be fully represented on the committee, so as to establish an active and an effective liaison between the practising and non-practising sides of the profession. Since its formation the activities of the committee have been extended beyond the literal interpretation of its original terms of reference; it has assisted the Council as a drafting and advisory body, working closely with regional committees. In the result, recommendations have been issued on a large variety of subjects, many of them highly controversial and in the form, not of instructions, but of advice to members as to the best practice. This is not the place to review them in detail but they include matters such as:

Depreciation of fixed assets.

The form and contents of accounts of estates of deceased persons and similar trusts.

Accounting in relation to changes in the purchasing power of money.

Presentation of balance sheet and profit and loss account.
Group accounts in the form of consolidated accounts.
Terms used in published accounts of limited companies.
Statements on auditing: General principles of auditing.
Stock-in-trade and work in progress.
Audits of building societies.
Internal control.
Responsibility of auditor of parent company where he does not audit the subsidiaries.
Professional ethics.

It may perhaps fairly be claimed that the impact of these recommendations on directors of companies and on all concerned with the preparation of accounts has been material and that in large measure they have been adopted.

In addition to the above, statements have been issued on various matters in connection with company law, taxation, costing, management accounting, mechanized accounting, business efficiency and other practical and technical matters.

The Institute publication which is of greatest use to members must surely be the *Members' Handbook*. A temporary short version was issued in 1950 but was replaced in 1958 by the handbook in loose-leaf form. Although there is still much material of an administrative nature to be incorporated in the handbook before it can be regarded as complete, the whole of the technical section has now been issued.

# Section 7: Examinations

THE FIRST essential of the Institute's examination system is to endeavour to ensure that no one shall embark upon articles unless his standard of general education can reasonably be expected to permit him to stay the course, and eventually enable him to attain the standard required of a chartered accountant. This is necessary as much in the interests of the articled clerk, to save waste of time and disappointment, as in the interests of the profession.

Before the country's educational and examination system became developed, it was essential for the Institute to run its own preliminary examination to test those, other than graduates, who wished to join the profession. For this purpose it was necessary to engage external examiners and largely to be guided by them as to the standard to be attained.

The introduction of the school certificate, and higher school certificate, examinations early in the twentieth century meant that the Institute came increasingly to recognize performances at these examinations as justifying exemption from the preliminary examination; the proportion of entrants taking the latter examination declined rapidly. This move was accelerated when the general certificate of education examination came into being in 1951; that examination became generally available in a great variety of schools and was also taken by a growing number of external and private candidates. In 1962, 3,510 certificates of exemption were granted, while the number of candidates sitting and passing the Institute's preliminary examination was 399 and 108 respectively.

It was, therefore, a natural development when, in 1962, the Council decided not to hold the preliminary examination after November 1963. Thereafter all entrants into articles have been required to obtain a certificate of exemption from the preliminary examination by reaching a required standard in an examination recognized for this purpose.

The following statement showing, at five-yearly intervals, the number of articles of clerkship registered, and the number of those clerks who subsequently succeed in becoming members of the Institute, indicates the growing extent of this examination problem:

| *Year* | *Articles Registered* | *Admission to Membership* |
|---|---|---|
| 1888 | 111 | 90 |
| 1893 | 162 | 148 |
| 1898 | 267 | 161 |
| 1903 | 244 | 192 |
| 1908 | 302 | 182 |
| 1913 | 415 | 258 |
| 1918 | 219 | 66 |
| 1923 | 850 | 362 |
| 1928 | 834 | 645 |
| 1933 | 838 | 584 |
| 1938 | 696 | 613 |
| 1943 | 474 | 72 |
| 1948 | 1,604 | 700 |
| 1953 | 1,361 | 890 |
| 1958 | 2,660 | 984 |
| 1963 | 3,549 | 1,731 |

These figures are shown in graph form opposite.

It may be of interest in itself, and also as an indication of the nature of the work of a chartered accountant, to note the subjects covered by the professional examinations since the date of the Royal Charter. The original bye-laws provided that the intermediate and final examinations (partly in writing and partly *viva voce*) should cover the following subjects:

1. Book-keeping and Accounts.
2. Auditing.
3. The adjustment of Partnership and Executorship Accounts.
4. The rights and duties of Liquidators, Trustees and Receivers.
5. The principles of the law of Bankruptcy.
6. The principles of the law relating to Joint Stock Companies.
7. The principles of Mercantile Law.
8. The principles of the law of Arbitrations and Awards.

As an additional subject candidates were required in 1922 to take one of the following:

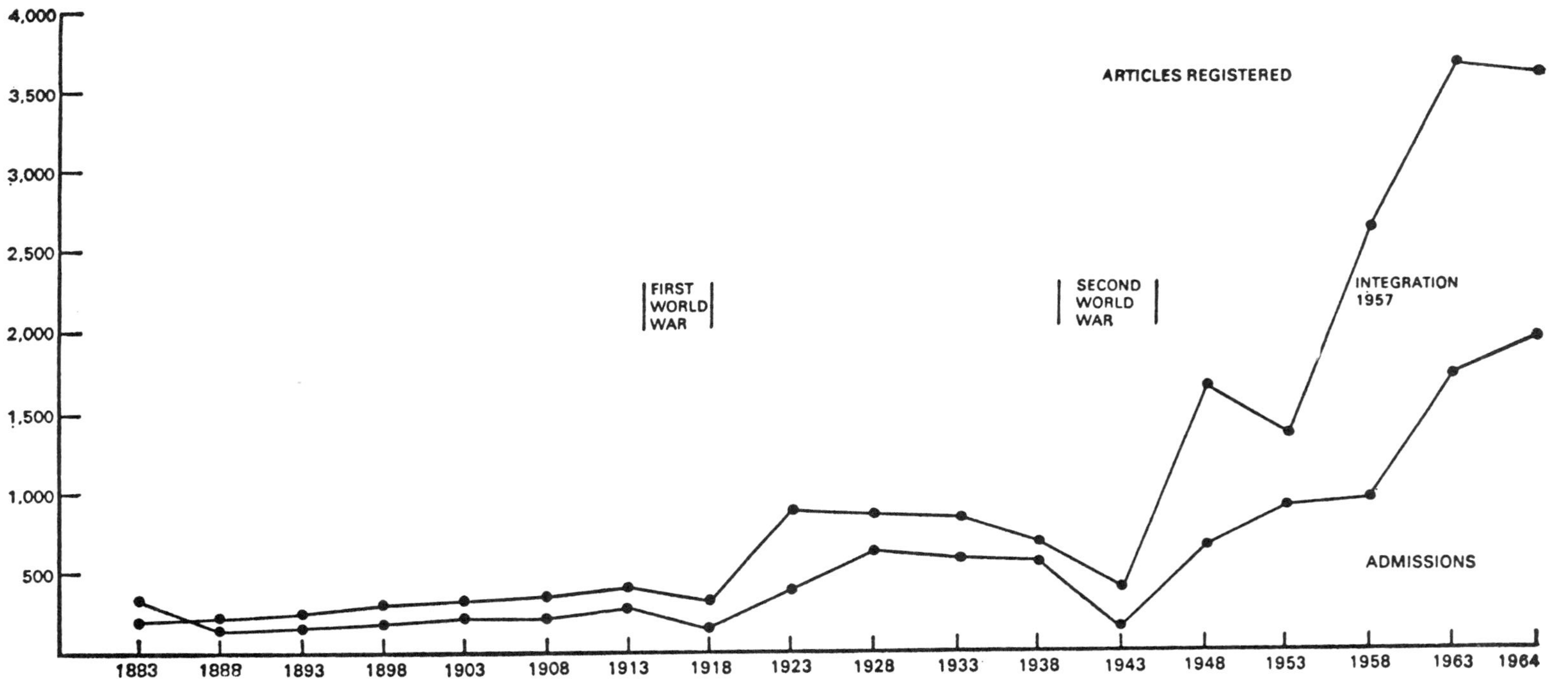


Graph showing number of Articles registered and of admission to membership of the Institute.

Economics, Banking, Currency and Foreign Exchanges, or Actuarial Science.

The records of the examination committee show that even in the early 1880s difficulty was being experienced with the *viva voce* examinations. At first these were left to the discretion of each examiner; then they were limited to further explanations on the printed questions and 'to take place after 4 o'clock'; then they were to be confined to the final examinations; finally they appear to have been dropped in 1892 when the revised bye-laws omitted all reference to them. One shudders to think what would happen if they had continued to the present time, with some thousands sitting twice yearly for each examination.

The general nature of the syllabus has remained remarkably constant, the only variations on the above list from time to time being largely related to the changes of emphasis, then current, on the subjects covered. Additions have been made to include subjects (or indeed separate papers) on taxation, costing, general financial and commercial knowledge and management accounting. Owing to the difficulty of putting 'a quart into a pint pot' (as the Parker Report put it), the final examination from 1965 will be taken in two parts.

As from 1966, a post-final examination is to be offered, to those members of the Institute wishing to take it, in management techniques. The Institute of Chartered Accountants in Ireland is hoping to join in this scheme and a Certificate is to be issued to successful candidates. Additionally (and indicating the growing importance of this field of the modern accountant's activities) a separate examination in management services (which term is intended to cover management consultancy in its widest sense, as well as accounting information) is to be organized, for persons having highly specialized knowledge of, and practical experience in this field, and for this a Diploma will be issued. The scheme will be sponsored jointly by the three Chartered Institutes, the Association and the Institute of Cost and Works Accountants. In the same way that until 1942 (as explained in Section 6) the Council had hesitated to offer guidance to members on technical matters, so it had felt that, as it must be an examining body, it should not itself get involved in responsibility for tuition. This latter duty has accordingly been largely delegated by principals to various tutorial establishments in supplementation of the training they themselves, and the students' societies (dealt with in Section 3), provide. The tutors have carried out their tasks by correspondence courses and by lectures. The accountancy members of their staffs have largely been drawn from the membership of the Institute and accordingly have had practical experience. Recently the Council has considered itself free to intervene, directly or indirectly, in the arrangements for study and tuition to such extent as may appear at any time to be necessary.

A cardinal principle of the examinations has been that, except for examiners in the law papers, the examiners and moderators (whose respective duties are referred to later) should be chartered accountants. This has been deemed necessary because the questions set cover practical points requiring practising experience and judgment.

A difficulty flowing from this decision has been to find individuals, largely from among those still in active work, who could find the time for the setting, and much more the marking, of the papers – and having, or acquiring, an aptitude for this special kind of task. As an indication of the size of the task involved, assume that 3,000 candidates sit at any given examination. A speed of marking of 400 papers each week (when the numbers are higher a greater speed is required in order to finish in the usual period of seven weeks for marking) involves substantially more than 100 hours per week of very concentrated work, apart from revision, summarizing and reporting. This can, of course, only be accomplished if the examiner has sufficient capable assistants, and carefully plans with them the distribution of the marking and standardization, retaining to himself an overall responsibility.

The heavy task of the examiners is occasionally relieved by a choice 'howler' from some bright spark such as the following:

An English paper set in the Preliminary during the war years produced a definition of 'abrasion' as being 'to see before, or mirage' and the attempt to incorporate the word in a sentence, as the question required, read 'The abrasion appeared before him as he walked up the passage but disappeared when he threw something at it.' An 'enigma' was described by one candidate as 'a serum inserted to relieve pain' and by another in an explanatory sentence which read 'That boy is a great enigma as all his internal organs are on the opposite side to those of a normal person.' 'Penury' was defined as a variation and polite form of expressing 'Hell'.

In the professional examinations, the chief examples appear in the general knowledge questions:

*King's Counsel* – A solicitor may act in the lower court but a K.C., *often a very wily man*, acts in the High Court.

*Life Assurance* – The natural joy of realizing the investment is offset heavily by the sorrow of the death of the insured. After the first premium has been paid the insured party may get knocked down or catch pneumonia with an easy mind.

*Insurable Interest* – . . . but the wife could not insure the life of the window cleaner unless she had an interest in him.

*Ex gratia* – Tips or gratuities not included.

If a gift is said to be *ex gratia*, then the person who received it does not have to pay for it.

*Ipso facto* – A sort of self-made man.

*Mandamus* – One of the Scottish Quarter Days.

*Prima Facie* – Something that is *prima facie* is something that seems to be something that on the face of it is something that it is not.

Perhaps the palm should go to the candidate who defined a 'trade cycle' as 'a type of bicycle generally used by errand boys'. One can only hope that he was given full marks.

In answering a question on winding-up, a candidate gave as an example the case of a company formed for the purpose of coaching candidates for the examinations of the Institute. He went on to say that 'as the Institute had been nationalized examinations had come to an end and the company could be wound up because its substratum had gone'. The examiner quoted this in his report to the moderators adding the words, 'See 1 Cor. 13. 9', which reads 'For we know in part, and we prophesy in part'. This is a fair example of the fact that examiners are not the soulless persons they are sometimes imagined to be.

The questions (and the suggested number of marks suitable for each) are in the first instance drafted by each examiner in consultation with his moderator. Subsequently a joint meeting, lasting most of the day, is attended by all examiners and moderators, they having first had a few days in which to study all the papers. Particular attention is given at this meeting to ensure fairness and suitability of questions, to regulate the length of papers, to challenge questions or phrases which could be regarded as ambiguous or as 'traps', to avoid duplication of questions in other papers for the same examination and to agree the allocation of possible marks for questions. The chairman of the examination committee presides at this meeting and a choice of techniques is available to him. He may either regard it as a refresher course and learn again details he has forgotten or he may weigh in and keep the pundits in order. There have been examples of both types of chairman. The examiners mark the papers and the moderators then review the results, paying particular attention to 'border-line' cases, and agree the pass list, the order of merit and the winners of the various prizes. This procedure had the effect that some members of the examination committee had neither themselves taken part in the setting or marking of the papers, nor in agreeing the results. It was accordingly decided in 1964 that the examination committee should consist solely of moderators whether members of the Council or not.

The original bye-laws gave unlimited freedom for those who failed the examination to sit again. Subsequently, and in order to protect a student from wasting his time unduly, the following changes have been made:

(a) The Intermediate is modified and brought forward earlier, in order to eliminate at an early date those not likely to make good. It must normally be passed during the period of articles.

(b) A 'Bad Failure' notice is given to a candidate whose papers call for this comment, and in the case of the Intermediate also to the principal so that discussions can take place between them.

(c) The principal can, in the case of a bad failure at the Intermediate, or if that examination is not passed at the third attempt, cancel the articles.

## Section 8: Hall, Library and Coat of Arms

AFTER MUCH controversy, many difficulties and delays, including the bankruptcy of the first builder, the Institute moved from the old offices at Copthall Buildings to the new hall opened in Moorgate Place on May 10, 1893. All its fine details are described in *A History of the Hall of the Institute of Chartered Accountants in England and Wales*, by John H. Stern. It is unnecessary now to give more than an outline of its main features and to try to convey some measure of this legacy from the past enjoyed by the profession for so long.

It should be remembered that the period in which it was erected produced a great deal of ugliness. Mixtures of wrought iron, marble and heavy woodwork were the rage. Comfort was almost sinful. The cost of labour was so low that efficiency was unimportant. In that age the Institute chose a design by an architect who was under the influence of Genoa and Venice and who was not impressed by contemporary architecture in England. Venice was also the source of another inspiration to the profession – Pacioli's book setting down the first exposition of double-entry book-keeping, referred to later.

Italian Renaissance in character, the building was designed by John Belcher, R.A., the plans being accepted after open competition. It has been the subject of much interest to architects and the public and is probably the best example of this style of architecture to be found in England. The *Dictionary of National Biography*, in recording Belcher's many achievements, states that 'the offices of the Institute of Chartered Accountants at once made his fame and became a landmark in City architecture . . .' It has been included in the list of buildings of special architectural or historic interest in the area of the City of London.

The principal impression given by the main front is a solid massiveness with a wealth of details. H. Bates was chosen to execute the corbel groups, the arms and supporting figures over the main door, and the terminals over the main piers of the ground floor. H. Thornycroft carried out the great frieze along the main front on to Moorgate Place and along the Swan Alley frontage as far as the side entrance where Belcher's and Thornycroft's work ends. Altogether this frieze is about 140 feet long.

Taking the original frieze as a whole from the left, there are facing Moorgate Place eight groups of figures representing Arts, Sciences, Crafts, Education, Commerce, Manufacture, Agriculture and Mining. Thornycroft continued on the Swan Alley side with Mining, Railways, Shipping, India, and the Colonies. At this point the frieze ceases to be interrupted by pillars and from the turret to past the side entrance it is only interrupted by the niche intended for a bust of Queen Victoria which never materialized. There are seventeen figures from surveyor and architect through all the various craftsmen employed in the building and ending with the Institute's solicitor. The figure of the architect is clearly Belcher and the solicitor is known to be H. Markby of Markby, Stewart & Co. who acted for the Institute. Very likely the others are also taken from life. To return to the Moorgate Place frontage, Bates provided over the main entrance the Institute Coat of Arms, described at the end of this section, and two figures holding a crown to represent the Royal Charter. Another rendering of the Coat of Arms appears below the oriel window on the corner and is borne by muscular Atlas-like figures which visually take the weight of the pillars supporting the dome on which Thornycroft's excellent figure of Justice is standing.

No description nor even a photograph can convey the very high standard of all the sculpture work, but a few examples of the representative figures chosen are worth mentioning. For Education the central figure is, like the others, treated allegorically and holds the label naming the subject. A mother is taking her child to the schoolmaster and a college student converses with a don. For Manufacture the central figure has, on her right, fabrics represented by a woman holding a roll of cloth, next to her the yarn maker with a spinning wheel behind her. On her left are a toolmaker and a blacksmith. For Shipping the central figure stands in a boat with

The Hall of the Institute, Moorgate Place, by Hanslip Fletcher.
*Reproduced by kind permission of The Sunday Times.*

The Library of the Institute, Moorgate Place, by Hanslip Fletcher.
*Reproduced by kind permission of The Sunday Times.*

garments floating in the wind. The left-hand figures are a P. & O. Captain with telescope and a dock labourer carrying goods on his back, and the right-hand figures are of a sailor drinking a parting toast to his sweetheart.

Great care was taken in 1930 with the extension beyond the side entrance in Swan Alley, and the newer part blends perfectly with the old. The architect was J. J. Joass, a pupil of Belcher's, and J. A. Stevenson did the terminals and the frieze, his work starting after the bearded and rotund Markby. Representatives of English architecture are Stevenson, Joass, Cockerell, Chambers, Wren and Inigo Jones. Joass is pointing to the extension shown on a site plan of the Institute, while Wren holds a model of St Paul's. Italian architecture is represented by thirteen figures including Michelangelo and Leonardo da Vinci, and a young boy is a symbol of the Renaissance. Then come three figures for Gothic, two for Byzantine, four for Roman, three Greeks, two Assyrians with a sacred bull, three Egyptians and, finally, prehistoric man. This later frieze extends to about 50 feet in length.

The entrance hall has a fine coffered ceiling, Tuscan pilasters with Ionic capitals, and a cushioned plain frieze over. On the main stairs there are four stained-glass windows. These are by Henry Holiday and add greatly to a well-lighted and dignified stairway.

The following portraits of past Presidents, giving their dates of presidency and the names of the artists, hang on the walls:

| | *Artist* |
|---|---|
| Frederick Whinney, 1884–8 | Sir William Llewellyn |
| George Walter Knox, 1896–7 | Sir William Llewellyn |
| John George Griffiths, C.V.O., 1897–9 | A. E. Emslie |
| Ernest Cooper, 1899–1901 | Frank Salisbury |
| Sir William Barclay Peat, C.V.O., 1906–8 | Herbert Olivier |
| Algernon Osmond Miles, 1909–10 | Sir William Llewellyn |
| The Lord Plender, G.B.E., LL.D., 1910–12 and 1929–30 | Sir William Llewellyn |
| Sir Horace Woodburn Kirby, 1913–16 | R. Bundy |
| Sir Edward Cecil Moore, BT., 1923 | Sir William Llewellyn |

| | |
|---|---|
| George Robert Freeman, 1925–6 | Frank Salisbury |
| Sir Arthur Francis Whinney, K.B.E., 1926–7 | Sir William Llewellyn |
| Sir Charles John Geoffrey Palmour, 1938–44 | Frank Salisbury |
| Sir Harold Gibson Howitt, G.B.E., D.S.O., M.C., 1945–6 | Frank Salisbury |
| Gilbert David Shepherd, M.B.E., 1947 and 1947–8 | Frank Salisbury |

There is also a portrait by Sir William Llewellyn of the Hon. George Colville, M.B.E., secretary of the Institute 1899–1935. Photographs of all past Presidents and Vice-Presidents hang in the Committee Room.

The Council Chamber is a room of outstanding design. The mural paintings are by George Murray to plans by the architect. The large panel occupying the space opposite the doorway illustrates Science bringing order with scales and rule to Commerce, which is typified below by a group of figures suggesting Eastern merchants. The panel over the clock represents the triumph of Law. In the central group, Time with a scythe, seated on a winged globe, is crowning Justice, who, with sword and scales, is accompanied by an attendant holding the tables of Law. The group on the left typifies Peace secured by Justice and that on the right Judgment with shield and flaming sword slaying Anarchy.

The pendentives represent Wisdom, Truth, Prudence, and Justice and worked into them are the arms of London, Liverpool, Sheffield and Manchester, in which cities were the five associations of accountants which formed the original membershipof the Institute.

Unfortunately, the acoustics are dreadful and all but raised voices ascend and get lost in the dome two storeys up. In less democratic days even this defect was held to have its points, as it rendered inaudible the asides of certain past Presidents among themselves, when any new member dared to get up and address the august assembly.

The library is reputed to have been Belcher's favourite room. It has a strong atmosphere of cloistered calm and quiet which takes immediate effect on all who enter it. The tall coupled Tuscan columns, supporting the council chamber and dome above, and the fine coffered ceiling give the room space, grace and proportion. The two main walls present a mass of books to the eye and the twin galleries along them, supported on cedar wood pillars with heavily curved capitals, are joined by a matching three-section bridge. This bridge is the striking feature of the room. It not only draws the two galleries visually together, it also serves the practical purpose of providing access between them.

The provision of a library has always been included as one of the principal objects of the Institute. The Institute of Accountants in Copthall Avenue had already established its own library when it amalgamated with the Society of Accountants in 1879 and there are to this day books in the library with the stamp of the Institute of Accountants in them.

There is little doubt that the most important influence, which laid the foundation of what has become the most complete library devoted to accounting and allied subjects in the world, was the appointment in 1893 of F. W. Pixley as the first chairman of the library committee, a post he held until 1933, and of Cosmo Gordon, who was librarian from 1911 to early in the First World War and again from 1933 until he retired in 1948. The Institute library of today owes a great deal to these two men, who between them set the Institute firmly on the path of buying all relevant early books on accounting which led up to the present unique collection. It would appeal to Pixley's professional interest in money values if he knew what a magnificent investment these purchases of old books have been. It would also appeal to Cosmo Gordon's love for old and beautiful books and to his Scottish sense of economy that not only did he play an important part in getting the collection together, but also was instrumental in purchasing, for the Institute Library, books at prices which today seem ridiculous.

One particular purchase deserves mention. In 1913 the widow of Karel Petr Kheil, a banker in Prague, offered for sale his entire library of books on book-keeping which he had collected during most of his life. The library committee sent Cosmo Gordon to

Prague to inspect with a view to purchase. The first offer was refused but the second of £690 was accepted. Today this sum does not even represent the value of some of the individual items acquired and a large number of the others are unique.

The Institute has a complete collection of all of Pacioli's known published works, including the two known printings of the first edition of his *Summa di Arithmetica*, which gave in print for the first time a complete exposition of double-entry book-keeping as practised in Venice in 1494, the second edition of 1523, his *Divina Proportione*, and his translation of Euclid. The collection includes also the very rare *Maner and Fourme*, by J. Peele, of 1553, printed by Richard Grafton who became Chief Master of Christ's Hospital where Peele was appointed clerk, and more recently it acquired from Moscow a micro-film of Ympyn, another work printed by Richard Grafton.

Books on accounting were working books used by teachers, accountants and merchants and their usefulness ended only when they finally fell to pieces. Of the three earliest books on accounting in English the only known copy of one was rediscovered in Moscow, having disappeared for forty years following the Russian revolution. Of the other two one has not survived at all and only one complete copy of the other is known.

One was originally translated from the Italian, probably a manuscript. It was first printed in Dutch and French and then in English. The details of this English version, which followed four years after the Dutch and French editions, are as follows:

> *A Notable and very excellente woorke, expressyng and declaryng the maner and forme how to kepe a boke of accomptes or reconynges. . . . Translated with great diligence out of the Italian toung into Dutche, and out of Dutche into Frenche, and now out of Frenche into Englishe*; by Jan Ympyn. 4to. 40 ll. London, Richard Grafton, 1547.

Another book was published in 1543. This was:

> *A profitable Treatyce called the Instrument or Boke to learne to*

> *knowe the good order of the kepying of the famouse reconynge called in Latyn, Dare and Habere, and in Englyshe, Debitor and Creditor*; by Hugh Oldcastle. 4to. London, John Gough, 1543.

No copy of the original edition has survived at all. It was republished with full acknowledgments by John Mellis in 1588 and it is from this and a few other references that it is known.

The other book published in English was:

> *The maner and fourme how to kepe a perfecte reconyng, after the order of the moste and worthie and notable accompte, of Debitour and Creditour. . . .*; by James Peele. Fo. 87 ll. London, Richard Grafton, 1553.

The only known copy of Ympyn is in the Lenin Library, Moscow. As has been said, Oldcastle's book has not, as far as is known, survived in the original at all and the last time it was recorded was at the end of the eighteenth century. Of Peele's book two copies have come down to us, one incomplete in the British Museum and a complete one which is in the Institute collection.

Copies of Pacioli's books are almost common compared with the earliest books in English published nearly 100 years later.

There are many other books of great rarity. But the library's main task is to gather together all the current accounting and legal text books, law reports, statutes and periodicals and to make them readily available to members. In recent years the useful material and the number of members requiring access to it have grown to a degree which could not have been foreseen in the 'nineties. Before the last war income tax used to occupy one library shelf and books on this subject now fill two whole cases of four shelves each. Many completely new subjects have been added. Attendances have increased from 2,898 in 1908 to a peak of 14,573 in 1963, after which there was a decrease owing to building operations. In 1960 a new library reference room was established in the east wing following the phenomenal increase in the use of the library which came immediately members of the former Society of Incorporated Accountants became eligible, on integration with the Institute, to use the library. Although not in the City, the library at their beautiful hall on the Embankment had served a useful purpose to members and students.

Scottish chartered accountants in London are allowed to use the members' rooms and the library.

It is realized that many of the details concerning the building, as set out above, may soon be out of date when the plans for extending and remodelling it are implemented. Still as a record they are, it is hoped, of historical interest.

By 1959 the Institute staff, the size and frequency of committees, and the whole administration of the Institute had completely outgrown the old Hall. Additional offices had to be leased in Moorgate and in London Wall until more permanent arrangements could be made. The age is again one of ugliness but at least it is functional. There are fine examples of modern libraries which achieve the same effects of atmosphere in different ways and by using new methods and materials. Because of the cost of the site and of building on it this is nowhere more difficult to achieve than in central London, where the centre of gravity of the profession lies and where the library must be situated.

The Royal Charter had conferred a professional status on public accountancy which justified an application to the College of Arms for a grant of Arms to the Institute. William Turquand accordingly presented a memorial to the Earl Marshal who, in August 1880, gave his authority to the application and, on January 22, 1881, Garter, Clarenceux and Norroy Kings of Arms granted and assigned the Blazon as follows:

> Argent on a Mount in Base in front of a Rudder in bend sinister a Female figure proper representing 'Economy' habited Gules mantled Azure about the temples a Wreath of Olive in the dexter hand a Rod and in the Sinister a pair of Compasses also proper a Chief of the second thereon a Balance suspended also Or . . . together with the Motto 'Recte Numerare'.

Already in this Section, in dealing with the architecture of the

Institute building, comment has been made about the then prevailing trend of taste for symbolism and complicated designs, often of Italian origin. It is, therefore, not surprising that inspiration for the devices on the shield can be traced to Rome. In 1603 a book had appeared, by Cesare Ripa, entitled *Iconologia*, which contained a woodcut of 'Economia' personifying good management (without the implication of frugality which 'Economy' carries perhaps in English), and introduced by the author as 'a matron of serious aspect, crowned with olives, holding a compass in her left hand and a rod in her right, behind her is a rudder, the rod signifying command, the rudder is the symbol of guidance'. The woodcut is reproduced as a plate facing page 147.

The Roman matron is, quite obviously, the heraldic 'female figure proper' more gallantly named 'The Institute Lady' by Cosmo Gordon in an article in *The Accountant* of November 6, 1948. The symbolism of the Balance in Chief is clear enough but it is not clear why, the scales being level, the indicator is not vertical but 'in bend sinister', like the rudder, with obvious disadvantages.

The motto, 'Recte Numerare', is not an inspiring one. Even in 1880, when accountants worked without benefit of computers, 'To Reckon or Number Rightly' was not the outstanding aim or chief skill of the profession. The same might equally be said of the more abstruse renderings which are 'To Account Correctly' or 'To Pay Honourably'.

The shield is the foundation of heraldry and the shield may be of any shape but, like the motto, the shape chosen for the Institute shield of arms is not ideal. Something would be gained by a change from an imprecise and tortuous outline to a clear and precise one more symbolic, if more symbols are sought, of the clarity and accuracy of presentation for which the profession strives in all its activities.

## Section 9: Public Appointments

A REFERENCE here should be made to the growing extent to which members of the Institute have been called upon for public services. A few of the earliest examples of such appointments are recorded in the chronological part of this history, but they are of necessity very incomplete. Among them were included reviews of the Companies Acts, of the law concerning bankruptcy and of the system of accounts of local authorities.

It was in the First World War that members began to be called upon for specific tasks and among these were the Controllership of enemy banks, Financial Secretaryships of Ministries (Treasury, Munitions and Food), Controllerships of various kinds, and appointments as advisers to Government Departments (including those responsible for all three military services) on accounting control, audit and costing.

Between the wars, much reorganization required to be done and help was given by members on commissions, committees and tribunals of various kinds and on subjects as varied as:

Coal Control, Sugar Commission, Coal and Oil Production, Nightwork in Bakeries.

Hospitals, Housing, Tithe Rents, Rural Housing, Water Acts, Local Government on Tyneside, National Health Insurance, Pensions, Child Adoption.

Agriculture, Marketing Schemes (Milk, Pigs and Hops), Cattle Committee, Livestock Commission, Land Fertility, Transport, Railway Rates, London Passenger Transport.

Aircraft Prices, Admiralty Contracts, the affairs of the British Legion.

Income Tax, Capital Issues, Trusts, Public Trustee, Trustee Savings Banks.

Colonial Development, the affairs of British North Borneo, the financial liabilities of Southern Rhodesia on attaining self government, Jamaica Banana Industry, Newfoundland Fisheries, Enemy Debts.

The Second World War, and the period immediately thereafter, called for an enormous amount of help from members of the Institute in every department of State. These special fields of service included:

First Parliamentary Secretary to Minister of National Insurance.
Financial Secretary, Ministry of Food.
Deputy Director of Progress and Statistics, War Office.
Member of Air Council.
Chairman, British Overseas Airways Corporation.
Colonial Economic Research Committee.
Adviser to Board of Trade on Price Control.
Central Price Regulation Committee.
Meat and Livestock Control.
Chairman of Committee on Long Distance Haulage.
Import Duty Advisory Council.
Membership of Royal Commission on Taxation.
Committee to deal with provisions for retirement (taxation).
Council of NAAFI.
Conference to consider scheme for dealing with war damage.
Tribunals to assess compensation on nationalization (Mining Industry, and Cables and Wireless).
Valuation Boards for Coal Industry on nationalization.
Committee to review terms of service of the professional classes in the Civil Service.

From the Second War onwards such appointments became customary, and from 1954 a list of those occurring during the year has been included in the Annual Report of the Institute. The number of them so recorded in the eleven years following, i.e. to December 31, 1964, amounted to well over 150 and of necessity the record is incomplete for want of information.

It would be tedious in a history of this nature to go into too much detail. All that is required is to indicate the diversity of the tasks involved. To achieve that object it was thought that it might be more informative to classify the appointments into groups such as (a) those calling primarily for accountancy skill; (b) those which involved collaboration with other experts and professions, and (c) those personal to the individual appointed.

On such an approach, however, it was found that the difficulty of choosing the proper classification was considerable, and the individual in question might have had other views as to the reasons for his selection. On balance, therefore, it has been felt preferable, whilst restricting the list of personal appointments and bodies to which members have been appointed since 1954 to those set out below, to group them under the names of the appointors; which grouping will, in part, indicate the classifications referred to.

*Her Majesty the Queen*
Governor-General of Australia.
Administrative adviser in Her Majesty's Household.
Postmaster-General and subsequently Minister of Transport and several previous junior Ministerial appointments.
Chief Secretary to the Treasury.
Restrictive Practices Court (three members).
Royal Commission on Local Government in Greater London.
National Incomes Commission.
Crown Estate Commissioner.
Commissioner under the Public Works Loans Act, 1875.
Transport Tribunal (two members).

*Archbishop of Canterbury*
Commission to inquire into the organization of the Church by Dioceses in London and south-east England.

*Prime Minister*
Council on Prices, Productivity and Incomes.
Council for Wales and Monmouthshire.
Advisory Commission on the review of the constitution of Rhodesia and Nyasaland.
National Portrait Gallery (trustee).

*Lord Chancellor*

Committee of Inquiry into the Public Trustee Office.
Advisory Committee under the Legal Aid and Advice Act, 1949.
Public Trustee.

*Chancellor of the Exchequer and Secretaries of State*

Advisory Committee in regard to Development Areas.
Advisory Council – Export Credits guarantee.
Tribunal of Inquiry under the Prevention of Fraud (Investments) Act, 1939.
Board of Referees (seven members).
Chairman of the Iron and Steel Holding and Realization Agency.
Committee of Inquiry into the practical effects of a Turnover Tax.
Inquiry to investigate prices agreed by Ministry of Aviation for guided weapons (and by the Minister of Aviation).
Committee to advise on a new hall on the Queen's Hall site.
Advisory Panel under the Income Tax Acts regarding applications by UK resident companies to emigrate (chairman).
Chief Industrial Adviser – Department of Economic Affairs (two members).
National Economic Development Council (two members) and subsidiary committees (Wool, Paper and Board Making, Electrical Engineering and Food Processing).
National Board for Prices and Incomes.
Regional Economic Planning Councils (five members).

*Home Secretary*

Investigation into costs of operating London taxis with a view to advising on revision of fares.
Committee on Levy on Betting on Horse Races.

*Colonial Secretary*

Tribunal to investigate allegations reflecting on the official conduct of the Premier of, and other persons in, the Eastern Region of Nigeria.
Committee of Inquiry into the financial structure of the Colonial Development Corporation.

*President of the Board of Trade*
Committee on Bankruptcy Law Amendment.
Board of National Film Finance Corporation.
Cinematograph Films Council (chairman).
Committee on Crown powers to use unpatented inventions and unregistered designs (chairman).
Companies Act Accountancy Advisory Committee (three members) and General Consultative Committee.
United Kingdom trade and industrial mission to Ghana.
Committee to review the Companies Act 1948 and the Prevention of Fraud (Investments) Act, 1958.
Monopolies Commission (two members).
Advisory Council on Export Credits Guarantees.
Committee of inquiry into Shipbuilding industry.

*Minister of Agriculture, Fisheries and Food*
Committee on Pig Production (chairman).
Committee of Inquiry into Horticultural Marketing.
Committee of Inquiry into remuneration of distributors of liquid milk.
Consumers' Committee for Great Britain (chairman).

*Minister of Transport*
Committee of Inquiry into Inland Waterways.
Inquiry into allegations concerning purchasing policy and specific contracts of the British Transport Commission.
British Railways Board.
Inquiry into shipping services between Great Britain and Northern Ireland (chairman).
Committee on replacement of 'Queen' ships.

*Minister of Labour*
Inquiry into working of Dock Labour Scheme.
Committee to review operation of the Truck Acts.
Industry Training Boards – Engineering and Wool (two members).

*Minister of Housing and Local Government*
Committee on Air Pollution.

Clean Air Council.
Committee on staffing of Local Government.
The Commission for the New Towns (two members).
Panel on remuneration of primary and secondary school teachers.

*Minister of Health*
Dental Rates Study Group (chairman).
Relationship of Pharmaceutical Industry with National Health Service.

*Minister of Power*
Committee of Inquiry into the Electricity Supply Industry.
Committee of Inquiry into the cost of distributing coal, coke and manufactured fuels (chairman).
Inquiry into allegations regarding disposal of scrap cable by the London Electricity Board.
Executive membership of Iron and Steel Board.
Committee on Coal Derivatives.

*Minister of Aviation*
Managing Director of British Overseas Airways Corporation.
Investigation of the position and prospects of the Corporation.

*Secretary of State for War*
Committee to investigate relationship of the Services and NAAFI.

*Minister of Supply*
Director of Contracts and Principal Controller of Costing.
To advise on methods of fixing prices paid for stores acquired by non-competitive contracts.
Reorganization of Ordnance Factories.
Royal Ordnance Factories Board.

*Minister for Science – and Education*
United Kingdom Atomic Energy Authority.
Committee to examine the nature, sources and effects of the problem of noise.

Committee on salaries and gradings in Colleges of Advanced Technology (chairman).
Sports Council.

*Minister of Commerce, Northern Ireland*
Committee to inquire into the cost of distributing coal, coke and manufactured fuels in Northern Ireland (chairman).
Investigation of the position and future of the railways and their effect on the transport system.

*Overseas Governments*

| | |
|---|---|
| *Fiji:* | Commission of Inquiry into the sugar industry. |
| *Gold Coast:* | Committee of Inquiry into the affairs of the Cocoa Purchasing Company Limited.<br>Mines board of inquiry. |
| *Kenya:* | Mission to advise on development of public water supplies.<br>Fiscal Commission. |
| *Malaya:* | Mission to inquire into the rubber industry. |
| *Malta:* | Council of Administration in connection with the Dockyard. |
| *Mauritius:* | Commission of Inquiry into the sugar industry. |
| *New Zealand:* | Statutory Board Controlling export of meat, dairy produce and fruit (chairman of London Trade Committee). |
| *Nigeria:* | Commission to inquire into the affairs of the Nigerian Coal Corporation. |
| *Singapore:* | Committee of Inquiry into the strike of the Singapore Traction Company. |
| *Uganda:* | Uganda relationships commission. |
| *West Indies:* | Fact-finding mission on citrus industry. |

Consultation has taken place from time to time in recent years between various Government departments and the Institute on matters such as: Taxation, Company Law, Bankruptcy and Liquidations, Nationalized Industries, Building and Friendly Societies, Powers of Trustees and Decimalization of the Currency.

This section has only dealt with public appointments in the official sense. No attempt has been made to cover the field of appointments to public – or indeed to private – limited companies. The number even of those which are publicly known would be far too voluminous to deal with here. They include chairmanship and membership of boards of directors, and executive appointments at all levels. It has become the rule, rather than the exception, for annual reports, prospectuses and similar documents to contain the names of members of the Institute in these various capacities.

In addition, the President of the year becomes a member of a committee to control transfer of ordinary shares of The Times Publishing Co. Ltd, in order to maintain the independence of that paper. He acts in the same way for the *Spectator*. He is an *ex officio* Governor of the Dominion Students' Hall Trust, a trust providing a hall of residence, London House, for post-graduate students from the United Kingdom, the Commonwealth and the United States of America. He was, while the body existed, one of the Appointing Trustees to select members of the London Passenger Transport Board. He is also often called upon to nominate suitable members as arbitrators.

## Section 10: Membership

THE HISTORY of the Institute is, after all, the history of its members. The remaining Sections will accordingly deal with them collectively, and with a few of them, and of their firms, individually.

This section, then, seeks to record the main changes which have taken place in the nature of the membership and in its size.

The original Charter of 1880 provided for the admission of two categories of member, Fellows and Associates. The basis on which the members of the five societies referred to in the Charter were accepted into these two categories is explained in detail in Chapter 1. Broadly it may be said that any person who had been in practice as a public accountant on January 1, 1879, and who, up to the date of his application, had been continuously in practice as a public accountant for five years was entitled to be admitted as a Fellow. All other persons elected by reason of their having prescribed professional experience were admitted as Associates, but were entitled to apply for Fellowship after having completed five years continuous practice as a public accountant.

This latter distinction continued until January 1, 1960, when Fellowship was granted automatically to any Associate ten years after admission to the Institute.

Women members were eligible on the same basis as men from 1919, the first woman being admitted in 1920.

A distinction is drawn between practising and non-practising members for subscription purposes and in the List of Members, but in all other respects no distinction is made. The non-practising members have increased in numbers very much in recent years and at the date of this history it may be said that about 53 per cent of the total membership is in commerce or industry and 18 per cent on the staff of practising accountants. The growing increase in the proportion of the numbers of members in commerce or industry has resulted in pressure from them for further representation on the Council.

The schemes of integration whereby members of the Society

of Incorporated Accountants became eligible for membership of the Institute of Chartered Accountants in England and Wales or, as appropriate, of the Institute of Chartered Accountants of Scotland or of the Institute of Chartered Accountants in Ireland, became effective as from November 2, 1957. As a result of the schemes four-fifths of the members of the Society became members of one or other of the three chartered institutes and were entitled to describe themselves as chartered accountants and, so far as this Institute is concerned, to use the designatory letters F.C.A. or A.C.A. Approximately one-fifth of the Society's membership, however, had not received the training in public accountancy in the United Kingdom which is a pre-requisite for admission to membership of the chartered institutes. These members were admitted to the English Institute as incorporated accountant members and continued to use their original designatory letters of F.S.A.A. or A.S.A.A. Further proposals in 1965 to deal with this situation are given in Section I.

Suggestions have from time to time been made that the designations 'Fellow' and 'Associate' should be dropped and that all members should be called 'Chartered Accountants' – perhaps with the designatory letters 'C.A.'. Such suggestions have not been popular in Scotland where these designatory letters are held to be the prerogative of those privileged to have been trained north of the border or, if south of it, by Scottish principals.

A firm may only describe itself as 'Chartered Accountants' if all its partners may be so described as members of the Institute or of any Institute or Society of chartered accountants in the British Commonwealth of Nations approved by the Council. If any such Institute or Society has been so approved, the approval does not necessarily cease to be effective by reason only of the country concerned having ceased to be within the British Commonwealth of Nations.

The growth of membership in its various categories is indicated by the graph on page 177. It is realized that the violent changes in the last few years, due to the two causes indicated, make any type of graph difficult, but it is thought that the simple type adopted best displays the actual variations. The total membership reached 40,000 in March 1965.

*Benevolent Association*

The Chartered Accountants' Benevolent Association assists those members of the Institute who fall by the wayside through illness or other misfortune and also the dependants of such members.

It was formed as long ago as March 24, 1886. Its first annual report issued in April 1887 showed that four applications for assistance had been dealt with and that a total of £45 had been expended on relief. The report for the year ended February 28, 1965, showed that assistance given since 1886 had amounted to about £400,000.

Over the years many benefactors have helped the Association to build up its finances, and at February 28, 1965, its invested funds were valued at over £562,000, including the assets of the Incorporated Accountants' Benevolent Fund taken over in 1962. Without wishing to particularize between benefactors it should perhaps be mentioned that a sum of no less than £173,981 has so far been received from the estate of a member, H. C. Merrett.

The Association is an independent organization, managed by a Board of Governors. The day-to-day management is in the hands of the secretary of the Association who refers urgent cases to its President or to another member of the Executive Committee so that immediate help may be forthcoming where necessary.

Over the last twenty years there have been several developments which are worth recording. In 1944 the Chartered Accountants' Benevolent Association Trustees was incorporated to act as custodian trustee. In 1949 the Association became a founder member of Crossways Trust Limited which provides homes for old people; it now has ten places in the homes of the Trust. Since 1950 food hampers have been sent to beneficiaries at Christmas and in appropriate cases gifts in kind have been made in addition to monetary grants. In 1951 the important decision was taken to invest a considerable proportion of the funds in other than fixed interest securities; this decision has paid handsome dividends.

Despite the great advances made in this country in the field of social security there is still a clear need for the type of assistance which can be given by the Association.

## Section 11: Founder Firms

THE EXPRESSION 'founder firm' is not a recognized title. A reference to the first List of Members of 1881 shows many names which have become household words, and it would be tempting to regard any existing firm, which still retains one of them, as being a founder firm. It would, however, be difficult to compile such a list and it might be too voluminous. It has, therefore, been thought more practicable to consider a founder firm, for the purpose of this section, as one which can claim continuous partnership descent from a signatory to the Charter or a member of the first Council.

The following notes on firms which appear to pass that test may be of interest, and reference is also made to any firm which can claim to have been in existence for at least 100 years:

BAKER (JOHN), SONS & BELL, *London*

The founder of the firm, John Baker, became a clerk to Jeremiah Harridge, Shipping Accountant, in 1846. In 1858 Harridge, as a shareholder in a bank which became insolvent, had to flee the country to avoid bankruptcy, because in those days shareholders were not protected by limited liability. In his absence, John Baker took over the practice. In 1864, it took the style of John Baker & Co., and after other changes in name took on its present style in 1929. The 1847 records include manuscript Voyage and Captain's accounts, when a voyage to the Far East and back appears to have taken two years.

BEEVERS & ADGIE, *Leeds*

In 1857 Charles Beevers entered the office of George Simpson, Public Accountant, who was himself successor to a practising accountant, William Marshall. This practice goes back to 1849. Beevers became a partner in 1870; William Adgie became a partner in 1892.

BEGBIE, ROBINSON & CO., *London*

The firm started in October 1837 when G. C. Begbie rented an office in Coleman Street. He immediately engaged as junior clerk a young man named Robinson. Thus commenced, through three generations of that family, a continuous connection of 119 years which was only broken by the death of the last member in 1956. A book celebrating the centenary of the firm and entitled, *A Hundred Years of Accountancy*, now in the library, recalls the state of London at that time – Queen Victoria just ascended the Throne; London–Birmingham and London–Croydon railways under construction; P. & O. Company starting their first ship on its maiden voyage with doubts as to whether a steamship could carry sufficient coal across the Atlantic; experiments in progress with a telegraphic signal from Euston to Camden Town, but typewriters and even copying presses unknown.

BLACKBURNS, ROBSON, COATES & CO., *Bradford*

The firm was founded in 1844 by H. W. Blackburn, who was joined shortly afterwards by his brother John Blackburn, a member of the first Council. His son, J. H. Blackburn, started with the firm in 1864, was admitted as a Fellow of the Institute of Accountants in 1879 and later became a member of the Council of the present Institute for fifty-one years, which is a record. For nine years from 1920, the firm was amalgamated with Barton Mayhew & Co.; thereafter it became Blackburns Coates & Co., until Sir Leonard Coates died in 1947, when it joined forces with Lawrence Robson & Co., taking on its present firm name. A circular letter written by H. W. Blackburn in 1869 was apparently free from the ethical standards later imposed by the Charter. Its last sentence reads:

> 'The great experience we have had in the winding up of Insolvent Estates now for more than twenty-five years, and the staff of assistants at our command, enable us with confidence to say we can efficiently serve the commercial public in this department.'

Those were the days!

# Notice

1. Godliness, Cleanliness and Punctuality are the necessities of a good business.

2. This firm has reduced the hours of work, and the clerical staff will now only have to be present between the hours of 7 a.m. and 6 p.m. on week days. The Sabbath is for worship, but should any man-of-war or other vessel require victualling, the clerical staff will work on the Sabbath.

3. Daily prayers will be held each morning in the main office. The clerical staff will be present.

4. Clothing must be of a sober nature. The clerical staff will not disport themselves in raiment of bright colours, nor will they wear hose unless of good repair.

5. Overshoes and top-coats may not be worn in the office, but neck scarves and headwear may be worn in inclement weather.

6. A stove is provided for the benefit of the clerical staff. Coal and wood must be kept in the locker. It is recommended that each member of the clerical staff bring four pounds of coal, each day, during the cold weather.

7. No member of the clerical staff may leave the room without permission from Mr Ryder. The calls of nature are permitted, and the clerical staff may use the garden below the second gate. This area must be kept in good order.

*continued over*

**Office staff practices 113 years ago.**

8. No talking is allowed during business hours.

9. The craving for tobacco, wines or spirits is a human weakness, and, as such, is forbidden to all members of the clerical staff.

10. Now that the hours of business have been drastically reduced, the partaking of food is allowed between 11.30 a.m. and noon, but work will not, on any account, cease.

11. Members of the clerical staff will provide their own pens. A new sharpener is available, on application to Mr Ryder.

12. Mr Ryder will nominate a senior clerk to be responsible for the cleanliness of the main office and the private office, and all boys and juniors will report to him forty minutes before prayers, and will remain after closing hours for similar work. Brushes, brooms, scrubbers and soap are provided by the owners.

13. The new increased weekly wages are as hereunder detailed:

| | s. | d. |
|---|---|---|
| Junior boys (to 11 years) | 1 | 4 |
| Boys (to 14 years) | 2 | 1 |
| Juniors | 4 | 8 |
| Junior Clerks | 8 | 7 |
| Clerks | 10 | 9 |
| Senior Clerks (after 15 years with the owners) | 21 | 0 |

The owners hereby recognize the generosity of the new labour laws, but will expect a great rise in output of work to compensate for these near Utopian conditions.

*(Reproduced from various publications throughout the world; source unknown.)*

BLEASE & SONS, *Liverpool*
The firm claims to go back for over 100 years as in 1849 John Stanley Blease was shown in *Gore's Directory* as an accountant. Subsequently, in the 1865 *Directory* he was shown again as a partner of Robert S. Blease whose son, Walter Blease, was a founder member of the Liverpool Society of Chartered Accountants. The present firm name was adopted in 1886.

CARLILL, BURKINSHAW & FERGUSON, *Hull*
The founder of the firm was J. G. Carlill and a letter of his to clients and 'prospective clients' in June 1835 establishes that the firm is just on 130 years old. The letter also establishes the delightful freedom of those days; it reads:

> 'I take the liberty to offer you my services as an Accountant, and should you or any of your friends be good enough to give me a trial in this way, my best attention shall be given to afford satisfaction. I have had a few years experience in Book-keeping and flatter myself I am qualified for the undertaking.'

It is even accompanied by a covering letter from Carlill's father saying that the son is 'fully competent and I feel assured will faithfully and satisfactorily execute any business of the nature referred to, which may be committed to his care'. The firm has lately become associated with Messrs Hodgson, Harris & Co.

CARTER & COMPANY, *Birmingham*
This firm can claim both to have been in existence for over 100 years and to be a founder firm in that its origin is known to be before 1840 and Edward Carter, who became a partner in 1860, was a member of the first Council. The firm amalgamated with Cooper Brothers & Co. in 1960.

CHALMERS, IMPEY & CO., *Liverpool*
This firm comes from two old stocks, Chalmers Wade & Co., which practised in Liverpool, and Impey Cudworth & Co., of Birmingham; they merged in 1961. Both C. H. Wade (then of Manchester) and

A nineteenth-century counting-house.
*Courtesy Radio Times Hulton Picture Library.*

A. W. Chalmers of Liverpool were petitioners for the Charter of 1880 and members of the first Council of the Institute. Their firm had had a continuous existence since 1796 when Joseph Redish, its founder, appeared in the Liverpool Directory as 'Accountant'. Both Chalmers and Wade had previously been members of the Incorporated Society of Liverpool Accountants, the first body of accountants to be formed in England, Chalmers being a signatory to its Memorandum of Incorporation in 1870. The Impey Cudworth business appears to trace its origin to a date unknown but prior to 1871, when Impey took over in Birmingham the business of a friend who had been practising as an accountant previously. The business in its earliest days was largely with Quaker clients. Impey was a keen sportsman especially in the hunting field and is said to have called all his hunters 'Business' so that his clients could be truthfully informed when he was away that he was 'on Business'. In 1965, the name of the firm changed from Chalmers Wade Impey Cudworth & Co. to its present style.

COOPER BROTHERS & CO., *London*

William Cooper began to practise as an accountant in his own name in 1854 and was joined in 1857 by one of his brothers, Arthur, when the firm became W. & A. Cooper. In 1861 the name was changed to Cooper Brothers & Co., so that for over 100 years its style has not been altered. Two other brothers, Francis and Ernest, became partners in 1872 and these four men between them had a significant influence on the formation of the Institute; the firm has since provided three of its presidents. The following extract from a letter written in September 1855, by William Cooper to an inquirer who wished to have his son instructed in accountancy, is of interest:

> 'The business of an accountant comprises the investigation and arrangement of all kinds of intricate accounts. The acquirement of a thorough knowledge of what is called the "double entry" system of accounts is the chief requisite. The duties of the young man would at first be very light. His salary after the

expiration of his term would depend upon his age and capacity but might probably commence at £50 for the first year. A good hand-writing would go far to recommend him.'

And again an account written in 1921 by Ernest Cooper of the early position of the profession as he remembered it:

> 'We could hardly, south of the Tweed, claim to be a profession. There was absolutely no organization or co-operation, no Institute or Society, no examinations, very few articled clerks, no newspaper, no library, no benevolent fund, and not even a dining club or a golf club. An accountant was regarded as associated with and dependent upon insolvency, and I well remember that to be seen talking to or having your office entered by an accountant was to be avoided, particularly in the stressful times of 1866.'

CURTIS, JENKINS, CORNWELL & CO., *Bristol*
The firm was founded by Robert Fletcher in 1818 under the style Robert Fletcher & Co. In 1839 John Curtis and William Vaughan Jenkins were admitted to the partnership. In 1861 the style of the firm became Curtis & Jenkins.

DELOITTE, PLENDER, GRIFFITHS & CO., *London*
This firm was founded by William Welch Deloitte at the age of 27 in 1845, and he presided over its destinies for fifty-two years thereafter. He and his later partner, John G. Griffiths, were both members of the first Council of the Institute. Much later the firm absorbed the business originally founded by William Quilter (referred to in Section 12) so that it has yet another contact with the founding of the Institute. The history of the firm up to 1956, written by Sir Russell Kettle and available in the Institute Library, gives a most interesting picture of London in the 1840s – gas lighting just commencing; the great railway mania; the steel pen supplanting the quill; envelopes unknown and letters sealed by wafers; public execution a form of entertainment; Income Tax re-imposed

and intended to be 'of a temporary character' – and of the development of accountancy in the last half of the nineteenth century. The normal daily hours of work in the early years were apparently nine; in times of urgency much more. Articles were not then in fashion and a letter in the office letter book to an applicant for employment reads, 'we consider that your services for the first twelve months would be amply remunerated by what you would learn in that time'. Audit clerks were provided with a 'baton' which in its three compartments contained pens and pencils, ink and india-rubbers. William Plender (later Lord Plender) became a partner in 1897 and so continued for forty-nine years. The firm's name has from time to time contained the names of other partners – Greenwood, Dever and Hollebone, but has been under its present style since 1905. It has provided six presidents of the Institute.

EDMONDS & CO., *Portsmouth*
This firm was founded in the 1850s by William Edmonds in Portsea, and has continued with his name ever since. It is now associated with THORNTON, BAKER & CO., which can itself trace its origin to 1865 in the same area.

GRACE, DARBYSHIRE & TODD, *Bristol*
The firm was established in 1818 by John Moxham. In 1822 he married into the Quaker community from whose descendants so many of the firm's partners were to come. Among these were the family of Grace and the firm was apparently renamed during the period 1857 to 1861 as James Grace & Son. In those days it went in for many activities and as James Grace says, 'We threw our net for business wherever we thought it would catch fish, or I should say make money.' The name of the firm was changed to its present style in 1920, having since 1861 practised as James & Henry Grace.

EDWIN GUTHRIE & CO., *Manchester*
Edwin Guthrie was a member of the first Council of the Institute and at that time was in partnership with Charles Henry Wade, also

a member of that Council; both were petitioners for the Charter. They later separated and Wade's firm joined up with Jones, Crewdson & Youatt. Edwin Guthrie is also one of the distinguished band of members of the Institute who did so much to develop accountancy in the early days in the United States of America. He founded there the firm of Barrow, Wade, Guthrie & Co. in 1883. Edwin Guthrie & Co. amalgamated with Peat, Marwick, Mitchell & Co. in 1955.

HARD, DOWDY & CO., *London*

The present partners have no doubt that the firm goes back over 100 years. A press copy book of 1879 records a bill rendered by H. G. Walter 'Accountant and Auditor' with principal's time charged at 42s per day and that of chief clerks at 21s. The firm's name in 1880 (the year of the Charter) was Kendrick & Walter, and by 1882 Walter & Gregson. The firm was acceded to by Edwin Hard in 1913 who then changed its name to Edwin Hard & Co.

HARMOOD-BANNER, CASH, STONE & MOUNSEY, *Liverpool*

The Harmood family settled in Liverpool in 1700 and became owners of the 'Golden Fleece', an inn which in later years was used for meetings of creditors; it is even possible that the sight of opulent attorneys may have been a factor in deciding the original Harmood-Banner to set up his accountancy practice in 1805, the year of Trafalgar. He was the son of a certain Thomas Banner who married the daughter of Captain Harmood, Commander of a frigate stationed in the Mersey; hence the double name. He was appointed in 1814 by George III 'A commissioner to take Bails' and it is interesting to note in those far-off days that his Royal Warrant of appointment after greeting him as 'our trusty and well beloved' refers to him as 'accountant'. The firm continued in the hands of later generations of the family until 1878 when they were joined by George Nicholson, which family also contributed three generations of partners. In 1946, they were joined by Lewis and Mounsey, another old Liverpool firm, which was founded in 1825 by Thomas Whinneray. The indenture of 1840 by which he took on

Edward Mounsey as an articled clerk shows that he undertook to provide the young man with 'good wholesome and sufficient meat, drink and lodging, becoming wearing apparel and the mending thereof'. In 1964 this firm was joined by Cash Stone & Co., one of whose first partners, William Cash, was a member of the first Council of the Institute. The present firm, therefore, can claim in two of its origins to go back over 100 years and in a third to be a founder firm. It is now associated with another founder firm, Stead, Taylor & Stead, referred to later.

HARPER, FEATHER & PATERSON, *London*

This firm, though not going back quite 100 years, can claim the distinction of having had two members on the original Council of the Institute, Alfred Cotton Harper and Edward Norton Harper. The firm name was, for many years, Harper Bros and both of them were members of the Society of Accountants in England before the Institute was founded, Alfred Harper being its secretary. At the date of his death in 1930, he was still a member of the Institute Council and sole survivor of the original Council. Shortly before his death, he wrote a little booklet entitled *I.C.A.*, giving a short sketch of the inception of the Institute detailing the meetings and troubles associated with that happening.

HART BROTHERS, REDDALL & CO., *London*

The founder of this firm, Edward Hart, was a member of the first Council of the Institute and died in 1895. The records of the firm substantiate that he had been in practice since somewhere around 1845. Edward Hart, Junior, articled to Frederick Whinney, joined his father in 1880 and on his death in 1950 the President of the Institute stated that he was the last original member admitted at the date of the Royal Charter, having previously been a member of the Institute of Accountants. Edward Hart, Junior, also established a practice in the United States of America in 1890 under the style of Hart Bros, Tibbetts, Heiron & Co., and is regarded as one of the fathers of the development of professional English accountancy principles in America.

HILL, VELLACOTT & CO., *London*

The actual date of origin of the firm is uncertain, but it claims direct partnership descent from Edward Thomas Jones, who in 1796, under a licence signed by George III, published his patented *English System of Book-Keeping*. It may, therefore, well be, as Lancelot Hill (President 1931–2 and 1933–4) was often heard to claim, that the firm is the oldest in the profession, certainly in London (although as noted later there is a Bristol firm who claim to go back to 1780). The firm continued under various descendants with the name Jones until A. J. Hill joined it in 1867 and W. E. Vellacott in 1878; the records not showing when the name of Jones was dropped. In 1878 a Manchester practice was established as a distinct partnership under the name Jones, Crewdson & Co., and a Leeds practice under the name of Theodore B. Jones & Co. Another firm, Edwin Jones & Co. of London, is descended from the original founder. The *English System* referred to above contains the following:

> 'I am not aware of one Book for teaching Book-Keeping in Schools, besides that published by myself, which gives any plan for avoiding serious errors, or for detecting the smallest mistake; much less do such treatises as I have seen offer any means of proving whether any set of Books be demonstrably correct or not.'

HODGSON, HARRIS & CO., *Hull*

The actual origin of this firm is uncertain, but the founder, Robert Hodgson, signed the balance sheet of his old employers in 1879. Though not in itself a founder firm it has, as noted earlier, in 1964 become associated with CARLILL, BURKINSHAW & FERGUSON, who go back over 100 years.

JACKSON, PIXLEY & CO., *London*

Many of the records of this firm were destroyed during the 1939–45 war. It is, however, clear that they can trace a partnership descent from William Edwards (the founder also of the firm of James, Edwards, Dangerfield & Co.) to the 1840s. In 1848 he took into partnership S. L. Price who was to become the founder of the firm of Price Waterhouse & Co. The partnership was dissolved in the following year and Edwards himself died in 1885. The firm, however, continued to practise under his name until 1892, when it adopted its present title.

JAMES, EDWARDS, DANGERFIELD & CO., *London*

The firm was founded in 1843 by William Edwards, who in 1855 took in A. A. James as his articled clerk and subsequently as his partner, practising as Edwards & James. In 1867, H. T. Edwards, the son of the founder, retired and formed a partnership with William Cash. He later rejoined his old firm along with his new partner, the firm becoming James, Edwards, Cash & Stone. In 1873 the firm divided and the four partners carried on their respective practices as James & Edwards and Cash & Stone. In 1922 the firm was amalgamated with Cates Brown & Harding, in 1933 with H. Garton Ash, and in 1963 with Dangerfield, Brewis & Co.

JOSOLYNE, MILES & CO., *London*

The founder, a Cornishman named Honey, had been practising in Ironmonger Lane for some years before he and his son moved, in 1832, to 28 King Street, Cheapside. The firm of Honey & Honey, and its successors, has occupied these premises since that date. The last Honey retired in 1875 and, in that year, J. A. Josolyne became a partner, joined in 1878 by A. O. Miles, who had been articled to the firm. The name was changed in 1886 to Josolyne, Miles & Co., which has remained, with temporary alterations, till the present. In 1965 the firm entered into an association with Cassleton Elliott & Co., under which, in addition to their own names, they carried on business in the joint name of both firms.

In the 'seventies the business was described as 'Public accountants, including the formation of public companies, private partnerships, arbitrators and fire-claims' and the partners also acted as valuers and, occasionally, as sharebrokers.

A. O. Miles was elected to the Council in 1895 and was President in 1909–10, celebrating his sixtieth year with the firm in 1932 and remaining an active partner till 1939. His commanding presence, which enabled him to quell many angry creditors' meetings, is perpetuated among the portraits in the Institute.

KEMP, CHATTERIS & CO., *London*

This firm represents the amalgamation (in 1921) of two firms which were both very active in the early days of the Institute – Kemp, Son, Sendell & Co. (founded in 1857) and Chatteris, Nichols & Co. (founded in 1848). Charles Fitch Kemp was a member of the first Council of the Institute as he had been of the predecessor Society of Accountants. He served as President for two years from 1894 to 1896 and his son, Harold Fitch Kemp, held that office in 1931. Chatteris, Nichols & Co. do not appear to have been so actively associated with the Chartered Institute, although Henry Chatteris was auditor of the Society of Accountants.

A diary kept by Charles Fitch Kemp in 1857 contains many entries which relate to the profession and City life at that time.

| | | |
|---|---|---|
| 1857 | *January* 27 | 'Met Turquand and conversed about my proposed partnership with him.' |
| | *February* 6 | 'Called on Linklater. . . . Chatteris at meeting.' |
| | *February* 18 | 'Met . . . and went to the Gresham Club with him – two bottles of claret "very naughty".' |
| | *October* 15 | 'Rode my Horse to Town and like him very well.' |

The possible partnership with Turquand never materialized but the early reference to Chatteris indicates the two firms had known each other for many years prior to the merger in 1921.

Since 1963 the practice of Kemp, Chatteris & Co. has been conducted in association with that of Touche, Ross, Bailey & Smart, whose founder, the late Sir George Touche, was also instrumental in founding the firms of the same name in the United States and in Canada. In 1964 this association was extended to include the long-established Scottish firm of Wilson Stirling & Co. of Glasgow.

LOVEWELL BLAKE & CO., *Great Yarmouth*
There is some speculation as to the true age of the firm, but it seems reasonable to suppose that Lovewell Blake set up in business in 1858, when he went into partnership with his father. He died in 1910, but the firm has throughout retained his name. He was a member of the Society of Accountants in England formed in 1872. An advertisement by him in *The Accountant* of October 1874 records that he 'attends and reports meetings of Creditors within twenty miles of Great Yarmouth free of charge. Proxies obtained and Accounts collected upon reciprocal terms'. It is pleasing to record that the principles of the firm improved so much over the years that a later partner became the first President of the Institute to be elected from East Anglia. In 1964 the firm became associated with Cooper Brothers & Co.

MELLORS, BASDEN & MELLORS, *Nottingham*
This firm celebrated its centenary in 1954. Its origin, however, goes back earlier than 1851 for at that date Robert Mellors at the age of 15 was articled to a Nottingham firm of accountants, Taylor & Mosley, and four years later was admitted to partnership. Robert Mellors lived to the age of 95 and became a great figure in the affairs of his native city, being known as its 'Grand Old Man'. Prior to admission to the Institute in 1880 he had been a Fellow of the old Institute of Accountants from 1872. The firm name was changed to his own in 1860, to Mellors & Basden in 1878 and to its present title when in 1887 T. G. Mellors joined the partnership. The firm has provided two presidents of the Institute.

C. M. MERCHANT & SON, *Bury*
C. M. Merchant started in practice prior to 1860, in the firm of Murray & Child. On the dissolution of the practice in that year, C. M. Merchant continued on his own and the firm's name has never been changed.

MORRIS, GREGORY & CO., *Manchester*
The founder of the firm was Alexander Morris, born about 1800;

he started life in the drapery business. The first mention of the firm is to be found in Slater's *Manchester Directory* for 1852, wherein is recorded:

> 'Alexander Morris & Son, Accountants and Agents to the County Fire and Provident Life Assurance Companies, 59 King Street.'

PEAT, MARWICK, MITCHELL & CO., *London*

The firm traces its origin to Robert Fletcher who, after an early period of his life in Aberdeen as a clerk in an insurance company, started an accountancy practice there in 1866. He came to London in 1867, where he became one of the pioneers of accountancy, and established the firm of Robert Fletcher & Co. His purpose in moving was to assist in the reorganization of the London, Chatham and Dover Railway. He took on as one of his clerks in 1870 W. B. Peat, admitting him to partnership in 1877. Fletcher retired in 1878 and died in 1883. After his retirement, the business carried on with Roderick Mackay as senior partner, who was a member of the first Council of the Institute; his other partners were E. E. Price and W. B. Peat and on the death of Mackay in 1891 the firm was taken over by the latter and its name changed to W. B. Peat & Co. It continued under that title until 1911 when, following a chance meeting between W. B. Peat and James Marwick on an Atlantic crossing, it became associated with the firm of Marwick, Mitchell & Co., which firm practised in the USA, Canada and on the continent as well as in the United Kingdom. This association was for a period abandoned, but later in 1925 the firms came together again and the title Peat, Marwick, Mitchell & Co. was adopted on both sides of the Atlantic and elsewhere. The firm has provided three presidents of the Institute.

EDWARD THOMAS PEIRSON & SONS, *Coventry*

Edward Thomas Peirson was a member of the first Council of the Institute and it is thought he actually started in practice in 1852. Since then the practice has been continued under his name and his descendants have throughout been in the partnership.

PRICE WATERHOUSE & CO., *London*

Samuel Lowell Price, a member of the first Council of the Institute, had previously been one of the moving spirits in the formation of the old Institute in 1870, and was a member of its Council also. He had been in practice as an accountant from at least 1848 and in 1865 was joined by two others, W. H. Holyland and Edwin Waterhouse, both of whom had been trained in the firm of Coleman, Turquand, Youngs & Co. From 1874 when Holyland retired, the firm dropped his name from its title and has ever since practised under the name now used. In 1871 it was asked by Monkhouse Goddard & Co., founded in 1868 in Newcastle upon Tyne, to press the Institute of Accountants to change its rules so as to admit provincial accountants. S. L. Price supported this in the Council and the rules were altered in 1873, with the result that the old Institute became a national body. Those then concerned could not have known that half a century later the Newcastle practice of the firm and that of Monkhouse Goddard & Co. were to be joined together and have since used the Price Waterhouse name.

It is interesting to note from the records of the firm that even as early as 1870 accountancy was not, as is so often thought, largely limited to bankruptcy work, but included investigations of the accounts of businesses in many parts of the world. Out of these activities arose the need for overseas offices; an example of this was the establishment of offices in North America where two outstanding partners, Arthur Lowes Dickinson and George Oliver May, in turn played leading parts along with other practitioners in the development of the accountancy profession. The firm has provided three presidents of the Institute.

PRIDEAUX, FRERE, BROWN & CO., *London*

The firm appears to have been started, at least by 1847, by William Henry Grey who, though he did not himself become a member of the Institute, took in as partner in 1858 Francis Greville Prideaux. Ernest Rowland Frere became a partner in 1883. Grey's business in the early days appears to have been largely in helping Foreign

Office officials with their accounts and advising the 'Landed Gentry'. He wrote a pamphlet entitled *A Few Words to the Wealthy on Household Accounts*.

SAFFERY, SONS & CO., *London*
The firm was founded in 1855 by Joseph John Saffery, who was a member of the first Council of the Institute. As President of the Institute in 1890, he laid the foundation stone of the Hall in Moorgate Place and the firm still has the ceremonial trowel in its possession.

SMITHSON, BLACKBURN & CO., *Leeds*
This firm can trace its origin to the 1840s when Edward Bolton was in business in Leeds as an accountant. The records in 1850 show that he was then receiving substantial audit fees. Except for an interval from 1885 till 1921 the next four generations of the Bolton family down to the present date have continuously been partners in the firm.

STEAD, TAYLOR & STEAD, *Liverpool*
The accountancy practice of this firm commenced in 1816 or 1817 by Thomas Crook, as Thomas Crook & Son. He retired in 1855 and the business was carried on as Taylor & Stead by his two senior clerks, Robert Taylor and Thomas Walton Stead. In 1857 John Charles Stead was admitted to the partnership and the firm became Stead, Taylor & Stead, which title has been retained ever since. The firm is now associated with Harmood-Banner, Cash, Stone & Mounsey.

J. & A. W. SULLY & CO., *London*
In 1865 James Wood Sully was in Sheffield where, on July 4 (exactly 100 years ago as this history goes to press), he entered into partnership with Alfred Allett, Public Accountant and Financial Agent, of that city. It would seem that this partnership was dissolved in or about the year 1870, and a new partnership between J. W. Sully and M. N. Girdlestone commenced in London in 1871.

In 1873 Alfred Willis Sully joined his uncle as a clerk and this eventually led to the partnership of J. & A. W. Sully practising in London and Bristol. J. W. Sully was admitted a Fellow of the Institute on the day of its incorporation.

Since these early days, and until 1960, the Sully family is much in evidence – Frederick Harold Sully (1899) – Frederick James Sully (1908) – Douglas George Sully (1913 – killed in action) and Alfred Victor Sully (1919), the last member of this family to be associated with the firm.

TRIBE, CLARKE & CO., *Bristol*

This appears to be the oldest established firm in the Institute. It was founded in 1780 by Josiah Wade with offices in Queen Square. These were destroyed in the Bristol riots of 1831 when the firm moved to its present offices in Albion Chambers. Wade had various partners in the early days, Bradley, Barnard and Thomas, whose names figured in that of the firm. It was joined in 1853 by Wilberforce Tribe. In 1871 E. G. Clarke joined the firm and since that date it has been known under its present style. S. L. Price (later the founder of Price Waterhouse & Co.) appears to have been employed by the firm in 1842 at a salary of £120 per annum. Early records show that the business was not chiefly of a bankruptcy nature, but included ordinary accountancy work, and an audit certificate, which nowadays seems to have much to commend it, reads simply:

'Examined and found right. Bristol, December 20, 1797.'

TURQUAND, YOUNGS & CO., *London*

It is thought that John and Alexander Young started practising in 1840. The business was joined by William Turquand and the first record of the use of the present firm name is in the year 1857. In 1859, James Edward Coleman was admitted, having himself been in practice since 1840. The firm has from time to time had other names in its style, namely, Coleman, Weise, Bishop and Clarke; also for a period up to 1938 it included the name McAuliffe, when it became associated with McAuliffe, Davis & Hope, largely interested in the Far East. It reverted, however, to its present style in 1951. Both William Turquand and John Young were members of the first Council of the Institute, William Turquand being its first president. The firm has provided two presidents and one vice-president for the Institute.

VINEY, PRICE & GOODYEAR, *London*

It is thought that the origin of this firm goes back to 1828, when it existed as 'Practising Accountants' under the name of Parrinton & Sons. The nature of the work was largely in connection with bankruptcies. The name Viney appears in the firm name from about 1860. Goodyear had been in partnership with E. E. Price, practising under the name of R. Mackay & Co. Price became anxious about the affairs of Robert Mackay and joined up with Viney, bringing Goodyear with him in 1892. The firm has continued under the name of these three individuals ever since.

WHINNEY, MURRAY & CO., *London*

The firm traces its origin to 1848 when Robert Palmer Harding, the first Vice-President of the Institute, entered into partnership with a Mr Pullein. Frederick Whinney was apprenticed to Harding and was taken into partnership in 1857 when his name was included in that of the firm. John Smith was admitted into partnership in 1893. In the following year the firm name was changed to Whinney, Smith and Whinney under which style it continued until in 1965, on closer association with Brown, Fleming & Murray, it changed to Whinney, Murray & Co. It has existed in Old Jewry and Frederick's Place ever since its foundation. It has provided five presidents of the Institute. A member of the Whinney family has been a partner since 1857, including a present great-grandson of Frederick.

* * *

Existing firms which, prior to integration with the Society, were Incorporated Accountants cannot be founder firms of the Institute, but the following notes are of interest concerning those which have been in existence for at least 100 years:

LANGTON & MacCONNAL, *Liverpool*

This firm practised as Chartered Accountants until 1905, after which date it became a firm of Incorporated Accountants until integration in 1957. One of the founders, William Mathison, appears to have been in practice in 1847 and was an original member of the Liverpool Society of Accountants in 1870. He joined forces in 1869 with H. C. Langton, who had also been practising on his own account for some years, to found the firm of Langton & Mathison. H. C. Langton died in the same year, and the firm was continued by William Mathison until his retirement in 1880. He was succeeded by Langton's managing clerk, John MacConnal, who, in 1864, had had an altercation with Langton to whom he refused access to the premises of his employer's business although Langton had been appointed its trustee in bankruptcy. This altercation led to respect and partnership. Since Mathison's retirement in 1880 the firm has carried on under its present style.

LITHGOW, NELSON & CO., *Liverpool*

The firm was started in 1856 by Thomas Heaps who called himself 'Surveyor, Collector, Estate Agent and Agent to Eagle Life Assurance Co.' He was joined in 1865 by his nephew W. J. Nelson. Later the firm merged with W. G. Lithgow of Southport when the present style was established. At one period C. Hewetson Nelson was a partner before he started his own practice. He and Bertram Nelson (a grandson of W. J. Nelson) were both presidents of the Society of Incorporated Accountants.

# Section 12: A Few Past Leaders

TO PREPARE a list of members on whom biographical notes should be included must obviously be a difficult task. Some must be mentioned because of the parts they played in the development of the Institute; the risk must, therefore, be taken that others of equal eminence, and equally deserving of mention, will be omitted. No doubt every member asked for a selection would prepare a different list.

To minimize as far as practicable the risk of invidious distinctions the names of members now alive have been excluded, as also have those of past members who had not shared actively in the government of the Institute itself. After much discussion this basis of selection has been applied strictly, though it has obvious disadvantages. Apologies are offered in advance to any who, or whose friends, may feel hurt thereby.

A single exception has been made on the insistence of those responsible, as it was felt that a history of the Institute which lacked a note about its editor-in-chief would be seriously defective. It goes without saying that Sir Harold Howitt neither suggested nor approved this decision.

The following notes prepared on the above basis of selection are presented in the order of the dates of the active professional lives of those with whom they deal. Their portraits follow page 146.

### WILLIAM QUILTER

Although he was not a President of the Institute or indeed on its Council, William Quilter was President in 1870 of the old Institute of Accountants and was very closely concerned with the foundations of the profession. He was a partner with Thomas A. Welton (in the firm of Quilter Ball & Co.) who was the honorary secretary of the old Institute, a member of the first Council of the present Institute in 1880 and eventually President in 1891–2. William Quilter appears to have deviated to the stockbroking business in which he formed the firm of Quilter Balfour & Co. in 1886, his accountancy practice continuing under the name of Welton & Bond and being, much later, absorbed by Deloitte's. On his death his son, Sir Cuthbert Quilter, founded a prize in the Institute examinations in honour of his father.

WILLIAM TURQUAND, *President* 1880–2

Turquand was a member of the old Institute of Accountants and its President from 1877. In that capacity in 1880, he was one of the petitioners to the Privy Council for the grant of the Charter and he became the new Institute's first President. He was the son of an official assignee of the Court of Bankruptcy, a fact which no doubt largely influenced him in the choice of his profession. He was appointed by the Board of Trade as one of the accountants, under the first Limited Liability Act, 1855, to report on the solvency of firms seeking its protection, at a time when 'limited liability' was only granted to those who could prove by this means that they were solvent. He was associated with most of the important liquidations during the last half of the nineteenth century, including in particular the Overend Gurney failure. His last liquidation was that of the West of England Bank. At his death in 1894, many tributes were paid to the leading part which he had taken in the formation of the Institute and the enhancement of its reputation and to his own personal qualities of ability and integrity.

FREDERICK WHINNEY, *President* 1884–8

As an active member of the Institute of Accountants, Whinney took the chair at the meetings with other accountancy bodies for the negotiations which eventually led up to the granting of the Charter. In a very direct sense, therefore, he is undoubtedly one of the chief founders of modern professional accountancy. The records show that at one time he strongly objected to taking in the members of the Society of Accountants on the ground that many of their members were not accountants 'pure and simple'. He was a member of the first Council of the Institute and was its President for four consecutive years, a record beaten only by a later partner of his firm in the Second World War. The early history of the Institute, as recorded elsewhere, is full of his robust advocacy of some form of registration for the profession, in which advocacy he was often hotly opposed by other stalwarts of those days. He took a great interest in students' societies, not only in encouraging their activities but also by personally giving many exceedingly able lectures. In his early career, he was largely concerned with bankruptcies and liquidations of various kinds, one of the earliest being the failure of Overend Gurney in 1866, when he acted along with Turquand. He retired from practice in 1905 and died in 1916 in his eighty-seventh year.

WILLIAM WELCH DELOITTE, *President* 1888–9
Before he set up as a practising accountant in 1845, Deloitte had for twelve years been on the staff of the Official Assignee in Bankruptcy. He was a member of the Council of the old Institute of Accountants and of the first Council of the present Institute. He was a founder member of the Benevolent Association and its President for many years. He died in 1898 and in his later years delighted in country life in Southall where he held considerable property. His name derives from his grandfather, a certain Count de Loitte in the household of Louis XVI. We have a picture of him from notes by John Gane, who left him in 1870, to form with Herbert Jackson the firm which has since borne their names. 'He was an alert, decisive little man, with just a touch of austerity in his manner – most particular in all things and dressed very carefully – his patience was sorely tried by the inability of the junior clerk to make head or tail of his handwriting.'

EDWIN WATERHOUSE, *President* 1892–4
Edwin Waterhouse was born in Liverpool in 1841; one of eight children of Alfred Waterhouse, partner in the firm of Nicholas Waterhouse & Sons, merchants and brokers, and a member of the Society of Friends. He was articled to Turquand Youngs in 1861, and in 1865, with S. L. Price and W. H. Holyland, founded the firm of Price, Holyland & Waterhouse. The firm adopted its

present title of Price Waterhouse & Co. in 1874. For seventeen years up to 1915 Edwin Waterhouse was President of the Chartered Accountants' Benevolent Association. He was one of the earliest members called upon to advise the Government of the day upon the accounting organization of Government Departments and was a member of the committee which framed the Companies Act, 1900. Apart from being one of the great founders of the profession, he combined great ability and strength of character with a particularly gentle nature. His interests were in music and art and a love of his countryside in Surrey.

GEORGE WALTER KNOX, *President* 1896–7

Of Scottish parentage, he was born in London and indeed graduated from its University as a prominent scientist. He abandoned science, however, for accountancy and started his professional career in Sheffield, where in 1872 he joined the Society of Accountants in England. He was a member of the first Council of the Institute and remained a member until the date of his death forty-six years later. He opened his London office in 1884 under the style of Knox Cropper & Co., which names have remained in the firm's title ever since. He was chairman of the examination committee for no less than eighteen years, and gave a considerable amount of his time to the interests and welfare of young people in many walks of life. His obituary notices and the speeches made at his death testify to a remarkably lovable character, and to one who had devoted his life largely to the interests of the Institute. His early scientific training did not apparently help him with 'modern inventions' as he called them, and, to his dying day, he referred to the telephone as 'the tube'.

ERNEST COOPER, *President* 1899–1901

Ernest Cooper was the youngest of a family of thirteen, four of whom founded the firm of Cooper Brothers & Co. of which he was the senior partner for thirty years from 1893. He had been a member of the old Institute of Accountants since its formation in 1871. In 1921 he read to the Autumnal Meeting of the Institute a most interesting account of his experiences in a paper entitled *Fifty-seven years in an Accountant's Office*. He took a leading part in the formation of the Institute and in the violent discussions on the subject of registration which went on in the early days. He was a member of the Council for thirty-three years and his contribution to its affairs and to the dignity of the profession was outstanding. He was somewhat of a forbidding figure with a reputation for absolute integrity. In dress and in manner he was Victorian and behaved as such. He was abstemious, blunt in approach and direct of speech. He was invariably dressed in a curious starched white shirt of his own design with short black coat and striped trousers and, after a business visit to Greece early in his career, he always wore a beard.

JOHN SUTHERLAND HARMOOD-BANNER, *President* 1904–5

He became head of the firm of Harmood-Banner & Son on the death of his father, the founder of the firm. In 1875 he had joined the Incorporated Society of Liverpool Accountants. He served on the Council of the Institute for forty-two years until the time of his death in 1927. Apart from his reputation in the profession, he took a great part in public affairs, being a Member of Parliament for the Everton division of Liverpool, and as Lord Mayor of that city was known as its Chancellor of the Exchequer. He was High Sheriff of Cheshire, was knighted in 1913 and created a baronet in 1924. He took on a large number of directorships and in 1919 was appointed a member of the Royal Commission on Income Tax. In build he was short and stout, and it is said that on rising after being dubbed a knight he broke his braces.

WILLIAM BARCLAY PEAT, *President* 1906–8

A devoted Scot, he sprang from a family near Montrose who had farmed land there since the sixteenth century. After school life at the Montrose Academy, he was indentured to a lawyer in that town. In 1870 his father sent him to London to earn his living, where he took to accountancy and joined the firm of Robert Fletcher & Co. and became a member of the old Institute. Soon afterwards, he was sent to Middlesbrough on an investigation and whilst there opened an office for the firm, being admitted as a partner in 1877. This was the period of early development of the steel industry on the north-east coast and he took a leading part in it. He returned to London in 1891 taking over the business on the death of its then senior partner, Roderick Mackay, and changed its name to W. B. Peat & Co. He remained as senior partner for thirty-two years, and was a great and beloved figure in the development of the profession and of the Institute. He was a member of the Council for thirty-seven years, and President for twenty years of the Benevolent Association to which he was a most generous benefactor. On his death, his son, Sir Harry Peat, also made a most generous donation to that Association, in honour of his father, for the education of children or dependants of members who fall on evil days. In addition, he gave generously in prizes for the Institute's examinations, one in particular being named after his first principal and partner, Robert Fletcher. As auditor of the Privy Purse he was honoured with a C.V.O., and he held several decorations conferred by foreign governments. He was knighted in 1912. He was appointed to many Government inquiries on a variety of matters, including hospitals, the future of Southern Rhodesia and agriculture, being chairman of a Royal Commission on the last-named in 1919. To the end of his days at the age of 83, he retained a lively interest in country pursuits and in his native Scotland. He delighted in quoting freely from many standard works, but chiefly his beloved *Robbie Burns*.

WILLIAM PLENDER, *President* 1910–12 *and* 1929–30, *later Baron Plender of Sundridge in the County of Kent*

In his day, Lord Plender was the doyen of the accountancy profession. From modest beginnings as the son of a grocer and draper near Newcastle upon Tyne, he climbed to eminence not only in the world of accountancy but in the sphere of public service. He received his education at the Royal Grammar School, Newcastle. Coming to London in 1884, after seven years' apprenticeship in the office of J. G. Benson of Newcastle, he rose to be senior partner in Deloitte, Plender, Griffiths & Co. Apart from his outstanding work for the Institute, of which he was a member of the Council for forty-three years and President on three occasions (being elected President also of the Fourth International Congress of Accountants in London in 1933), his public services were prodigious as evidenced by the phenomenal number of Royal Commissions, Government and other committees and inquiries relating to financial, industrial, scholastic and charitable matters upon which he was invited to serve. He was honoured by membership of many educational and benevolent bodies to whose advancement he contributed much.

Of modest demeanour he nevertheless impressed his personality on all those with whom he came into contact and at international accounting conferences he was an outstanding figure. In his private life, he was a keen student of historical and humanitarian literature which he could quote on appropriate occasions in speeches remarkable for their felicity. He acquired a notable collection of etchings and in his later years became interested in antique furniture. In his home at Ovenden in Kent, and at his town house, nothing pleased him more than to entertain his large circle of friends. His interest in the young was a prominent feature in his character as evidenced by his twenty-nine years as President of the Chartered Accountant Students' Society of London, and to those whom misfortune had overtaken he was universally kind. One who knew him for upwards of forty years has described as his chief characteristics the virtues of humanity, kindness and tolerance. Honours came thick upon him; he was knighted in 1911, G.B.E. 1918, Baronet 1923, Baron 1931, and he had many others including High Sheriff of the County of London and of Kent and President of Kent County Cricket Club. It was sad at the end, when both his homes had been destroyed by enemy action, to see him finishing his days uncomplainingly in a nursing home at Hove.

CHARLES JOHN GEOFFREY PALMOUR, *President* 1938–44

Palmour joined in 1901 the firm of Whinney, Smith & Whinney with which he remained throughout his life, being its senior partner from 1927 until his death in 1948. He was elected to the Council in 1927 and likewise remained a member until his death. He became President in 1938 and had the unique distinction of holding that position for six years, during which period he had to cope with all the exacting problems of membership which arose in war conditions. In 1938 he led the British delegation to the International Congress of Accountants in Berlin at the time of the Munich crisis, and though he behaved with dignity and decorum in public, his colleagues were frightened behind the scenes that he would bring on war a year earlier than happened. It was said of him that he belonged to an age when the British Government was able to send a gunboat to enforce payments of debts or bonds that fell into arrear. His zeal for, and his pride in, the Institute were unbounded and it was no doubt with memory of the efforts which his forbear in partnership, Frederick Whinney, made towards registration of the profession that he himself took such a prominent part in the negotiations for its co-ordination during his years of presidency. He was a forceful and picturesque character, with a manner as blunt as his heart was kind. He was a very prominent freemason, holding the rank of Past Grand Warden of England. He was knighted in 1946.

HAROLD GIBSON HOWITT, *President* 1945–6

Within a few years after the death of Lord Plender, Sir Harold Howitt, G.B.E., D.S.O., M.C., D.C.L., LL.D., D.L., became by general recognition the doyen of the accountancy profession in the United Kingdom. Born in Nottingham in 1886, he was educated at Uppingham School, of whose governors he was later to become chairman, and after serving under articles in the city of his birth joined in 1909 the London staff of W. B. Peat & Co., now Peat, Marwick, Mitchell & Co., in which firm he became a partner in 1911 and so continued until his retirement in 1961. He had an outstanding record of service in the 1914–18 war, being awarded for his courage and leadership the D.S.O. and the M.C. and mentioned four times in dispatches. In the Second World War he was a member of the Air Council and the Air Supply Board and engaged with the greatest distinction and success in a variety of other activities in the public service. Before and after that war his services were in constant demand for important public work of a most varied character, including numerous Government committees and inquiries. Knighted in 1937, he became a G.B.E. in 1946. He received the honorary degree of D.C.L. from Oxford University in 1953 and that of LL.D. from Nottingham University in 1958. He rendered services of the greatest importance to the whole accountancy profession and to the Institute, of whose Council he was for twenty-nine years a distinguished and active member. During that long time he contributed at professional meetings a number of important papers and speeches on a variety of subjects. President of the Institute in 1945–6, he was chosen by common consent to be President of the Sixth International Congress on Accounting held in London in 1952, and by his conduct in that office did much to ensure the successful resumption of international co-operation among accountancy bodies which had been interrupted by the 1939–45 war.

Throughout his busy professional life Sir Harold has displayed the greatest concern for young people and an active interest in social work and education. An effective and lucid speaker, a patient, courteous and humorous negotiator and chairman, a man of infinite charm and capacity for friendship, he is beloved by all who know him. His character, moulded in the stresses of two world wars, finds its basis in a happy home and family life.

# Section 13: Past Presidents

| | |
|---|---|
| 1880–2 | William Turquand, *London* |
| 1882–3 | Robert Palmer Harding, *London* |
| 1883–4 | Arthur Cooper, *London* |
| 1884–8 | Frederick Whinney, *London* |
| 1888–9 | William Welch Deloitte, *London* |
| 1889–91 | Joseph John Saffery, *London* |
| 1891–2 | Thomas Abercrombie Welton, *London* |
| 1892–4 | Edwin Waterhouse, *London* |
| 1894–6 | Charles Fitch Kemp, *London* |
| 1896–7 | George Walter Knox, *Sheffield* |
| 1897–9 | John George Griffiths, *London* |
| 1899-1901 | Ernest Cooper, *London* |
| 1901–2 | Walter Newton Fisher, *Birmingham* |
| 1902–3 | Alfred Augustus James, *London* |
| 1903–4 | Francis William Pixley, *London* |
| 1904–5 | John Sutherland Harmood-Banner, *Liverpool* |
| 1905–6 | John Gane, *London* |
| 1906–8 | William Barclay Peat, *London* |
| 1908–9 | John Ball Ball, *London* |
| 1909–10 | Algernon Osmond Miles, *London* |
| 1910–11 | William Plender } *London* |
| 1911–12 | Sir William Plender } *London* |
| 1912–13 | Jarvis William Barber, *Sheffield* |
| 1913–15 | Horace Woodburn Kirby } *London* |
| 1915–16 | Sir (H.) Woodburn Kirby } *London* |
| 1916–17 | Arthur Henry Gibson, *Birmingham* |
| 1917–19 | Frederick John Young, *London* |
| 1919–20 | John William Woodthorpe, *London* |
| 1920–1 | John Gordon, *Leeds* |
| 1921–3 | William Cash, *London* |
| 1923 | Sir Edward Cecil Moore, BT., *London* |

1924–5 Thomas Galland Mellors, *Nottingham*
1925–6 George Robert Freeman, *London*
1926–7 Sir Arthur Francis Whinney, K.B.E., *London*
1927–8 Richard Henry March, *Cardiff*
1928–9 Sir Nicholas Edwin Waterhouse, K.B.E., *London*
1929–30 Sir William Plender, BT., G.B.E., *London*
1930–1 Harold Fitch Kemp, *London*
1931–2 Henry Lancelot Hingston Hill, *London*
1932–3 Clare Smith, *Bristol*
1933–4 Henry Lancelot Hingston Hill, *London*
1934–6 Arthur Edwin Cutforth, C.B.E., *London*
1936–7 Roger Neale Carter, *Manchester*
1937–8 Frank Lindsay Fisher, C.B.E., *London*
1938–44 Charles John Geoffrey Palmour, *London*
1944–5 Harold Montague Barton, *London*
1945–6 Sir Harold Gibson Howitt, G.B.E., D.S.O., M.C., *London*
1946 Edward Furnival Jones, *London*
1947–8 Gilbert David Shepherd, M.B.E., *Cardiff*
1948–9 Bernhard Heymann Binder, *London*
1949–50 Sir Russell Kettle, *London*
1950–1 Harold Garton Ash, O.B.E., M.C., *London*
1951–2 Charles William Boyce, C.B.E., *Bradford*
1952–3 Thomas Buston Robson, M.B.E., *London*
1953–4 James Blakey, *Manchester*
1954–5 Donald Victor House, *London*
1955–6 William Speight Carrington, *London*
1956–7 Arthur Seymour Hamilton Dicker, M.B.E., *Norwich*
1957–8 William Halford Lawson, C.B.E., *London*
1958–9 William Leonard Barrows, *Birmingham*
1959–60 Charles Urie Peat, M.C., *London*
1960–1 Sidney John Pears, *London*
1961–2 Paul Francis Granger, *Nottingham*
1962–3 Percy Frederick Carpenter, *London*
1963–4 Robert Pearson Winter, C.B.E., M.C., *Newcastle upon Tyne*
1964–5 Wilfrid Guy Densem, *London*

## PAST PRESIDENTS

At the annual meeting of the Institute in May 1965, Robert McNeil (Hove) was elected President and Sir Henry Alexander Benson, C.B.E. (London), Vice-President.

# Bibliography

*General Histories*

*Professional Accountants: an historical sketch*, by B. Worthington. 1895. (Gee.)

*A History of Accounting and Accountants*, by R. Brown. Edinburgh, 1905. (T. C. & E. C. Jack.)

*Chapters in the History of Bookkeeping, Accountancy & Commercial Arithmetic*, by D. Murray. Glasgow, 1930. (Jackson, Wylie.)

'The Institute Lady', by C. Gordon. *The Accountant*, November 6, 1948, p. 371.

*A History of the Hall of the Institute of Chartered Accountants in England and Wales*, by J. H. Stern. 1953. (Gee.)

*A History of the Chartered Accountants of Scotland from the earliest times to* 1954. (Institute of Cahrtered Accountants of Scotland.) Edinburgh, 1954.

*English Accountancy: a study in social and economic history:* 1800–1954, by N. A. H. Stacey. 1954. (Gee.)

*Fifty Years: the story of the Association of Certified and Corporate Accountants* 1904–54. (Association of Certified and Corporate Accountants.) 1954.

'The Development of the Profession in Ireland', by G. Brock. *The Accountant*, August 25, 1956, p. 182.

'Steps in the Evolution of the Profession in the United Kingdom: (dates of principal events, 1853–1957).' *The Accountant*, November 9, 1957, p. 544.

'Eighty Years of Service: (Institute of Chartered Accountants, eightieth year).' *The Accountant*, October 15, 1960, p. 465.

*History of the Society of Incorporated Accountants*, 1885–1957, by A. A. Garrett. 1961. (Oxford University Press.)

'The British Accounting Tradition in America', by Mary E. Murphy. *Journal of Accountancy*, April 1961, p. 54.

'The Singular Case of Double Entry', by C. O. Merriman. *The Accountant*, December 23, 1961, p. 823.

*The History of the First Fifty Years of The Society*, 1963. (South Wales and Monmouthshire Society of Chartered Accountants.) Cardiff, 1963.

*A History of Accountants in Ireland*, by H. W. Robinson. Dublin, 1964. (Institute of Chartered Accountants in Ireland.)

*Histories of Individuals and Firms*

*War Memorial of the staff of Messrs Deloitte, Plender, Griffiths & Co.: Roll of Honour and record of service in the Great War* 1914–19. (Deloitte, Plender, Griffiths & Co.) 1920.

*Fifty-seven Years in an Accountant's Office:* a paper, by E. Cooper. 1921. (Gee.)

*A Hundred Years of Accountancy* 1837–1937. (Begbie, Robinson, Cox & Knight.) 1938.

*Deloitte, Plender, Griffiths & Co.: some notes on the early days of the firm*, by J. Kilpatrick. 1942. (Wyman.)

*History of the Firm: the first fifty years* 1850–1900, by G. E. Richards. 1950. (Price Waterhouse & Co., typescript.)

*Price Waterhouse & Co., in America: A History of a Public Accounting Firm*, by C. W. DeMond. New York, 1951. (Comet Press.)

*Towards the Centenary: notes on the origin and history of an accountancy practice.* (J. & A. W. Sully & Co.) 1951.

11 *Ironmonger Lane: the story of a site in the City of London*, by D. Dawe and A. Oswald (Offices of Peat, Marwick, Mitchell & Co.) 1952. (Hutchinson.)

*A History of One Hundred Years of Accountancy Practice* 1852–1952. (Morris, Gregory & Co.) Manchester, 1953.

*A History of Cooper Brothers & Co.:* 1854 *to* 1954. (Cooper Brothers & Co.) 1954. Batsford.

*Accountant's Journal: debit and credit*, by J. Mitchell. Gateshead on Tyne. 1954. (Northumberland Press.)

*I Remember*, by C. F. Bird. 1955. (Hutchinson.)

*Seventy Years of Progress in Accountancy Education*, by H. Foulks Lynch & Co. Ltd, 1955. (H. Foulks Lynch & Co. Ltd.)

*A Short History of Grace, Darbyshire and Todd: Chartered Accountants of Bristol*, 1818–1957. (Grace, Darbyshire and Todd.) 1957.

*Kingsfords*, by Kingsford, Garlant and J. B. Marks. 1957.

*Deloitte & Co:* 1845–1956, by Sir R. Kettle. 1958. (Oxford University Press.)

Robert H. Montgomery. *Lybrand Journal No.* 3, 1959, p. 89.

*The Story of the Firm* 1864–1964: *Clarkson, Gordon & Co.*, by A. J. Little. Toronto, 1964. (University of Toronto Press.)

# Index

*The names of individual members referred to in the body of the History are not indexed.*

# *List of Titles*

## Accounting History and the Development of a Profession

***Management Accounting Research: A Review and Annotated Bibliography.***
Charles F. Klemstine and Michael W. Maher. New York, 1984.

***Accounting Literature in Non-Accounting Journals: An Annotated Bibliography.***
Panadda Tantral. New York, 1984.

***The Evolution of Behavioral Accounting Research: An Overview.***
Robert H. Ashton, editor. New York, 1984.

***Some Early Contributions to the Study of Audit Judgment.***
Robert H. Ashton, editor. New York, 1984.

***Depreciation and Capital Maintenance.***
Richard P. Brief, editor. New York, 1984.

***The Case for Continuously Contemporary Accounting.***
G. W. Dean and M. C. Wells, editors. New York, 1984.

***Studies of Company Records: 1830–1974.***
J. R. Edwards, editor. New York, 1984.

***European Equity Markets: Risk, Return, and Efficiency.***
Gabriel Hawawini and Pierre Michel, editors. New York, 1984.

***Transactions of the Chartered Accountants Students' Societies of Edinburgh and Glasgow: A Selection of Writings, 1886–1958.***
Thomas A. Lee, editor. New York, 1984.

***The Development of Double Entry: Selected Essays.***
Christopher Nobes, editor. New York, 1984.

***Papers on Accounting History.***
R. H. Parker. New York, 1984.

***Collected Papers on Accounting and Accounting Education (in two volumes).***
David Solomons. New York, 1984.

***The General Principles of the Science of Accounts and the Accountancy of Investment.***
Charles E. Sprague. New York, 1984.

***Selected Papers on Accounting, Auditing, and Professional Problems.***
Edward Stamp. New York, 1984.

***Factory Accounts.***
John Whitmore. New York, 1984.

***Sourcebook on Accounting Principles and Auditing Procedures: 1917–1953 (in two volumes).***
Stephen A. Zeff and Maurice Moonitz, editors. New York, 1984.

***The First Fifty Years 1913–1963.***
Arthur Andersen Company. Chicago, 1963.

***Paciolo on Accounting.***
R. Gene Brown and Kenneth S. Johnston. New York, 1963.

***The Early History of Coopers & Lybrand.***
Coopers & Lybrand. New York, 1984.

***Report of the Trial . . . Against the Directors and the Manager of the City of Glasgow Bank.***
Charles Tennant Couper. Edinburgh, 1879.

***Development of Accounting Thought.***
Harvey T. Deinzer. New York, 1965.

***The Principles of Auditing.***
F.R.M. De Paula. London, 1915.

***The Accountant, or, the Method of Bookkeeping Deduced from Clear Principles, and Illustrated by a Variety of Examples.***
James Dodson. London, 1750.

***A Common Sense Method of Double Entry Bookkeeping, on First Principles, as Suggested by De Morgan. Part I, Theoretical.***
S. Dyer. London, 1897.

***Economics of Fatigue and Unrest and the Efficiency of Labour in English and American Industry.***
P. Sargant Florence. London, 1923.

***Haskins & Sells: Our First Seventy-Five Years.***
Arthur B. Foye. New York, 1970.

***The History of the Society of Incorporated Accountants, 1885–1957.***
A. A. Garrett. Oxford, 1961.

***The Game of Budget Control.***
Geert Hofstede. Assen, 1967.

***The History of The Institute of Chartered Accountants in England and Wales 1880–1965, and of Its Founder Accountancy Bodies 1870–1880.***
Sir Harold Howitt. London, 1966.

***History of the Chartered Accountants of Scotland from the Earliest Times to 1954.***
Institute of Chartered Accountants of Scotland. Edinburgh, 1954.

***Accounting Thought and Education: Six English Pioneers.***
J. Kitchen and R. H. Parker. London, 1980.

***The Evolution of Corporate Financial Reporting.***
T. A. Lee and R. H. Parker. Middlesex, 1979.

***Accounting in Scotland: A Historical Bibliography.***
Janet E. Pryce-Jones and R. H. Parker. Edinburgh, 1976.

***A History of Accountants in Ireland.***
H. W. Robinson. Dublin, 1964.

***The Sixth International Congress on Accounting.***
London, 1952.

***The Accomptant's Oracle: or, Key to Science, Being a Compleat Practical System of Book-keeping.***
Wardbaugh Thompson. York, 1777.

## Accountancy in Transition

***The Tangled Web of Price Variation Accounting: The Development of Ideas Underlying Professional Prescriptions in Six Countries.***
F. L. Clarke. New York, 1982.

***Beta Alpha Psi, From Alpha to Omega: Pursuing a Vision of Professional Education for Accountants, 1919–1945.***
Terry K. Sheldahl. New York, 1982.

***Four Classics on the Theory of Double-Entry Bookkeeping.***
Richard P. Brief, editor. New York, 1982.

***Forerunners of Realizable Values Accounting in Financial Reporting.***
G. W. Dean and M. C. Wells, editors. New York, 1982.

***Accounting Queries.***
Harold C. Edey. New York, 1982.

***The Development of Accounting Theory: Significant Contributors to Accounting Thought in the 20th Century.***
Michael Gaffikin and Michael Aitken, editors. New York, 1982.

***Studies in Social and Private Accounting.***
Solomon Fabricant. New York, 1982.

***Bond Duration and Immunization: Early Developments and Recent Contributions.***
Gabriel A. Hawawini, editor. New York, 1982.

***Further Essays on the History of Accounting.***
Basil S. Yamey. New York, 1982.

***Accounting Principles Through The Years: The Views of Professional and Academic Leaders 1938–1954.***
Stephen A. Zeff, editor. New York, 1982.

***The Accounting Postulates and Principles Controversy of the 1960s.***
Stephen A. Zeff, editor. New York, 1982.

***Fiftieth Anniversary Celebration.***
American Institute of Accountants. New York, 1937.

***Library Catalogue.***
American Institute of Accountants. New York, 1919.

***Four Essays in Accounting Theory.***
F. Sewell Bray. London, 1953. *bound with*
***Some Accounting Terms and Concepts.***
Institute of Chartered Accountants in England and Wales and The National Institute of Economic and Social Research. Cambridge, 1951.

***Accounting in Disarray.***
R. J. Chambers. Melbourne, 1973.

***The Balance-Sheet.***
Charles B. Couchman. New York, 1924.

***Audits.***
Arthur E. Cutforth. London, 1906.

***Methods of Amalgamation.***
Arthur E. Cutforth. London, 1926.

***Deloitte & Co. 1845–1956.***
Sir Russell Kettle. Oxford, 1958. *bound with*
***Fifty-seven Years in an Accountant's Office.***
Ernest Cooper. London, 1921.

***Accountants and the Law of Negligence.***
R. W. Dickerson. Toronto, 1966.

***Consolidated Statements.***
H. A. Finney. New York, 1922.

***The Rate of Interest.***
Irving Fisher. New York, 1907.

***Holding Companies and Their Published Accounts.***
Sir Gilbert Garnsey. London, 1923. *bound with*
***Limitations of a Balance Sheet.***
Sir Gilbert Garnsey. London, 1928.

***Accounting Concepts of Profit.***
Stephen Gilman. New York, 1939.

***An Introduction to Merchandise, Parts IV and V (Italian Bookkeeping and Practical Bookkeeping).***
Robert Hamilton. Edinburgh, 1788.

***The Merchant's Magazine: or, Trades-man's Treasury.***
Edward Hatton. London, 1695.

***The Law of Accounting and Financial Statements.***
George S. Hills. Boston, 1957.

***International Congress on Accounting 1929.***
New York, 1930.

***Fourth International Congress on Accounting 1933.***
London, 1933.

***Magnificent Masquerade.***
Charles Keats. New York, 1964.

***Profit Measurement and Price Changes.***
Kenneth Lacey. London, 1952.

***The American Accomptant.***
Chauncey Lee. Lansingburgh, 1797.

***Consolidated Balance Sheets.***
George Hills Newlove. New York, 1926.

***Consolidated and Other Group Accounts.***
T. B. Robson. London, 1950.

***Accounting Method.***
C. Rufus Rorem. Chicago, 1928.

*Shareholder's Money.*
Horace B. Samuel. London, 1933.

*Standardized Accountancy in Germany. (With a new appendix.)*
H. W. Singer. Cambridge, 1943.

*The Securities and Exchange Commission in the Matter of McKesson & Robbins, Inc. Report on Investigation.*
Washington, D. C., 1940.

*The Securities and Exchange Commission in the Matter of McKesson & Robbins, Inc. Testimony of Expert Witnesses.*
Washington, D. C., 1939.

*Accounting in England and Scotland: 1543–1800.*
B. S. Yamey, H. C. Edey, Hugh W. Thomson. London, 1963.